Eyewitness to World War II

Eyewitness to World War II

Edited and with an introduction
by Stephen W. Sears

HOUGHTON MIFFLIN COMPANY

BOSTON / NEW YORK

Library of Congress Cataloging-in-Publication Data
Sears, Stephen W.
Eyewitness to World War II : the best of American heritage /
edited and with an introduction by Stephen W. Sears.
p. cm.
ISBN 0-395-61902-5
1. World War, 1939–1945 — Personal narratives,
American. I. Sears, Stephen W. II. Title: Eyewitness
to World War 2
D811.A2E94 1991 91-226362
940.54'8173 — dc20 CIP

Printed in the United States

AGM 10 9 8 7 6 5 4 3 2

CONTENTS

INTRODUCTION

E very month, writes an *American Heritage* editor, a flood of first-person accounts of the Second World War reaches the magazine's offices. "It is a seemingly endless flow and endlessly interesting," he goes on, for each person's view of the event witnessed is different from every other person's. "World War II is an old story only if you have read the same version before. . . ."

The eyewitness accounts of the war that follow, from the pages of *American Heritage*, are indeed unique. Each of the men (and in the case of "Rosie the Riveter Remembers" each of the women) witnessed the war as an individual and from an individual's perspective. These perspectives are enormously varied—that of a general in the field and an admiral on the bridge, that of a Marine corporal, a seaman second class, a mess cook, a civilian caught in the trap of war. Some are the vital raw materials of history. Others are thoughtful and expert interpretations that comprise the stuff of history. Everyone in these pages was *there*, seeing, recording, remembering, adding to our store of knowledge of this greatest war in history.

There is here, too, a unique consciousness of the importance of history, of getting the story right and setting the record straight. A Navy interrogator seeking to fill out the record of the loss of the light cruiser *Juneau* off Guadalcanal captures from Allen Heyn, seaman second, a tale as harrowing as any in the literature of the sea. General James Gavin, then a colonel commanding the 505th Parachute Regimental Combat team, tells of the chaotic airdrop on Sicily and the equally chaotic battle for Biazza Ridge, one of those small-unit actions with vitally important consequences for the campaign. General Gavin also offers here his informed perspective on that ghastly battle in the Huertgen Forest that (he says) was fought for no good reason.

Halfway around the globe from Huertgen, Admiral Kemp Tolley, then a youthful lieutenant, suggests that there was something strange—very strange—about the windjammer U.S.S. *Lanikai*'s proposed voyage into Far Eastern waters in early December of 1941, something that should be on the historical record. Edward L. Beach wants the historical record to show the "culpable negligence" that for so long put so many American submariners at risk, buttressing his argument with his own experiences on war patrol.

Events of war are seen from unusual angles. Hughes Rudd overlooked the European Theatre of Operations at 75 miles an hour from the cramped cockpit of an L-4 artillery spotter known with scant affection as a "Maytag Messerschmitt." Herbert Mitgang witnessed the ETO from behind a typewriter, telling it like it was for the Army. Sybil Lewis, a brave black woman in a white man's world, manned a rivet gun in a California aircraft factory. John Burroughs, literally a citizen in arms, passed the ammunition on Wake. Nineteen-year-old Stephen Young's first experience of war was entombment in the capsized *Oklahoma* at Pearl Harbor. David Davidson, playing a role in a morality play, had to distinguish the good Germans from the bad Germans. William Manchester recorded Marine private Whitey Dumas playing a role in the Pacific war that was, well, different.

Celebrated battles are here as well. Two of the greatest air combats of World War II are remembered by men in the pilot's seat—Lewis Ellis in the B-24 *Daisy Mae* over Ploesti, and Lester Rentmeester in a Flying Fortress, one of the more than 650 that took off for Berlin that day in March 1944. Few soldiers have described infantry combat better than Charles Cawthon, who records here the odyssey of the 2nd Battalion, Stonewall Brigade, on D-Day and in the subsequent breakout from the Normandy beachhead. Admiral Jocko Clark, called by Marc Mitscher his best task group commander, recounts the spectacular carrier air battle off the Marianas—and laments he did not gamble for total victory in that engagement.

Ex-lieutenant G.D. Lillibridge remembers one of the grimmest names in Marine Corps annals, Tarawa, a name with the same terrible ring that Shiloh and Antietam had to an earlier generation. Lillibridge, revisiting Tarawa twenty-five years later and remembering the many who never left that tiny atoll, thinks that "not forgetting may be the only heroism of the survivor."

Thanks to these eyewitnesses, none will ever forget.

Stephen W. Sears
May 1991

THE STRANGE MISSION OF THE *LANIKAI*

by ADMIRAL KEMP TOLLEY

F.D.R. contemplates war with Japan.

O n March 18, 1942, eighty-two days out of Manila, all
sails set, rigging taut, a small, green, weathered schooner entered the port of Fremantle, Western Australia. Atop her
afterdeck house a small-caliber, slim-barrelled cannon sat on a
brass pedestal. Faded, tattered Philippine and United States
flags whipped from her spanker gaff. Above them, at the main
peak, floated a wisp of bunting that the intrigued onlookers
aboard the Allied warships present thought might be a man-o-
warsman's commission pennant.

The windjammer's name, U.S.S. *Lanikai*, sparked instant
recognition at headquarters—twice during the last three
months she had been reported overdue and presumed lost.
Chief of staff Rear Admiral William R. Purnell met her skipper
with appropriate astonishment: "My God! What are *you* doing
here? You're supposed to be dead!"

My introduction to *Lanikai* took place on December 4,
1941, when as a young lieutenant I was called into U.S. Asiatic
Fleet headquarters on the Manila waterfront and told I was her
commanding officer. Orders were oral, informal, and brief.
"Commission her as a U.S. man-of-war, get a part-Filipino
crew aboard, arm her with a cannon of some sort and one
machine gun," said Fleet operations officer Commander Harry Slocum, adding that she was to be ready for sea in forty-
eight hours, provisioned for a two-week cruise.

Having been brought up in a Navy where one planned in
detail and requisitioned in quintuplicate after many confer-
ences and much coffee, I was relieved to be set straight on the

1

new, streamlined procedure. "The rules do not apply here," Slocum explained. "The Navy Yard has been directed to give you highest priority—anything you ask for within reason—without paperwork of *any* kind. Of this you can rest absolutely assured; the President himself has directed it."

The presidential directive (to which of course I was not privy) triggering all this had been addressed to the commander in chief, U.S. Asiatic Fleet: PRESIDENT DIRECTS THAT THE FOLLOWING BE DONE AS SOON AS POSSIBLE AND WITHIN TWO DAYS IF POSSIBLE AFTER RECEIPT THIS DISPATCH. CHARTER THREE SMALL VESSELS TO FORM A QUOTE DEFENSIVE INFORMATION PATROL UNQUOTE. MINIMUM REQUIREMENTS TO ESTABLISH IDENTITY AS UNITED STATES MEN-OF-WAR ARE COMMAND BY A NAVAL OFFICER AND TO MOUNT A SMALL GUN AND ONE MACHINE GUN WOULD SUFFICE. FILIPINO CREWS MAY BE EMPLOYED WITH MINIMUM NUMBER NAVAL RATINGS TO ACCOMPLISH PURPOSE WHICH IS TO OBSERVE AND REPORT BY RADIO JAPANESE MOVEMENTS IN WEST CHINA SEA AND GULF OF SIAM. ONE VESSEL TO BE STATIONED BETWEEN HAINAN AND HUE ONE VESSEL OFF THE INDOCHINA COAST BETWEEN CAMRANH BAY AND CAPE ST. JAQUES AND ONE VESSEL OFF POINTE DE CAMAU. USE OF ISABEL AUTHORIZED BY PRESIDENT AS ONE OF THE THREE BUT NOT OTHER NAVAL VESSELS. REPORT MEASURES TAKEN TO CARRY OUT PRESIDENTS VIEWS. AT SAME TIME INFORM ME AS TO WHAT RECONNAISSANCE MEASURES ARE BEING REGULARLY PERFORMED AT SEA BY BOTH ARMY AND NAVY WHETHER BY AIR SURFACE VESSELS OR SUBMARINES AND YOUR OPINION AS TO THE EFFECTIVENESS OF THESE LATTER MEASURES.

Proof that the White House had spoken was soon evident. "Sign this receipt for 'one schooner' and tell me what you want," said Commander R.T. Whitney, captain of the Yard. There was no time for the usual small talk or coffee. Telephone calls to ordnance, supply, hospital, communications, and personnel mobilized the Yard's resources. A Spanish-American War three-pounder "quick firer" already was being bolted to the afterdeck-house roof, the biggest cannon it was felt could safely be fired without collapsing the twenty-seven-year-old ship's structure. A half dozen Filipino-American seamen were on their way to the dock. The native crewmen who had come in a package with the ship had just been sworn into the Navy. Speaking little English, they were at a loss to understand what it was all about, but they cheerfully accepted the bags of uniforms, proudly donned the little round white sailor hats, and turned to, loading stores, ammunition, and the bags of rice and cases of salmon that were their bread and meat.

Chief Boatswain's Mate Charlie Kinsey arrived at the dock with his jaw dropped down. He walked forward and squinted at the ship's nameplate, then called down to Chief Gunner's Mate Merle Picking, who already was checking out his "main battery," the three-pounder.

"I've got orders to the *Lanikai*," said Kinsey in a thick Georgia drawl, "but this *cain't* be *it!*"

The President's message, carrying highest-secrecy classification and precedence, had said his order was to be executed "as soon as possible and in two days if possible." So ready or not, on the forenoon of December 7—still December 6 in the United States—I reported for final instructions. "Open these orders when you are clear of Manila Bay," said Slocum. "I can say for your ears only that you are headed for Indochina. If you are queried by the Japanese, tell them you're looking for the crew of a downed plane."

Lanikai's radio receiver worked, I reported, but the transmitter did not. The water supply concerned me, too. Aboard a ship designed for a crew of five there were nineteen. "You have a set of international signal flags, don't you?" said Slocum ironically. "If you run short of water, signal any passing Japanese man-of-war for some."

Lanikai sailed the fifteen miles out to Manila Bay's entrance that afternoon and anchored, awaiting dawn to transit the minefield channel. Her crew, worn out from frantic last-minute preparations for sea, found their bunks early. Topside, in the soft tropical night, I watched the hundreds of lights twinkling in the clear air over the great fortress of Corregidor, "The Rock," bulking huge and black nearby. Tomorrow those sealed orders would be torn open and the great adventure revealed.

Slocum had confided that *Lanikai* would relieve the U.S.S. *Isabel* on station; she had left on December 3 for Camranh Bay's entrance. "Izzy" was a trim, white, nine-hundred-ton yacht taken into the Navy during World War I. For the last decade she had served as holiday flagship for the commander in chief of the Asiatic Fleet. Her age and flyweight military muscle clearly made her the most easily expendable unit in the Fleet, but she possessed in addition a striking attribute for this mission: as a Navy buff Roosevelt could plainly see, in the copy of *Jane's Fighting Ships* he kept handy, that *Isabel*'s white hull and buff upperworks, configuration, and wholly inconspicuous little battery of four 3-inch guns made her look like any typical small merchantman that used the China coast. So F.D.R. had designated *Isabel* as one of the "three small ships" that were to be used—the others to be chartered locally. And, as the President had "suggested," a token five Filipino seamen were put aboard before her precipitous departure. She was to remain painted white, Admiral Thomas C. Hart, commander in chief, Asiatic Fleet, directed her skipper in a personal briefing. Her running lights were to be dimmed at night to give the appearance of a fishing craft.

At 7 A.M. on the fifth *Isabel* was forty miles from Camranh Bay and its big concentration of Japanese warships when a Japanese plane closed her. *Isabel* was shadowed the remainder of the day, planes sometimes coming so close that their identification numbers could be made out. At 7:10 P.M., on Hart's urgent orders, she reversed course and headed back to Manila Bay.

Replying to the President's message, Hart radioed: "HAVE OBTAINED TWO VESSELS. ONE NOW ENROUTE INDOCHINA COAST. SECOND ONE SAILING SOON AS READY. AM CERTAIN SHOULD NOT OPERATE THEM SOUTH OF PADARAN. ISABEL RETURNING. WAS SPOTTED AND IDENTIFIED WELL OFF COAST HENCE POTENTIAL UTILITY OF HER MISSION PROBLEMATICAL. HAVE NOT YET FOUND THIRD VESSEL FOR CHARTER." The "one now enroute" was *Lanikai*; the second was never commissioned, the plan having been overtaken by events at Pearl Harbor.

The eighth of December, 1941, was only three hours old when a radioman nudged me awake from fitful slumber on a rubber mat atop the afterdeck house. The message he carried read "ORANGE WAR PLAN IN EFFECT, RETURN TO MANILA," the "orange" being a supposedly secret euphemism for "Japanese" that was recognized Navywide. But there was no need to awaken the crew until daybreak.

In today's frame of reference, which tolerates the Korean and Vietnam wars having been fought without constitutional legitimacy, it is difficult to appreciate F.D.R.'s dilemma in 1941. He was sentimentally attached to China, whence Grandpa Warren Delano, a traditional Old China hand, had thrilled the young Franklin with tall tales of clipper ships, pirates, mandarins, and perhaps even something of the opium operations that had contributed a million dollars to the family fortune. The powerful China lobby, plus Secretary of War Henry L. Stimson, a lifetime Japanophobe, reinforced the Rooseveltian leanings. And with advisers like Secretary of the Treasury Henry Morgenthau, Supreme Court Justice Felix Frankfurter, and man for all seasons Harry Hopkins to encourage the President's liberal tendencies, he naturally felt deeply opposed to the Nazi-Fascists.

But the President found himself mired in a swamp of national apathy. Army draftees drilled with wooden rifles, stovepipe "cannon," and "tanks" improvised from trucks. Their typical view of Army life was made clear in messages chalked on the fences and in the latrines: "OHIO"—over the hill in October (i.e., desertion). The general beer-hall and backyard bull session attitude was "Let those European bastards beat each others' brains out!"—sentiments strongly reinforced when Germany fell on the U.S.S.R. in June. What ordinary American wanted to die defending Singapore? or Surabaja (if he had ever heard of it), or blitzed London? or even Manila? But Roosevelt was a determined man as well as a consummate political strategist; despite public unconcern he had aligned the nation against Hitler by means of heavy congressional approval of the Lend-Lease Act on March 11, 1941.

On August 3, 1941, F.D.R. left New London, Connecticut, aboard his yacht U.S.S. *Potomac*, taking great pains to give the appearance of a fishing holiday. Transferred secretly at sea to the cruiser U.S.S. *Augusta*, he arrived at Argentia, Newfoundland, on August 8 for a four-day initial face-to-face meeting with Winston Churchill, also on a fishing expedition and a desperately urgent one. Britain was broke. Her lone ally, Russia, was reeling backward. It was 1917 all over again.

What F.D.R. promised Churchill over the nuts and wine perhaps never will be fully known, but a reference Churchill made in the House of Commons in January, 1942, gives a clue: ". . . the probability, since the Atlantic Conference, at which I discussed these matters with Mr. Roosevelt, that the United States, even if not herself attacked, would come into the war in the Far East. . . ."

Verbal promises to Churchill were one thing, but commitments in black and white were quite another. During mid-1941 the finishing touches were put on *Rainbow* 5, a world-encompassing war plan hammered out in Washington by American planners after a series of secret Anglo-American military consultations officially referred to as ABC-1 (American-British Conversations). The U.S. Congress, which then still jealously guarded its treaty- and war-making prerogatives, had no inkling of the plan's existence, let alone the fact that it gave first priority to the survival of Great Britain rather than to the defense of U.S. territories in the Pacific.

Roosevelt had verbally approved *Rainbow* 5 for distribution to the major commands, but it was to be inoperative "until we get into the war," as chief of Naval operations Admiral Harold "Betty" Stark later testified F.D.R. had said. Roosevelt also took the precaution, considerably to the disappointment of the British, of not officially approving the ABC reports in advance, instead of making this contingent upon a United States declaration of war.

On July 7 the President made a more open move toward war; by executive order, and with the agreement of the Icelandic government, American forces occupied Iceland. Rear Admiral Richmond Kelly Turner, chief of the Navy War Plans Division, asked the President if this didn't conflict with his October 30, 1940 speech in Boston, where he had ringingly proclaimed that "I have said this before, but I shall say it again, and again, and again; your boys are not going to be sent into any foreign wars!" According to Turner, the President answered not a word but leaned back, his long cigarette holder elevated at a jaunty angle, and gave vent to a hearty chuckle.

On September 4 the technically neutral U.S. destroyer *Greer* assisted a British patrol plane in a fight with a German submarine about 175 miles from Iceland. A week later the President issued his "shoot on sight" proclamation, authorizing and presumably legalizing American warships' firing on German or Italian warcraft wherever met in the western Atlantic.

On October 17, in response to the new doctrine, the U.S. destroyer *Kearny* attacked a U-boat west of Iceland and managed to survive a German torpedo. Germany did not declare war but countered off Iceland: on October 31 the U.S. destroyer *Reuben James* was sunk, with the loss of most of her crew. But to F.D.R.'s discomfiture these events apparently did little to stir the American public out of its lack of interest in Europe's war.

Before the shock of Pearl Harbor finally and dramatically

reversed the course of U.S. opinion, before Congress became aroused enough or informed enough to ask embarrassing questions about commitments, much less become aware of such rather informal Naval operations as conducted by *Isabel* and *Lanikai* in the western Pacific, a sequence of events had with inexorable urgency filled the five weeks preceding December 7. In the lexicon of a later age the countdown approached zero in the following fashion:

November 5. Unknown, of course, to the Americans, a Japanese combined-fleet operation order directed that war preparations be completed by early December.

A memorandum from Army chief of staff General George Marshall and Admiral Stark warned the President that the U.S. Pacific Fleet was inferior to Japan's fleet and could not take the offensive:

November 7. Stark wrote to Hart that although the Navy was already at war in the Atlantic, the country didn't seem to realize it and was still apathetic.

November 10. Churchill said in a public speech that in case of war between Japan and the United States a British declaration would follow "within the hour."

November 17. United States Ambassador Joseph C. Grew, in Tokyo, warned Washington to guard against "the probability of the Japanese exploiting every possible tactical advantage, such as surprise."

November 19. The State Department warned U.S. citizens in the Far East to get out.

November 20. Japanese envoys Nomura and Kurusu conveyed to Secretary of State Hull Japan's demands for the preservation of peace: the United States must keep hands off China, resume trade relations with Japan, help Japan get supplies from the Netherlands East Indies, and stop American Naval expansion in the western Pacific.

November 21. Things looked black to Hull, but the day was brightened somewhat by Kurusu's telling him Japan would not necessarily be bound by the terms of its tripartite mutual assistance pact with Italy and Germany.

The Pearl Harbor attack force assembled at Hitokappu Bay, Kuriles.

November 22. Roosevelt suggested a *modus vivendi* with Japan to last six months, having already been sounded out by Ambassador Nomura on the subject on the tenth. This was to include among other things the resumption of economic relations between the two countries; a suspension of Japanese troop movements to Indochina, Malaya, and the Netherlands East Indies; and American encouragement of nonhostile conversations between Japan and China. Reactions to these suggestions from the Chinese, the British, the Australians, and the Dutch varied from bitter opposition to nervous skepticism.

An intercepted message to the Japanese envoys in Washington revealed that the previous deadline for meeting Japan's demands, November 25, had been extended to midnight of the 29th, after which there would be no possibility of an extension and "things are automatically going to happen."

November 24. United States forces occupied Dutch Guiana. All top U.S. military commands were alerted that a "surprise aggressive movement in any direction including attack on the Philippines and Guam is a possibility."

November 25. The War Council—Roosevelt, Hull, Secretaries of War and the Navy Stimson and Knox, Marshall, and Stark—met for a long discussion. Stimson, the meticulous diarist, noted that Roosevelt felt the attack might come as soon as December 1, "for the Japanese are notorious for making an attack without warning, and the question was what we should do. *The question was how we should maneuver them into the position of firing the first shot without allowing too much danger to ourselves*" (italics supplied). Nevertheless the *modus vivendi*'s final terms were smoothed out. The whole show left Stark up in the air. Somewhat distractedly he wrote to commander in chief U.S. Fleet Admiral Husband E. Kimmel at Pearl Harbor: "I won't go into the pros and cons of what the United States may do. I will be damned if I know. I wish I did. The only thing I know is that we may do most anything and that's the only thing I'm prepared for; or we may do nothing—I think it is more likely to be 'anything.' "

A very large Japanese expedition was sighted at sea below Formosa, moving south.

November 26. An intercept from Hanoi to Tokyo, dated the twenty-fifth, ominously noted that "no doubt the Cabinet will make a decision between peace and war within the next day or two." There was a parade of worried diplomats in and out of the State Department and White House. The Chinese ambassador, along with Chiang Kai-shek's influential, rich troubleshooter, T.V. Soong (Chiang's brother-in-law), called on

Roosevelt, bitterly protesting the proposed *modus vivendi* and threatening that it would wreck the Chinese will to continue resistance. Ignoring all normal protocol and lines of diplomatic communication, the Chinese had been soliciting senators, bankers, and private citizens in their campaign to promote support of Chiang.

Secretary Stimson telephoned Roosevelt the news of the big Japanese force headed south and was nearly blasted loose from his handset. The President "fairly blew up," Stimson recorded. "Utter lack of good faith. It changes the whole situation!" F.D.R. angrily shouted.

Kurusu and Nomura, invited over at teatime by Hull, no doubt happily anticipated good news on the *modus vivendi*. But the tea was bitter. Hull handed them what variously has been called a peace proposal, a modified *modus vivendi*, and an ultimatum. Far from acceding to Japan's demands of November 20, it called for Japan to get out of China and Indochina and respect the status quo in the Pacific. There was a heated two-hour discussion during which the Japanese envoys said it would be useless to send such a thing to Tokyo. In their message doing just that, they expressed the view that negotiations were a closed issue and that the United States could be expected to occupy the Netherlands East Indies as they recently had Iceland and Dutch Guiana.

The Japanese carriers of the Pearl Harbor attack force were on their way from the Kuriles toward Hawaii.

November 27. Stimson had got wind of something big going on, so during the forenoon he telephoned Hull to find out what it was. "I have washed my hands of it!" said Hull testily. "It is now in the hands of you and Knox—the Army and the Navy."

That same morning the war warnings that have been the subject of so much dispute went out to the major field commanders. The Army message contained a sentence missing from the Navy warning: "IF HOSTILITIES CANNOT, REPEAT CANNOT, BE AVOIDED, THE UNITED STATES DESIRES THAT JAPAN COMMIT THE FIRST OVERT ACT." This was inserted on direct order to Stimson by the President, whose sensitive political nerve ends reminded him that even after the recent destroyer incidents in the Atlantic, the American public was stone cold to the idea of going to war with *anybody*.

November 28. Having been handed the baton by Hull, Stimson was itching to crack somebody over the head with it and suggested to Roosevelt that MacArthur's planes bomb the Japanese task forces passing by the Philippines. Stimson never had forgiven the Japanese for humiliating him in 1931, when as Hoover's Secretary of State he had tried unsuccessfully to fling the Japanese out of Manchuria without the force to turn the trick.

The War Cabinet, totally unaware of the Pearl Harbor attack force, met at noon to discuss the major Japanese expedition now heading south off Indochina. As usual, Stimson recorded the gist of the proceedings; it was the opinion of everyone that "if this expedition was allowed to get around the southern point of Indochina and to go off and land in the Gulf of Siam . . . it would be a terrific blow at all of the three Powers, Britain at Singapore, the Netherlands, and ourselves in the Philippines. *It was the consensus of everybody that this must not be allowed*. . . . that if the Japanese got into the Isthmus of Kra, the British would fight. It was also agreed that if the British fought, we would have to fight."

There was some chat about the U.S.S. *Panay* incident, and it may be assumed that the President's elephantine memory gave him total recall of the worldwide furor provoked when this tiny Yangtze gunboat was sunk by trigger-happy Japanese aviators on December 12, 1937. There was not much hope of inflaming American public opinion or Congress sufficiently to support a declaration of war, judging from their apathetic reactions to the Atlantic incidents. *But it was essential that Roosevelt have at the very least a legal reason to commit American forces.* Perhaps pondering this, the President left to escape the pressure briefly at Warm Springs, Georgia.

December 1. The Japanese cabinet secretly made the final decision for war. An intercepted Tokyo message told Japanese diplomats in London, Hong Kong, Singapore, and Manila to destroy their code machines.

The Japanese envoys in Washington, following their orders, made one more appeal to an unreceptive Hull, suggesting a second-level meeting at Hawaii—Wallace or Hopkins versus Prince Konoye or Viscount Ishii.

Having been urged by Hull to return from Warm Springs, Roosevelt arrived at the White House from Union Station about noon. Hull was already there. Stark arrived at 12:50 and left at 1:25, overstaying the President's lunchtime by twenty-five minutes. Obviously what went on was too hot for the telephone, as Roosevelt's alter ego and prime counsellor, Harry Hopkins, had to come from his U.S. Naval Hospital bed for a belated White House snack and a post-mortem on the conference. He tottered in just as Stark was leaving. There is no record of the proceedings. Roosevelt, Hopkins, Hull, and Stark are not known to have mentioned the matter afterward; Stark adroitly fielded questions in investigations or sat mute when interviewed on the issue.

Admiral Stark hurried back to his office and handed his assistant chief of Naval operations, Rear Admiral Royall E. Ingersoll, the bare, specific requirements laid down by F.D.R. that resulted in the commissioning of the *Lanikai*, but gave him no background information whatever. By about 7 P.M. the message Ingersoll had labored on and conferred over during the afternoon went to the code machine for transmission to Manila. The events of the week that followed soon became a page of history that closes with those well-remembered words—Pearl Harbor.

Following the unexpected outbreak of a very clearly expected war, *Lanikai* fell into a sort of limbo, her *raison d'etre* dissolved by the "incident" at Pearl Harbor. A heavy Japanese air raid on December 10 destroyed Manila's Cavite Navy Yard and ended any possibility of *Lanikai*'s being fitted with submarine-listening gear. So for a week she patrolled under sail outside the harbor entrance. To everyone's genuine surprise nothing collapsed when several test rounds were fired from the three-pounder. Monster cockroaches and ancient debris tumbled out of crannies, but if there were any rats aboard, no one saw them. More likely, in the wise ways of ships' rats, they got the gist of F.D.R.'s message and left *Lanikai* for better duty elsewhere.

Blundering through the minefield channel twice daily— even though the mines were "friendly"—clearly was a greater menace to *Lanikai* than her patrols might be to the Imperial Navy. So on December 24 she was called alongside the pier to help evacuate Navy headquarters.

With the Asiatic Fleet falling back on Java, there was no point in Hart's remaining; he turned over local Naval command to Rear Admiral Francis W. Rockwell, commandant 16th Naval District, and departed southward on December 26. The day before, a very unmerry Christmas, Hart's flag lieutenant, Lieutenant Commander Charles Adair, jumped down to *Lani-*

kai's deck and, without much trouble located me.

"Skipper, I've got a proposition," Adair told me without preamble. "How'd you like to take a crack at running the blockade to Java? The boss is leaving by submarine. No space for staff. It's a long chance and your ship. What do you say?"

My reply was instant: "When do we start?"

Admiral Rockwell having reluctantly given permission, *Lanikai* hurriedly took in provisions, fuel, and water. "Go to sea in *that* thing?" goodnaturedly gibed a sailor who was not a member of the crew. "You gotta outboard motor?" There was assorted advice, including a reminder to blow up our water wings before starting.

"Departed Corregidor 1940 (7:40 P.M.), destination unknown"—*Lanikai*'s log entry for December 16—gave her crew of eighteen and six passengers not the mildest clue that during the next three months four thousand perilous miles would pass under the keel while all hands labored under the well-founded suspicion that the Japanese navy might be expected behind the next island.

It had been a grueling day, rounding up supplies and swabbing on green paint, but there was no lack of eager lookouts straining all senses to catch a whiff of smoke, spot a feather of bow wave, hear the clang of a slammed hatch or a dropped tool. Sounds carry far on a still night at sea, and there was the certain prospect that anything afloat or aloft would have to be enemy. Aboard *Lanikai* there was only the creaking and groaning of the hull, the slap of blocks and rigging, and the gentle *pffut-pffut-pffut* of the auxiliary.

So began *Lanikai*'s hegira, beating her five- or six-knot way south, sailing by night and holing up by day as close to island greenery as depth of water allowed. Her fresh meat was the scrawny chickens bartered for shotgun shells and the fish caught alongside, all washed down with rainwater and coconut milk.

One remembers with a little chill the might-have-beens: the near-miss bullets and bombs—fire on board—passing almost under the Japanese guns at Jolo—groundings that could have been the end of the road—sighting enemy warships against the sunset sky—near-disaster south of Java when a great Japanese carrier force swept around *Lanikai*, which was saved by her own insignificance, just another slightly larger whitecap on a typhoon-tortured sea.

There had been good moments too. "Dot Nederlander of yourss hass got a zuspicious aggzent!" bellowed the skipper of a small Dutch warship, her guns trained out, when Lieutenant Paul Nygh, Royal Netherlands Navy, a *Lanikai* passenger, answered his hail. "Doc" Cossette, pharmacist's mate, slacked fire during a Surabaja air raid long enough to shake his fist at the Dutch cruiser *Tromp* alongside. "You squarehead bastards!" he cried, "You've cut our foresail halyards with your goddamn popguns!" To engineer Crispin Tipay, a near-miss meant only one thing: "Queek, boyss! Get the dinghy. Thot bomb just keel a lot of feesh!" There was a pleasant interlude on the island of Bali. Then, at last, Australia, with its hospitality and rough humor. Baskets of groceries came aboard without bills, sometimes with a forbidden bottle of brandy hidden beneath. "Year foitin' fer *us*, airen't ye now, mite? There's nao price tag to *thot!*" they said.

Over the decades that followed, my suspicions first aroused by Commander Slocum's apparent cynicism—his suggestion about asking the Japanese for water continued to grow. A clue here, a conversation there, gleanings from the archives declassified bit by bit, brought into clearer focus the intent that lay behind the President's message. Over thirty years later Slocum, now a rear admiral, wrote: "I feel sure you realise that when you were ready to sail ... most of us understood time had almost run out, and that whatever 'FDR had in mind' could in all probability never be carried off." What indeed *did* FDR have in mind?

It seems clear that the part of the message beginning with "AT THE SAME TIME" was Stark's addition, conveying to his close friend and frequent correspondent Hart that he was innocent of any complicity in the actual as opposed to the stated purpose of *Lanikai*'s assignment. On his own, Hart had commenced overflights of Camranh Bay on about November 23, and on November 30 Ingersoll sent him a dispatch "legalizing" this. His hand-written rough draft bears an "OK, Stark" and "Read to the President and he approved." The resulting information was flowing in, and it was in fact the abundance of intelligence on Japanese movements that caused Hull's urgent call to Roosevelt at Warm Springs to hurry back to face the obvious crisis. There was no need for a "defensive information patrol"—but at the same time the almost constant American reconnaissance of the waters in which the patrol was to operate would have produced a quick report if *Lanikai* (for example) had been attacked by the Japanese.

One of the first in whom suspicions were aroused was Representative Frank B. Keefe, of Wisconsin, who told the Joint Committee on the Investigation of the Pearl Harbor Attack in 1945:

. . . Admiral Hart was already conducting reconnaissance off that coast by planes from Manila. So far as the Navy was concerned, sufficient information was being received from this air reconnaissance. Had the Japanese fired on any of these small vessels, it would have constituted an overt act on the part of Japan.

Grilled by Michigan's Senator Homer Ferguson before the same body, Admiral Ingersoll repeatedly testified that the message was wholly the President's idea; that Admiral Stark would not have initiated such a movement and was satisfied with the information Hart already was furnishing; that if the President gave Stark any reasons, including for the "suggested" use of Filipino crewmen, Stark did not pass them on to him. Ferguson's final question was, "Could you tell us whether or not these were really men-of-war, so that if they had been fired on it would have been an overt act against the United States?" "It would have been," replied Ingersoll.

Admiral Hart testified also. In July, 1967, he wrote me: "I was a full day on the stand before that Committee. In a long forenoon of it, Ferguson, Brewster and Keefe took a lot of time shooting questions at me. All were pretty clumsy, not having much in their minds to go on." This was unfortunate, as in October, 1970, Admiral Hart wrote me that "only Admiral Stark could have *known* anything more of the inception—the whys and wherefores—of the picket ship idea (than I)."

Sumner Welles, F.D.R.'s Undersecretary of State, in 1950 pointed up Roosevelt's agonizing dilemma:

He did, however make it very plain to me that he thought the immediate danger was an attack by Japan upon some British possession in the Far East, or even more probably upon the Netherlands East Indies. What worried him deeply was that, though it might be impossible to persuade either the Congress or the American people . . . it was tantamount to an attack on our own frontiers and justified military measures in self defense. He felt, however, that Japan would not attack the United States directly until and unless we found ourselves in the European war.

Roosevelt was equally unsure of the Philippines and their mercurial president, Manuel Quezon. So on November 26, 1941, he directed U.S. High Commissioner Francis B. Sayre to consult Quezon "in great confidence" to try to determine if the Philippines would support the United States in the event she found herself at war with Japan. Those Filipino crewmen aboard the "three small ships" might just help Quezon and his countrymen make up their minds in case of any Japanese attack.

Would Roosevelt have gone for an incident? In December, 1971, the British released the minutes of an August 19, 1941, cabinet meeting, indirectly quoting Churchill's remarks covering his Argentia conference with Roosevelt a week earlier:

He (Roosevelt) obviously was determined that they should come in. . . . If they were to put up the issue of peace or war to Congress, they would debate it for months. . . . The President had said that he would wage war but not declare it and that he would become more provocative. If the Germans did not like it, they could attack American forces. . . . The President's orders to these (convoy) escorts were to attack any German U-boat which showed itself even if it were 200 to 300 miles away from the convoy. *Everything was to be done to force an incident* (Italics supplied).

There seems to be no reason to suppose that after Hull's tough message to the Japanese on November 26 Roosevelt's idea of forcing an incident was not applicable to the Pacific and the Japanese as well as to the Atlantic and the Germans.

Some respected historians, such as Samuel Eliot Morison, have seized on Roosevelt's proclivity for dabbling in Naval affairs as an explanation of his "three small ships" directive. Morison, using as an example the cruisers that F.D.R. earlier had proposed "to keep popping up here and there, and keep the Japs guessing," brushes off the "picket boats" episode with a footnote:

The President's later proposal to Admiral Hart to operate river gunboats *[sic]* as picket boats in the South China Sea does not stem from the same idea, but from a desire to supplement the work of our patrol planes in reporting Japanese ship movements. The suggestion made at the Pearl Harbor Inquiry that this was an international provocation was disingenuous; the United States Navy has a right to send its ships anywhere on the high seas.

Why then "ISABEL.... BUT NOT OTHER NAVAL VESSELS"—only ships that did not *look* like Naval vessels? Why those "MINIMUM" tokens of a Naval vessel that "WOULD SUFFICE"? Why Filipino crewmen when F.D.R. knew that Hart had seven thousand U.S. seamen to draw on? Neither Morison nor any of the many witnesses questioned on the subject before the congressional investigating committee provided any satisfactory answers. And as for silence, it is far more eloquent than words.

In May, 1952, Rear Admiral John B. Heffernan, director of Naval History, asked Admiral Hart to review Morison's book and offer corrections. Included in the latter was one on the footnote covering the "three small ships" episode: "Footnote 20 should be rewritten to accord with facts or be entirely omitted; it is not a piece of history of which to be proud."

One spring day in 1970 I was having a prelunch sherry with Admirals Harry Hill and Thomas Hart. "I once had the unpleasant requirement to send this young man on what looked like a one-way mission," Hart told Hill in explanation of our past association. Then he recounted *Lanikai*'s narrow escape from the dragon's mouth. "Would you tell Admiral Hill if you think we were set up to bait an incident, a *casus belli?*" I asked him.

"Yes, I think you were bait!" said Admiral Hart. "And I could prove it. But I *won't*. And don't *you* try it, either!"

We *are* trying, Admiral Hart. And in remembrance of your near clairvoyance in foreseeing the shape of coming events in the Far East, we can only hope that in looking down from an old sailor's snug retreat you will approve of setting the record straight.

—June 1984

"GOD, PLEASE GET US OUT OF THIS"

by STEPHEN BOWER YOUNG

A carefree Sunday lay ahead for the Oklahoma's mess cook. His pockets jingled, and a pretty girl awaited him for a picnic on a warm, white beach. Minutes later he lay entombed at the bottom of Pearl Harbor.

The world was my oyster that Sunday morning in December, 1941. I was nineteen, breakfast was over, and liberty would be starting in an hour or so. A quick look out a second-deck porthole of our battleship, the U.S.S. *Oklahoma,* confirmed my feeling that this was going to be a glorious day. There were still some early morning clouds, but the sun was warm, with just a breath of trade wind ruffling the waters of the harbor. I turned to swab down the deck around me. Someone had spilled coffee there.

I would be happy to get this three-month tour of mess-cooking over with so that I could get back on deck again. Topside had been my cleaning station for the past year, ever since I had come on board ship in Long Beach. I liked being out in the weather, scrubbing and holystoning decks, scraping and painting the bulkheads or gun-turret sides, shining brightwork, splicing line, rigging boat booms, and working at the aviation crane, aft. I had made seaman first as soon as I was eligible and expected to make cox'n in the spring. But I often wondered whether I should strike for gunner's mate instead. The 14-inch guns in the division's massive No. 4 turret aft fascinated me. My battle station was in the upper starboard powder-hoist room where we rolled the heavy powder bags through flameproof doors into the turret chamber to feed the guns.

The *Oklahoma* was old, but she had a kind of dignity, with her broad beam and tripod masts. The home of a thousand sailors, she had never fired a gun in anger, not even in World War I. Her cruising speed was only ten knots or so, but when she left the Golden Gate behind and began to push her ponderous bulk into the Pacific swells, you could feel her strength. I was proud to be a sailor in her crew.

All non-rated hands had to take their turn as mess cooks before going up for a rate. It was compulsory, but I had managed to avoid it until I had no choice. Now, only a few more weeks remained of lugging steaming tureens of chow up and down ladders from the midship galley to the living compartment aft where the fourth-deck division messed as well as slept. It always seemed a long way back and forth to our fantail hatch, a trip I made a dozen or so times a meal, not counting runs for seconds. But in a heavy sea, while balancing a tureen of soup in one hand and a platter of baked ham in the other, it seemed even longer. Setting up tables and carrying racks of dirty dishes to the scullery was no fun either, but the six of us who had the duty worked hard and made the best of it. It had been pretty easy this morning, for the boys had been on the town in Honolulu last night and were sleeping late. Everyone was up now, though, and I was anxious to make that first liberty launch ashore. One of my buddies grinned, "Don't hurry, your girl will wait."

"We're going on a picnic," I told him, as, together, we heaved up the last mess table and secured it.

My girl and I were going to Nanakuli, where the surf was much better than Waikiki and the beach not nearly so crowded. For once I had plenty of money—a ten and a one-dollar bill. Nice going at fifty-four bucks a month with a week of the month already gone.

The compartment rocked with shouts and laughter—with only a muffled undertone of growls from the duty-section men who had to stay on board and derive most of their day's amusement from the Sunday funnies.

I looked at my watch. Two minutes to morning colors. I started toward my locker.

Suddenly the bugle blared over the PA system. The sound filled the compartment. The first few notes told me it was not colors or calling away a motor launch. I stopped and listened. It was the call for gun crews to man their antiaircraft stations.

The word was passed, "Man the antiaircraft batteries!" Not my station, I thought. And what a crazy time to hold a drill!

"What's going on?" we asked each other. But no one knew, and we returned to whatever we had been doing.

Again the bugle tore the air. Now it was the call to general quarters! A voice boomed throughout the ship—"All hands, man your battle stations!" What the hell was this? Drills on Sunday? They knew we were all waiting to go ashore.

The harsh, excited voice on the PA system froze us in our tracks. "All hands, man your battle stations! On the double! This is no drill! Get going—they're real bombs!"

I headed for my turret battle station. Everyone was running and pushing. The ship shuddered as she was hit somewhere forward. I stumbled, but managed to stay on my feet. The lights went out just as I reached the ladder going down to the deck below. I groped my way, and as I hit the deck the emergency lights went on dimly. Another ladder to go. Another hit. Close by, this time. The deck heaved, but I hung on. The emergency lights went out momentarily. Obviously, we were being badly hit.

Finally, I made it down the ladder, slipping and sliding on the rungs following the man in front of me and avoiding the feet of the sailor behind, through the barbette and into the turret. The crew was milling around manning stations and scrambling up inside the turret to the guns above. I climbed up to the shell deck on my way to the hoist room. The officer in charge—the same one who had passed the word—ordered, "Stay below, men. Below the armored deck. These 14-inch guns are no good against planes. I'm going topside to see what's going on!" He never returned.

On the way back to the powder-handling room, I stumbled over a kneeling figure, fumbling at a shoe lace. He looked up and I saw that he was crying. He was a petty officer, a real tough guy, merciless in his treatment of the crew. I moved on.

The powder-handling room was crowded. Indistinctly I could see the faces of my friends, frightened, anxious, and unbelieving. Standing against the bulkhead, I grabbed for support as another hit made the deck beneath us jump. Until now, we supposed they were bombs, and felt almost safe below the armored deck. No one had thought yet of torpedoes tearing away a ship's side.

Then someone yelled and pointed to a spot where water

was pouring in through the lower portside bulkhead. The ship was listing slightly. Horrified, we watched the water rise and felt the deck slipping from under us as the list became more pronounced. Gear of all descriptions commenced to tumble about, and sailors began to scramble for the ladder leading upward. "All our breakfast dishes must be breaking!" I blurted. There was some nervous laughter from the few who knew I was a mess cook. "Don't laugh," I said. "They'll take it out of my pay."

We tried to get up the ladder to the next deck above. A few men attempted to wriggle up through an emergency escape tube which was only two or three feet wide. But it was useless: they got stuck before they could make it out. I raised my head above the shell-deck level just as the *Oklahoma*'s enormous shells, weighing a ton apiece, broke loose from their moorings and rolled wildly down the slanting deck where sailors were fighting to stay on their feet. There was no possible escape for these men, and I recoiled from the terrible sights and sounds.

Ducking back down into the handling room, I shouted, "They're just counterflooding to get us back on an even keel so they can fire the guns." This information seemed to calm the men for a few moments, but as the list increased, their excitement mounted. Sailors fell down the deck and met their deaths violently. Numbly I watched two friends of mine, arms and legs waving wildly, as they and the gear which had knocked them off their feet smashed into the debris at the bottom of the slanting deck. By the faint light I could see that they had joined others—floating face down in the water.

I clutched at the bulkhead, barely able to stay on my feet as the water flooded in. That was when the dreaded phrase was passed from man to man throughout the ship, "Abandon ship! Abandon ship!"

More shells broke loose. I could see them coming and yelled to a cox'n friend across the tilting deck, who was hanging onto the powder hoist, "Catch me! I'm coming over!" It was terribly clear to me that if he were unable to catch me, or if I were to lose my grip, I would slide helplessly down the deck and be slammed into the farther bulkhead either to drown or be crushed by those shells.

Desperately, I leaped across the space between us. He caught my outstretched arm as I vaulted from the path of the rolling shells. I think I thanked him as I grabbed the powder hoist and hung on. Looking up, I saw the head and shoulders of a sailor hanging upside down from the hatch above. His arms hung limply, swaying slightly. I had known him. We had gone through training together in Newport, played baseball there and in the Fleet. I looked away from his inverted eyes.

We could not get out. We were being hit again and again, dreadful, tearing hits. We realized all at once that these were not bombs, but torpedoes. And the ship was wide open, no watertight integrity at all. Every compartment, every void space, was open to the sea once the hull was torn apart. It had never happened that way before that I could remember, but there was an inspection scheduled for the next day and all spaces had been ordered opened.

The list rapidly increased until it seemed that the ship was almost lying on her side. With awful certainty we knew that we were sinking. Suddenly the ship lurched! The deck slipped out from under me and my hands snatched at empty air. As she rolled over, I was pitched into a mass of dead and dying and, with them, buffeted and tossed about. Then the dark waters closed over me as the ship came to rest upside down on the bottom of the harbor.

Eventually I surfaced, gulped for air, and swam desperately in the darkness, surprised to find myself alive. Random shouts mingled with cries for help; then quiet fell abruptly. Water gurgled as it made its way into the ship. I thought we were done for.

Suddenly, a voice I recognized cried, "Help! I can't swim!"

Someone switched on a battle lantern. It still worked, thank heaven. The light shone eerily in the darkness. The handling room was a shambles. Loose gear and dead bodies were floating everywhere.

I swam to the man who had called and grabbed him by the hair to hold him above water. An opening was spotted leading to a passageway, and we all swam for the hatch with my friend safely in tow. We gained the passageway and found it was only partly full of water. A hasty head count showed thirty of us huddled there.

I volunteered to take a look around and jumped along a half-submerged ladder to take the lantern. "It's a good thing this has waterproof batteries," I observed. "Everybody knows how dependable they are." We smiled a little, remembering the magazine advertisements and illustrations of people in tough spots who were saved by their trusty flashlights. "Don't go away," I added. "I'll be back." No one said anything except that they knew there was no way out.

Taking a deep breath, I ducked under water, reached another compartment, and surfaced. Flashing the light around, I saw that I was in a flooded living compartment. It was difficult to orient myself. There should be a porthole or escape hatch here, but I could see nothing except floating mattresses and bodies. When I finally found a porthole, there was a body stuck in it, a plump body. I grabbed the feet and yanked, but couldn't budge him. The irony of it! Slim as I was, I could have made it through. Everything else was blocked and jammed. I found my way back to the passageway and broke the bad news to the men.

Other areas were investigated, but we found no way out. We were in a pocket of air that had been trapped as the ship went down. Although our space was only partially flooded, we knew it was simply a matter of time until the air gave out and the water took over. It was rising slowly. We settled back to wait. Rescue seemed neither probable nor possible. I was sure that if the Navy could rescue us, it would. But by now, for all we knew, the Japs might have taken over Pearl Harbor anyway. The situation seemed hopeless.

"No talking," ordered a voice out of the dark. "We've got to save the air."

"For what?" another asked. No answer.

We had turned off the light to conserve the batteries. The voice was right: unnecessary talking would use up the air, so we remained silent in the darkness. The men settled back with their thoughts. I lay curled up on a piece of metal overhang. Others sat on the half-submerged ladder or against the upper bulkhead. Although we were upside down, the ship was not quite perpendicular to the bottom. There was an angle of thirty degrees or so. We were fortunate in that respect: we could keep out of the water somewhat.

Only a short time had passed since the bugle had called us to action, and my watch was still ticking. The ship must have gone down in fifteen minutes. It happened too quickly for us to have known much fear, too quickly for us to get out. On the other hand, it had seemed like a lifetime.

Time crawled. The water rose slowly as the air was used, steadily pushing its way into the broken ship. The bodies of our shipmates bobbed against the handling-room entrance to the passageway. It seemed as if they wanted to join the living there. We moved them behind some wreckage. There was nothing we could do for them, nor they for us. Sooner or later we would join our dead comrades. Perhaps others were joining me in silent prayer, "God, please get us out of this."

The taste and smell of fuel oil was sickening. Occasionally a man would move off, determined to seek some way of escape. None returned, however. But each man's life was all he had, and he was entitled to try to save it as best he could.

There were less than twenty of us left, but, incredibly, there was no panic. The hours passed by. The water level rose inexorably, inch by awful inch. I thought of home. Days of growing up. People I had known. Long summer days of hard farm work, but with lots of time for fun. Swimming, fishing. Pleasant thoughts. Even now, in the darkness, the memories brought a smile. My family. They were a source of strength to me.

It had been more than a year since I had seen them. They had all waved goodbye as I walked out of the yard that morning. How would they take the news of my death? With sadness, certainly, but with a reserved pride. I hoped they would be all right.

My watch stopped finally. Time did not matter. I dropped it in the water with a splash. Then I took out a pocketful of change and dropped the coins absently into the water. There was a place in town where *Oklahoma* sailors met to drink beer, sing songs of the Navy, tell sea stories, dance with their girls, laugh, and fight with sailors from other ships. Remembering it, I couldn't resist saying aloud, "How about a cold beer? I'm thirsty."

"Set 'em up, all the way around," a sailor replied.

"Join the Navy and see the world—from the bottom of Pearl Harbor."

No one seemed to mind the wisecracks. It was crazy, maybe, but everyone seemed to relax a bit.

The hours moved on. It was probably dark above us now, and it seemed darker here, somehow.

Breaking another long silence, one of the men recalled that there was an escape hatch here. "It's narrow and goes straight down, thirty feet or so to the main deck. Let's give it a try." I had to orient myself because "up" was now "down," and we were actually sitting on the overhead. I hadn't even known there was such a hatch right here. We turned on the light.

However, since it was more than three decks down the hatch, all under water, across the main deck and then up to the surface, escape did not seem probable. No one could hold his breath that long, and there might very well be obstructions, too. The hatch was only as big around as a man's body. But we had nothing to lose and any action was welcome. A man volunteered to try. We took off our skivvy shirts and made a sort of life line to guide him back. "So long," he said. He disappeared and did not return. Other men tried, but none of them returned. Soon the skivvy-shirt string hung slack. I decided to wait, although I didn't know why. It was as if someone had told me to wait, because somehow I was not afraid.

Time went by. As the water rose, the air became more and more foul. I felt a longing to break the silence again.

"Willy," I said, "I'll bet you a dollar we'll suffocate before we drown." "Okay, you're on," agreed Willy. "I say we drown first." We each produced a soggy dollar bill, after which we lapsed again into silence.

Once we heard firing way above us; it sounded strange coming down through the water in the darkness and the silence. I tried to imagine what was going on up there. It must be night, because more than half a day had passed. The Japs had really caught us napping, but that was the extent of our knowledge. We had seen nothing before the *Oklahoma* went down. Had the other ships also been sunk? Were the Japanese landing troops? Not knowing was terrible.

My thoughts were kaleidoscopic—school, family, my Navy life. I thought of pretty girls, laughing, full of life. I felt terribly alone, and blurted, "Damn it, I'm not even twenty and I'll never know or love a girl again!" At that moment this loss seemed stronger than any other. No one said anything, presumably out of silent agreement.

"It's getting worse," a voice said out of the dark, "we'll have to move. The Lucky Bag compartment [the ship's lost-and-found locker] is right next to us. Let's try to get in there if it isn't flooded."

This compartment went nowhere, but at least it would be more comfortable, with stacks of mattresses and peacoats to lie on. We turned on the flashlight and tested for air through a hole in the compartment bulkhead. There was no evidence of water so we opened the hatch and moved in. I kicked off my shoes and stretched out on a pile of clothing, lying there in what remained of the uniform of the day—oil-stained shorts. The dollar bill was safely tucked away in my watch pocket. I lay next to the bulkhead, along the slant of the deck, feet toward the water in the lower part of the compartment. It was rising slowly.

Sudden shouts through the bulkhead told us there was another group like ours in the adjoining space. We talked to them, briefly. Their situation was similar to ours; they, too, were trapped.

Water lapped over the hatch opening into the passageway. By now, we were only vaguely aware of time as we fell again into silence. Each of us was alone with himself in our living tomb.

Suddenly, anger rumbled within me. Why couldn't we have died in the sun where we could have met death head on? That was the way to die, on your feet, like a man. But instead, it was to be a slow, useless death, imprisoned in our dark iron cell.

Still, perhaps to die like this required a special kind of courage. Could I meet the test? "Oh, God," I prayed, "relieve us of our torment. If it is Your will that we die here, please watch over our families and comfort them. We are delivered unto You and ask to be forgiven for our sins."

The hours passed. . . .

Unexpectedly, and from a great distance, came the sound of hammering. Metal against metal! Our hearts jumped. The sound stopped, and we held our breaths. It started again, closer, and died away once more.

"What is it?" someone asked. "Is it possible they can reach us?"

"No. I don't know," said another.

"Quiet. Listen."

We looked around, not seeing anything in the dark, of course, but looking anyway. Ears strained for the sound to begin once more. It seemed an eternity. Was help on the way? Then the noise began again, not sporadically, but like the knock of an automatic tool. Did it mean rescuers? Why was the sound fainter now? It stopped again. Were they unable to find a route to us through the sunken ship? I dared not hope, but my heart pounded.

We hammered at the steel bulkhead with a dog wrench. Three dots—three dashes—three dots—SOS!!

We must let them know we're here. It had to be a pneumatic air hammer! It had to be! Or were the spaces over us and under us so flooded that we were sealed away? There it was again. Louder! Much louder now. Then, suddenly, silence.

"They're trying to get us," someone said. We rapped out the SOS again. Ten of us are still alive in here. We've been here a day—a whole twenty-four hours in this awful place. We were thirty, but now we're ten. The others are gone.

We yelled to the men in the next compartment. The noise had been coming from that direction. Their excited replies told us they, too, thought rescue was on the way. Now the rapping started again, closer, stopped, starting once more. We waited in an agony of suspense.

Abruptly, the silence of our compartment was broken as a yell sounded from the next compartment. Workers had broken through to them! They shouted to the rescue party that there were others trapped—us! We knocked frantically against the bulkhead! A voice was heard shouting above the clamor, "Can you stand a hole? We'll drill a small one through."

"Yes, yes, go ahead and drill!" A sailor flashed on the battle lantern. A hole appeared halfway up the bulkhead as the drill bit through the metal and then retreated. There was a loud hissing as the air pressure within and without equalized. The water began to pour in as the air rushed out! We had never thought of this. We could see the water flooding in through the hatch. Men jumped swiftly across the deck to close the hatch and dog it down. They secured it top and bottom, but water sprayed through the sides.

"Keep calm, fellows," a worker called. "We'll get you out!"

They began to cut through the metal. I watched, fascinated, tortured by the slow progress as the cut was made horizontal to the deck. We could see the blade push the cut along. Someone yelled, "Burn us out!" They replied, "No, you'd suffocate. Hold on! Hold on just a little longer!"

The water had risen to our knees. "Hurry! Hurry up!" we shouted as the downward cut began. I turned to look at the hatch. It was bulging inward at the center. Even that heavy metal could not withstand so great a water pressure. Would we all drown like rats at the last minute, just when rescue was at hand? It was going to be close, so close!

"Please hurry, for God's sake! We can't stop this flooding!" The cutting tool began its progress down the third side of the square. We watched, hypnotized. It was maddeningly slow. The water was now waist high. Would the hatch hold?

"We're going to bend it out," a voice spoke through the bulkhead. So close, yet a world away, separated from us by a quarter of an inch of steel, or less. It was the difference between life and death. Fingers pulled at the three-sided metal cut. I pushed at it. It was bending. There was no time to complete the cutting job. Gradually the opening widened as the water pushed at us from behind. It would be just wide enough to scrape through.

"Okay! Come on through!" voices called. We entered the opening in a flood of water. Friendly hands reached for our oil-slicked bodies and pulled us into the next compartment. We were free! Gratefully I searched the faces of our rescuers—big Hawaiian Navy Yard workers and some sailors. The Navy indeed took care of its own.

"Here, up on my shoulders, boy," said one of the men in the accent of the Islands. He smiled and I smiled back. "Thanks a lot," was all I could say. They boosted me from man to man and from space to space up through the bottom of the ship. Finally I emerged from out of the cold darkness into the warm sunshine of a new day. It was 0900, 8 December.

Standing on the upturned hull, I gazed about me. It was the same world I had left twenty-five hours before, but as I looked at the smoke and wreckage of battle, the sunken ships *Tennessee, West Virginia,* and *Arizona* astern of us, I felt that life would never be the same, not for me—not for any of us. I took a few drags on a cigarette. Someone said to put it out because of all the oil around.

A launch came alongside to take us to a hospital ship. As I stepped into the boat, I looked down at the ship we had lived in, the ship we had come so close to dying in, the tomb of friends and shipmates who were gone forever. The mighty *Oklahoma* was no more. The flag, the colored signal pennants would never fly again. Her guns were silent, her turrets full of men and water. How strange that never in all her life had she ever fired at an enemy.

The launch chugged along out into the harbor. Turning to the sailor who had bet a dollar with me on how we would die, I grinned at him. "Put the buck away for a souvenir, Willy. We both lost."

—April 1966

THE SIEGE OF WAKE ISLAND

by JOHN R. BURROUGHS

The doomed defense of a Pacific outpost, as seen by a civilian construction engineer who endured sixteen days of hell.

On Monday morning, December 8 (Wake Island time; it was December 7 at Pearl Harbor), 1941, we reported for work at seven o'clock as usual. At about eight, my friend Bob Bryan, a clerk in the engineering office, came to my desk, greatly excited.

"There's a report coming in on the radio that the Japs have attacked Pearl Harbor, and are bombing and machine-gunning Schofield Barracks!" he exclaimed.

I heard trucks rumbling over the Peale Island bridge. (Wake Island is actually an atoll composed of three islands: Peale, Wilkes, and the largest, Wake.) Looking out of the window, I saw the usual working party of marines who were building machine-gun pits on the windward side of Peale Island pass by. For the first time they were in full battle dress, with packs, helmets, and rifles. This gave me pause for thought, but still the urgency of compiling my reports in time to get them aboard the eastbound clipper was uppermost in my mind.

The radio reports persisted, however. Men began leaving their drawing boards and desks and circling about the engineering office uneasily. The China Clipper had taken off that morning, continuing its routine flight to Guam; but soon after its departure I was astounded to see it circling in from the west, low on the horizon.

Just about noon, a loud explosion occurred, followed by a series of similar ones that shook the building, violently rattling the windows in their casements. The first thought entering my mind was that the drill crews had set off some particularly heavy charges in the lagoon—for they had been at work for the past month blasting coral-heads to clear the seaplane runways. But outside, the lagoon was placid in the sunlight.

I joined a group of men from my department and from the engineering office who were running into the hall and toward the exterior door. Then for the first time I heard the drone of engines and the rapid staccato of machine-gun fire. Someone yelled, "Hit the floor!"

I crawled to the door on my hands and knees to look out. All along the water front clouds of black smoke were pouring upward; crossing the lagoon at an altitude of five or six hundred feet, headed in our direction, were three squadrons of two-engine bombers in tight V-formations. It flashed through my mind that very probably they would bomb our camp. "Outside!" I yelled, and running down the steps, I raced across the road and threw myself under a stunted tree.

Men were running in all directions seeking what sparse cover there was in the area. All around us, machine-gun bullets were kicking up little spurts of dust like the impact of heavy raindrops on a dirt road. I heard a swift tearing sound directly overhead and looked up into a shower of shredded leaves. At the same time, as though a sharp stick had been drawn across the ground, a stream of bullets cut a line in the dirt parallel to, and scarcely eight inches distant from, my body. The Japanese planes were flying so low that I could plainly see the crewmen peering out of the cockpits.

By now, Pan American's buildings and installations, as well as many of the permanent establishments that we had built on Peale Island, were roaring infernos of flame and smoke corkscrewing into the sky. Evidently the Japanese had expended their bomb load on our land-plane runway, for they passed over our camp strafing but not bombing. After they disappeared, I stood up, feeling queer in the knees. I looked at my watch. It was twelve o'clock "straight up." From beginning to end the attack had not lasted more than four or five minutes.

I ran back into the office, grabbed the cost ledgers, shoved them in a filing cabinet, and closed and locked the drawer. Reynold Carr, one of my clerks, called, "Hey, look at this!" A bullet had drilled a neat hole through the seat of his chair. He had missed death by seconds. We found other holes in the floor and walls.

Leaving the office, I walked toward the mess hall. It being near mealtime, scores of men had been on the mall when the attack came, and yet, miraculously, none of them had been hit. Men were now scattered about in little groups, talking in hushed voices, some squatting on their heels intently digging in the ground with pocketknives in search of bullets. Williamson, the assistant steward, came out of the mess hall and climbed on a table. "There'll be no seating today," he said. "We'll serve lunch cafeteria-style. Get in line. Pass through the kitchen to get your grub, then go outside—and don't bunch up."

I gulped the food, returned the utensils to the mess hall, and crossing to my bunkhouse, hurriedly made up a bedroll. I looked at the pictures on the shelf, hesitated a moment, and decided to leave them and my other possessions where they were. Shouldering the bedroll and pocketing toothbrush, tooth powder, and some chocolate bars I had purchased at the canteen, I left. I never entered the bunkhouse again. It was bombed out of existence the following day.

My bunkhouse was situated on a side road debouching on the arterial road which led to the Peale Island bridge. As I approached the main road, I saw two trucks and a pickup crossing the bridge very slowly; I stepped aside to permit them to turn down the side road to the hospital. The truck swung around the curve, a corner of its tail gate passing within a foot of my face. Its bed was covered with wounded, dying, and dead men, sprawled on rumpled, bloody quilts. Nearest me, his head, neck, and shoulder a lacerated mass, was a man whose arm was connected to his body by the merest shred of flesh. Half of his skull had been blown away, and his brains were oozing through the jagged aperture onto the quilt. The second truck and the pickup carried the same grim cargo.

Work parties were being made up in front of the contractor's office. I remember Lieutenant Commander Elmer Greey, the Navy's resident officer in the construction camp, asking me if I was arranging transportation back home and my reply that I was scheduled to report to the Marine camp with a party of volunteers. We tossed our bedrolls onto a truck and climbed in.

Our immediate task was the decentralization of .30 and .50-caliber machine-gun ammunition. Speed was imperative. The heavy cases were stacked in great piles high under the rafters of a long, sheet-iron warehouse building. Men swarmed up these piles while those of us below formed two lines. The cases began moving out rapidly. We shoved them aboard a truck, which transported them out to the parade ground where they were unloaded and hastily buried.

Before we had completed the decentralization of the small arms ammunition, ten of us were assigned to a detail engaged in trucking three-inch antiaircraft shells from temporary frame magazines to the gun batteries. Above five o'clock, we finished supplying the Wilkes Island battery, and headed in our truck for the contractor's camp. As we crossed the east-west runway of the airfield, a sad sight, formidable in its implications, met our eyes. Seven of our twelve Grumman Wildcat fighters were broken in two, their empennages and radial engines pointing skyward at sharp angles. Four of them had been set on fire by machine-gun strafing, and three were damaged beyond repair by close bomb hits. An eighth plane had been damaged but was in repairable condition.

Our Marine aviation personnel had also suffered heavy casualties. Of the pilots, First Lieutenant George Graves and Second Lieutenants Frank Holden and Robert Conderman had been killed, and Second Lieutenant Henry Webb severely wounded. The casualties had been proportionately heavy among the members of the ground crew. The loss of these pilots, as well as seven of our twelve fighter planes, on the first day of hostilities was the worst possible blow to our defenses.

All the planes had been aloft most of the morning; at the time of the attack, however, only four were up, the others having returned to base for refueling. Had the enemy delayed twenty minutes, we would have had eight planes in the sky, with two more ready to take off.

The initial success of the Japanese in taking the island by surprise can be attributed to the skill with which they made use of cloud cover. All morning the sky had been overcast, and a long dense cloud bank lay parallel to and directly above Wake's lee shore. Apparently the Japanese came in high, and while still far out to sea, cut their engines. They glided in, darting out of this cloud bank at an altitude of a thousand or fifteen hundred feet, and were over our airfield before we were aware of their existence.

At ten o'clock that night I found myself a member of a crew unloading antiaircraft shells near the extremity of Peacock Point. Fred Hauner, one of the men from my department, was with me. When we had unloaded the truck, Fred and I headed down the trail toward the Five-Inch battery. A sentry challenged us. "This is Burroughs," I answered. "Where is Lieutenant Baringer?"

Sergeant Boscarino, gun captain on gun No. 1, came up. "We've fixed up foxholes for you men. That's what we were doing during the bombing. We didn't waste any time. Come on and I'll show you where they are."

Fred and I followed, stumbling in the inky blackness, our feet catching on the creeping vines.

"There it is," Boscarino said, pointing to a smudge one degree blacker than the enveloping night. There was hardly room enough for the two of us to squeeze inside the foxhole. The "floor" was covered with coral cobbles the size of a man's fist. We each had a blanket, a sheet, and a canvas bedcover. I was too exhausted to fall asleep. For a long time I lay twisting on the pernicious coral, trying to avoid the drip of the rain that had begun to fall, and listening to the ominous boom and rumble of the nearby surf.

Fred and I awoke at daybreak and crawled out of our hole. In the west, smoke still ascended from the preceding day's holocaust. We had learned that Pan Am's casualties were ten men—mostly Chamorro boys from Guam—dead, and that some thirty service men had been killed or wounded in the attack on the airport. An undetermined number of contractor's men were casualties. The hospital was full, and the contractor's surgeon, Dr. Lawton Shank, and the Navy medical officer, Lieutenant Gustave Kahn, had operated without rest all during the afternoon and night of December 8.

Fred and I went down to Battery A's range finder and passed the time of day with the marines. Boscarino quickly instructed us in the use of a .30-caliber machine gun, and showed us which foxholes we were to occupy in the event an air raid caught us while we were working around the battery. A klaxon which could be heard all over the point had been rigged up to give the alarm when enemy planes came in sight. Lookouts equipped with binoculars were posted on the range finder shelter, and on top of Lieutenant Baringer's battery command post.

Dead tired from the excitement and the work of the preceding day, and from a sleepless, rain-drenched night, I stretched out on a rock and was nearly asleep when the klaxon sounded. As distant as the drowsy hum of bees on a sultry summer day I could hear the engines of the approaching planes. This time the Japanese did not have the advantage of a surprise attack. First I heard the rapid staccato of our .50-caliber machine guns, and then the close, loud, hollow-sounding "pung-pung-punging" as the AA battery under the command of Lieutenant William Lewis went into action. Fred and I crouched against the rear wall of our foxhole, as far back as it was possible to get from the brilliant splash of sunlight on the white rocks at the entrance.

The enemy flight was passing directly over Peacock Point. Above the ever-present pounding of the surf a new sound came to my ears: first, a swift rustling as of heavy silk; then a shrill thin scream culminating in a shattering explosion. I shrank back, instinctively throwing my arm in front of my eyes. The ground shuddered. Rock fragments were falling on the roof of our foxhole like the steady pounding of heavy rain. A rock the size of my head catapulted into the opening and rolled against my feet. As the sound of bursting bombs grew fainter and fainter, I crawled to the door and looked out.

Nearby, the leaves on the shrubbery were gray-coated with dust. Fred came out of the hole, and we stood on the rocks watching a huge conflagration in the contractor's camp. Soon all of Peale Island and the northwesternmost tip of Wake were blanketed by flame and smoke. Now and then a new wisp of light-gray smoke would rise and mingle with the black, as another frame building took fire.

We went down to the battery command post. Bit by bit, disastrous news came over the wire. The contractor's warehouse in Camp Two had been hit. Our machine shop and adjacent oil and gasoline stores had been completely wiped out. The explosive and incendiary bombs had cut a swath right through the center of the contractor's camp. The Nipponese had succeeded in bombing and burning the company hospital, which was crammed with men wounded in the preceding day's attack. I learned later that my bunkhouse had burned to the ground in this raid, leaving me bereft of all my possessions except the clothing I wore.

One fact of these raids struck me as peculiarly significant. The Japanese had carefully avoided destroying the power-houses in the two camps, the bridge connecting Wake and Peale islands, and the nearly completed Naval Air Station barracks building on Peale. This seemed strange, for without the powerhouses, the fresh water distilleries could not be operated, and without the distilleries we soon would be forced to capitulate because of thirst. But it also occurred to me that perhaps the Japanese were bent not so much on our destruction and the eradication of Wake Island as an effective link in our aerial communications with the Philippines, as they were in preserving our most essential installations for themselves. Of course this meant but one thing: landing parties—an attempt to storm the island—and this posed a serious personal problem to all civilian personnel.

The marines on the island were, essentially, a working party, many of them not long out of boot camp. The first full-strength defense battalion, it was rumored, was not due to arrive until January 9, 1942. Even the servicemen on the island were under-armed. Let me emphasize that the terms of our working agreements with the contractors prohibited our bringing personal weapons to the island. Yet there we were— 1,200 unarmed men—living like rats in the middle of a battlefield! A weapon in a man's hands gives him confidence. We did not have weapons. All we could do was crouch behind rocks and scoot from foxhole to foxhole.

On the morning of December 10 the raid alarm sounded about ten forty-five. This time, 26 planes came over, bombing from Peacock Point to Kuku Point, the heaviest attack having been reserved for the Marine camp, which was ablaze. The water-front oil dump also was on fire.

Just before dawn on the eleventh, I was awakened by shouting outside our foxhole. I heard my name called, and caught the words "all civilians down on the guns."

In the east the sky was slightly less black than total night. I felt the morning mist on my face. Men were emerging from the foxholes and running in the direction of Peacock Point. We followed, stumbling over the sharp coral boulders.

Lieutenant Baringer, a shadowy figure, stood upright on the roof of his command post. He was peering out to sea through his binoculars. I heard him say, "I can't make out what they are. . . ." There were ships lying offshore.

Sergeant Poulousky was coming up the trail. "I want you to take charge of the powder magazine," he said quickly. "Come along." The magazine looked exactly like a big vine-covered coral boulder. In reality the "boulder" was a large tarpaulin stretched over a wooden framework; under this camouflage a rectangle of sandbags outlined a trap door at ground level. We raised the trap door and propped it open. "Watch your head," Poulousky said.

"The shells are on this side," he explained, "and the powder canisters over here. See these shells?" He took my hand and guided it to several shells standing in a vertical position on the floor. "There's nine star shells here. For God's sake don't send *them* up."

I straightened up, bumping my head.

"If we go into action," Poulousky continued, "pass up two shells—one for each gun. Then two powders—understand?"

I followed him back up the ladder. Johnny Clelan and several other civilians were grouped about the entrance.

Poulousky turned to Clelan. "If we go into action, you stand at the head of the ladder here and take the stuff from Burroughs. Send a powder and a shell to gun No. 1, then a powder and a shell to gun No. 2—keep alternating."

We squatted around the magazine on our haunches talking in low tones about what might be "out there." We had heard that contractor's personnel on Johnston, Palmyra, and Midway islands had been evacuated several days previously. Thus we were inclined to think that the ships offshore had brought reinforcements, and, happiest thought of all, probably there would be an aircraft carrier in the flotilla. This optimistic trend of thought was shattered abruptly by Lieutenant Baringer's steady voice: "There's a red ball on her funnel."

Poulousky came tearing from the brush, yelling: "All right, you civilians, break out those shells. . . ." I dived down the ladder and fumbled for the first tier in the darkness. I grasped a shell. Johnny Clelan was crouching in the aperture above. I heaved upward, first a shell, then a powder canister. I could hear Tony Poulousky shouting excitedly: "Come on, you God-damned civilians, hurry up with those shells"; heard the heavy breathing of the men, and the sound of running feet on the coral.

"Okay down there," Poulousky yelled, "we've got

enough stuff on top. Come up for a breather."

I climbed up the ladder, lifted the canvas, and crawling outside, sat down on a rock. A series of long flashes far out at sea lightened the horizon. Seconds later a sound like distant thunder reached my ears. Suddenly flames, followed by a thick column of black smoke, arose in the vicinity of the marines' camp.

The sky was light now, and I could distinguish the outlines of three ships inshore from the horizon. Following closely on the flashes from the enemy guns, I heard Lieutenant Baringer's voice: "Range four thousand. . . ." He was squatting on his heels, binoculars intent on the target, and his voice calling the range came easily. Major Potter, commanding the five-inch gun positions, wisely had given orders to the battery commanders to hold their fire until the Japanese were close in.

Our initial target was a light cruiser broadside to us. The first shot from our gun No. 1 fell far short due to defective range setting, whereas gun No. 2 overshot the target; we were without electrical or compressed air control, and the gun captains were firing by lanyard. On the second salvo both guns fell short; the ship was moving out. Then, methodically, our battery built up to the target until, eight or ten minutes after we had gone into action, we scored a direct hit at a range of about 7,000 yards. It struck square amidship and right at the water line.

First a wisp of white emanated from the warship, followed by a big puff of steam. Brown smoke began billowing from her belly.*

From the smoke rising over the island, I could tell that the Japanese bombardment had set more of our oil tanks afire. Opposite the entrance to the small boat channel between Wake and Wilkes, a transport was hastily drawing off in flames. Far out at sea a small ship had been hit and seemed to be sinking.

The east was crimson and orange now, the earth-curve etched against the sky by the rolling Pacific. Each enemy unit stood clearly limned in the new light. Just beyond the trans-

---

*Lieutenant Baringer's battery had hit the light cruiser *Yubari,* flagship of the Japanese invasion force.

port, a smaller warship was falling apart.

I heard Lieutenant Baringer say: "They're drawing off. . . ." Then: "Range 17,500!" A thrill of enthusiasm ran through me. The Japanese had attacked in considerable strength—there had been at least two cruisers, four or five destroyers, and several auxiliary craft in their flotilla, with a possible fire-power of fifty or sixty naval rifles running up to ten- or twelve-inch caliber available against us—and we had beaten them off with three batteries of five-inch guns!

One of those freakish happenings that sometimes occur in battle chalked up an additional warship for Lieutenant Baringer's battery. From our position we were unable to see a Japanese destroyer lying beyond, but in the same azimuth as the cruiser at which we were firing. At his command post down on the reef, Lieutenant Robert M. Hanna could see this destroyer, however. He told me that the first shot fired from our gun No. 2, which overreached the cruiser, plopped squarely into this destroyer.

In their overconfidence the Japanese had walked into a trap, heaving-to to send in and to cover landing parties within a triangle formed by our land batteries and an American submarine which lay hidden on their seaward side. Our aviators, too, had scored heavily, ferrying bombs with which they smeared the enemy throughout the engagement. Except for the burning of tanks, the Japanese guns had done little damage. From the first shot to the last, not more than an hour had elapsed. For some time smoke and flames still were visible far at sea mingling with the heavy white smoke screen thrown out by their remaining destroyers.*

I put the magazine in order and then walked down to the range finder. The men in the range section were jubilant. Sergeant Boscarino came up from his gun. His face was grimed and black with powder smoke. He still wore the protective pad on his left forearm with which he wiped the "mushroom" on the breechblock after each round had been fired. Everyone congratulated each other.

At nine thirty the next morning, the Japanese raided

---

*In the engagement of December 11, the Wake Island shore batteries sank one Japanese destroyer and badly damaged several other warships. Thirty miles southwest of the atoll, the Grumman fighters sank a second destroyer. It was the last time in the Pacific War that coast defense guns repelled an amphibious landing.

Wake Island again. There seemed to be more planes than usual—I learned later that thirty bombers had come over—but they dropped fewer bombs. When they had passed over, I ventured out of the foxhole. Our few planes already were in the sky, and were diving into the enemy formations. The AA batteries on Peacock Point and on Peale Island opened up. The shells burst high in the sky, leaving white puffs intermingled with the tiny birdlike specks that were the enemy planes. Our few Grummans buzzed in and out of the enemy formations like hornets, oftentimes following the Japanese bombers amid the bursts of our own antiaircraft fire.

One evening shortly after the sea attack, I went down to the water to bathe. Lying on my back in a shallow pool, and listening to the pounding of the surf on the outlying reef, I felt perfectly safe. So far all air raids had come in the forenoon, and we had arrived at the conclusion that the Japanese planes—which, we presumed, were coming from the Marshall Islands, some six hundred miles to the south—found it inexpedient to return to their bases after nightfall.

I had come out of the water and was reaching for my towel when I heard someone shout. Looking up, I saw two marines running full tilt along the shore. It suddenly occurred to me that I was upwind from the range finder, and very possibly had missed the air raid alarm. Even with this thought I heard the sound of engines rising above the roar of the sea. I jerked on my shoes, snatched up my clothing, and ran for cover. As the first bombs fell, I scrambled into our foxhole, stark naked. It was a rather close call, but I had put on a good show for the other boys, and the explosion of the bombs was punctuated by their laughter.

Day followed day. There was no telling now when the Nipponese air arm would strike. Sometimes the klaxon awakened us at dawn. Again it sounded in the mid or late afternoon. Sometimes the enemy attacked twice in the same day; and as time wore on, one question loomed in the minds of civilians and servicemen alike: "Where, in Christ's name, was the U.S. Navy?" When would our people send reinforcements?

Life had been reduced to its simplest elements: we ate when food was available, slept, bathed infrequently, answered our nature calls. This life was lived in an atmosphere of ever-increasing apprehension. The feeling of exhilaration arising from our success in the battle of December 11 had worn off. The air raids continued. Though casualties were slight, and little damage was done, the damnable persistence of the Japanese had the effect of disrupting any attempts at large-scale reorganization for effective defense work.

Late on the afternoon of December 20, a United States PBY flying boat arrived at Wake Island. Word reached us over the grapevine that it had come for the purpose of delivering sealed orders to Commander Winfield Cunningham, who was in charge of the small naval detachment on the island.

The insouciance of the three aviators, their ignorance regarding the plight we were in, and their nonchalant request to be conducted to the Pan American Hotel, left us a little flabbergasted and vastly discouraged.

The PBY took off on the return trip at seven o'clock the following morning carrying Major Baylor, USMC, as a passenger. He was the last man to get away from the island. Two days later we were prisoners of the Japanese.

At eight fifty A.M. the inevitable alarm sounded. It was only a matter of seconds until we realized that this was no ordinary raid: the nerve-shattering roaring of the engines close overhead was exceeded only by the repetitive swish and scream and crashing crescendo of the falling bombs. Each ear-splitting detonation shook the timbers in our dugout. There was no surcease, no breathing spell between explosions.

Dive bombers were unloading their cargoes on us in sticks of four. Dropped at water's edge, the fourth bomb to fall was intended for the Peacock Point installations. We would hear the explosions of bombs one, two, and three, and then, when our turn came, the beams rattled and shook, the earth trembled, and dirt and gravel sifted down on us while we lay stiff with fear.

Lieutenant Baringer was worried. The presence of the dive bombers using heavy bombs indicated that an aircraft carrier was in the vicinity, and the presence of a carrier only too clearly signified the presence of a considerable enemy flotilla.

The following day, December 22, the dive-bombing started at twelve thirty-five and lasted for forty minutes. Evidently the Nipponese had our gun positions, for they hit Peacock Point hard. A large-caliber bomb had hit within twenty feet of gun No. 2's dugout, and nineteen marines had been pinned against the wall by heavy timbers. Had the concussion been a trifle heavier, all of them would have been crushed to death.

Our last two planes, piloted by Captain Herbert Freuler and Lieutenant Carl Davidson, went into the air that morning to meet the dive bombers coming in from the sea. There was dogfighting all over the sky.

After destroying one Japanese plane Captain Freuler looked up in time to see another coming at him intent on *kamikaze*. He gave it a burst of bullets, jerked back on the stick, and zoomed upward, barely avoiding a head-on collision. As he passed over, the enemy plane blew up. The force of the explosion stunned Freuler. Looking down he saw fragments of the disintegrated plane splashing all over the lagoon. A third plane was coming in on his tail. The force of the explosion had loosened the fabric on the ailerons and stabilizers, and Freuler's plane responded to the controls sluggishly. Before he could pull away, the Japanese flier had him. Badly wounded, he put his Grumman into a sideslip and made for the airport. His plane was behaving erratically. He made a pass at the field, but the Jap bombers were working it over and there was no chance to land. He made a wide circle and again came in. By this time he had lost a great deal of blood, and was weakening rapidly and feeling faint. Finally, on the fourth pass, he managed to set his plane down on the field. A fellow pilot, who was at the airport at the time, described Freuler's condition:

We found him slumped unconscious in a pool of blood, a big chink shot out of the flesh of his shoulder. Another bullet had penetrated the gas tank, pierced the back of the seat, the folded parachute pack, Freuler's clothing, and lodged against his spine. We found a .60 caliber slug in the engine. The oil-line was cut. The fabric of the controls was lying in folds. Everything—Freuler, the motor, the plane—"conked out" at the same time!

Lieutenant Carl Davidson was the last American pilot in the air over Wake Island. He chased an enemy plane out to sea and did not return.

On the gun positions the marines were grim and silent. This sort of thing could not go on indefinitely. Everyone sensed the coming of a crisis.

The decisive action at Wake Island began shortly after one o'clock on the morning of December 23. I was awakened by Lieutenant Baringer's runner, Jesse Nowlin. I pulled on my shoes, hastened outside, and roused the civilians in the adjacent foxholes. All along the water front on the lee side of Wake and Wilkes islands, ascending red flares described graceful arcs against the Stygian background. At sea, completely encircling the island, searchlights were at work, flash succeeding rapid flash, the long streamers of light cutting the sky into angular black chunks as the ships busily signalled to each other. Suddenly the entire beach on our side of the island was momentarily bathed in white light. This was from one of our own searchlights. It went out as suddenly as it had come on. From all directions came the clamor of machine guns, periodically punctuated by the hollow sound of our three-inch guns. From the powder magazine on Peacock Pint we were unable in the darkness to make out any of the targets which attracted this voluminous fire. The number of red flares increased. They came closer and closer, breaking over the island in ragged lines, bathing it in an eerie crimson glow. The sky now was a mosaic fashioned by tangled searchlight beams. The firing increased to a steady drumming sound. The .50-caliber nests nearby on the windward side of Peacock Point opened up. Bullets zinged close overhead, and we ducked for cover behind the sandbags protecting the magazine.

At the time the final attack came, approximately 450 servicemen were available to defend the island. These men had been on the alert at battle stations for fifteen consecutive days and nights without relief. With the exception of the plane which Captain Freuler had piloted on the afternoon of the twenty-second, and which, while repairable, would be out of commission for several days, we had lost all of our small squadron of airplanes.

As nearly as we could ascertain, the Nipponese were attempting to land all along the lee shores of Wake and Wilkes islands in motor-driven barges and boats. Throughout the night, flares also were seen over the lagoon. On Peale Island shortly before 2 A.M. the gun crews were ordered to take small arms and stand by to repel a possible landing sortie from the lagoon side. Except for reconnaissance patrols in their area, the troops on Peale Island were inactive until seven o'clock on the morning of the twenty-third when they were transferred to

Wake Island to join a skirmish line protecting the command post.

On Wilkes Island, however, it was a different story. Throughout the night, flares burst over the island and our machine guns fired constantly. In bombing Wilkes Island on December 10 the Japanese had hit a big cache of dynamite. The force of the terrific explosion damaged the big searchlight unit concealed in the brush nearby to such an extent that it went out of order after only a few seconds of use on the morning of the twenty-third. Consequently the defense against the landing parties was undertaken in total darkness.

The fighting on Wake Island was widespread, extending from the small boat channel eastward along the lee shore to within 150 yards of our Peacock Point positions, taking in the airport, and extending as far north as the communication center. The best way to tell the story of the melee on the lee shore of Wake, and in the brush between the road and the airport, is to relate the amazing exploit of Lieutenant Bob Hanna.

Lieutenant Hanna, being the American farthest out on the beach, was the first to discern the shadowy shapes of the Japanese landing craft silently gliding shoreward. A crew was to have been formed to service the nearby three-inch gun, but they had not arrived. Hanna got on the phone and was informed from command post that no crew was available to man this gun. Although he was a machine-gun specialist, Hanna asked for and obtained permission to man the three-inch gun himself. Assisted only by civilians Robert J. Bryan and Paul Gay, who had been trained on machine guns and who knew absolutely nothing about the operation of a three-inch gun, Hanna got busy.

It was pitch black and everything had to be done by "feel." Hanna told Bryan to bring the gun to bear on the target—a shadowy hulk close in, and approximately a hundred yards upshore from his position—while he proceeded to cut the fuses on several shells, making them as short as possible for a two-second burst.

Hanna loaded the three-inch piece, attached the lanyard and fired. The first shot went high. In laying the piece on the target, Bryan had sighted along the top of the barrel as one sights a shotgun or a sporting rifle. Hanna quickly lowered the muzzle and "bore-sighted" the gun. The next shot took effect.

Hanna could not recognize the nature of the target—whether it was a landing barge, a longboat, or what. As its stern receded into the blackness of the night and the Pacific, he put two more shots into her. The Japanese aboard the craft, probably to give their shock troops a brief glimpse of the terrain ashore, then did a foolish thing. Momentarily they turned on a hooded spotlight on the ship's bow. It was enough. For an instant the entire structure—it was a patrol craft—was silhouetted. Hanna quickly swung the muzzle of his gun to the left. A shot—there was a muffled roar—and clouds of steam rose upward. A second shot found the ship's magazine and she went up: small-arms ammunition covered the sky with red traceries; larger shells exploded making exquisite red and white flower pots; grenades feathered out like sparklers.

The "show" was visible all over the island. By its light Hanna discovered a second ship of the same class in the immediate vicinity, and succeeded in putting several shots into her. In the haste with which it had been placed, the platform of the gun he was firing had not been seated firmly on the ground, but rested in part on some tough, springy ironwood brush. Each time it was fired, the gun jumped about like an unruly mustang, and it was necessary to check the aim before again firing. The position was exposed, and Hanna and his crew were utterly without sandbags or any other type of protection.

Dawn found twelve men defending the beach in the vicinity of Hanna's position: Hanna, Bryan, Gay, Major Putnam, Corporal John Painter, who had given an excellent account of himself as a mechanic on the airport, Marines L. V. Murphy and Baumgardner, civilians Eric Lehtola and J. C. Smith, and three other civilians whose names are not available. Bryan was manning a .30-caliber machine gun. In addition, the party was armed with a Thompson submachine gun, a Browning automatic rifle, Springfields, and a few side arms.

Early in the war our draglines had gouged deep recesses into the bank paralleling the south side of the east-west runway for the protection of our planes when they were on the ground. Under the cover of darkness, a number of Japanese had infiltrated into these recesses, and when dawn came they gave Hanna's embattled group plenty of trouble with manually operated grenade throwers. These small mechanical mortars, with a very high trajectory, were surprisingly accurate.

Across the road from Hanna's party, in a narrow strip of brush paralleling the runway, Captain Frank Tharin and Captain Elrod were in charge of another group of skirmishers, their personnel including civilian mechanics Yeager, Gibbons, Gibbons' son, the contractor's structural steel superintendent, Pete Sorenson, and a structural steel foreman named L.H. Peterson. This patch of brush was full of Japanese and the fighting was at close quarters. Men maneuvered an inch at a time to get a shot at the Japs lying behind rocks and brush not more than twenty or twenty-five feet from them.

Hanna's party tried several times to abandon their exposed beach position and join Tharin's group in the brush, but were prevented from doing so by a Japanese machine gunner who commanded a full view of the open road which they must cross. Sorenson and Peterson, the first armed with a tommy gun, the second with a Springfield rifle, crouched behind an overturned AA carrier about fifty yards from Hanna. They too were practically in the open. They were kneeling about six or seven feet apart, when a grenade burst directly between them. By some strange freak of fortune neither man was injured. They separated, and within seconds the Jap mortars on the airport scored direct hits on each man, killing them instantly.

Bryan did yeoman service with his machine gun before a bullet pierced his forehead. Gay was killed by a machine gun burst which raked his chest, and an almost simultaneous grenade hit which practically disemboweled him. Hanna saw a Japanese firing at Major Putnam at close range. The bullet hit a three-inch shell and ricocheted harmlessly. Before the Jap could fire again, Hanna had dropped him with his .45.

In the brush across the road, Captain Elrod and young Gibbons had been killed. Captain Tharin and a companion ensconced in a bomb crater, each with a Thompson submachine gun, were having a wonderful time. A fringe of Japanese faces peered above the crater's rim—a spraying motion of the tommy guns—and the faces disappeared. When the surrender came, Tharin's foxhole literally was ringed by dozens of Japanese dead.

Just how the Japanese flanked our Wake Island positions is not entirely clear. Evidently under cover of darkness they entered the lagoon over the reef in rubber boats and secreted themselves in the thick brush along the lagoon side of Wake Island. Men attached to Lieutenant Lewis' AA battery reported that early in the morning they were fired on from that direction. After the surrender, a Japanese officer told one of the contractor's engineers whom he had put to work straightening out blueprints in the office, that further resistance on our part would have proven futile in any event; that there were over 150 Japanese naval vessels within an hour's call of Wake Island that morning.

The island was surrendered unconditionally about eight o'clock on the morning of December 23, a few hours less than sixteen days after the Japanese launched their first attack from the air.

It is interesting to know that the Japanese landing parties were a long way from defeating the American garrison in the field. Actually, throughout the early morning hours, we had them beaten. The main American skirmish line defending the command post, extending across Wake Island from the lagoon to Windy Beach, never did engage the enemy. On the lee shore of Wake, the parties commanded by Captain Tharin and Major Putnam were holding their own, and on Wilkes Island the force under Captain Platt had completely eliminated the attackers.

Practically alone in the command post, throughout the early hours of the morning of December 23 Major Devereux received reports from his officers in the field regarding enemy strength. Fifty to a hundred planes of all classes were in sight, and estimates of enemy vessels offshore ranged from sixteen to twenty-five or thirty with, undoubtedly, other units lying out of sight beyond the horizon.

In view of enemy strength, the ultimate outcome of the engagement was not in doubt. The opinion of the Marine officers and noncommissioned officers was that we would have been able to withstand the Japanese attacks throughout the day of the twenty-third, but that they would have overrun the island the following night under conditions that would have made formal surrender impossible.

In my estimation Commander Cunningham and Major Devereux showed rare good judgment, and saved the lives of the men on the island, by timing the surrender when they did. No doubt a sense of responsibility toward us civilians was a factor figuring in the capitulation.

Throughout the night, nine of us civilians on Peacock Point had lain under the camouflage on top of the trap door to Battery A's powder magazine, squeezed between the sandbags for protection from the bullets streaming overhead. With the first faint glimmer of daylight, enemy planes, coming in low, swooped over our position. Retreat to the dugout was impossible; for all we knew, our battery might go into action at any moment, in which event we would be needed.

There was only one thing to do. Hastily we raised the trap door and the nine of us tumbled into the magazine, where we crouched between the tiered powder canisters and the racks of shells.

Time passed. The sky lightened. The steady drumming of machine guns came from all sides. I looked through the small screened vent at ground level and was surprised to see the long tube of our gun No. 1 stripped of camouflage, ready for action. None of the marines was in sight. Fortunately for us unarmed civilians, the Japanese landing parties avoided the strong rip-tides off Peacock Point, and passed a hundred yards to the west of our position on their way to the airport.

The sun was up now. A plane dived directly on us, passed close—scarcely a hundred feet overhead—and, miracle of miracles, nothing happened. Then we noticed a significant lull in the firing of the machine guns. I risked a glimpse top-side. Overhead a multitude of planes of all types were flying low over the island. Our two naval rifles, stripped of their camouflage, were naked and cold-looking in the early morning sunlight. They were glaring targets, but the Japanese airmen ignored them. I couldn't figure it out.

After the hours of incessant gun fire, the sudden absolute quiet was awesome. We whispered in muted tones, or kept quiet, admonishing others to do likewise by sign language. Except for the soft murmur of a quiet sea lapping at the coral pebbles on the beach, Peacock Point was absolutely still.

At long last a man appeared in the clearing in the rear of our guns. It was Sergeant Warren. Approaching the magazine, he called: "You people can come on up. It's all over. The island's surrendered."

I don't know just what I did expect, but I hadn't expected *that*. The thing that must not happen, the thing we dreaded most—more than mutilation or death—had happened. In a benumbed state of mind, I automatically took out the small notebook in which I had been keeping a diary, tore it into small fragments, and scattered them among the powder canisters. Loosening my belt, I removed the only weapon I possessed—a clasp knife with a four-inch blade—and tossed it beside a rack of shells. I crawled outside, and, unutterably weary, stood on unsteady legs.

Slowly, we made our way to the range finder. The skirmish line had broken up, and men were coming out of the brush from all directions. Some of the marines were busy opening tinned food. "Eat all you can," Lieutenant Baringer admonished, "it may be a long time to the next meal." He turned toward us. "You civilians get away from the battery. The Japs may class you as guerrillas if they find you here."

"Let's go up on the road and see what it's all about," I said to Johnny Clelan.

Johnny and I shook hands all around with the marines, and started up the trail. We came out on the road, and walked in the direction of the contractor's camp.

The rounded dirt-covered crests of the four high-explosive magazines loomed ahead. A Japanese flag floated on top of one of them. Someone had left a half-full number ten can of pineapple rings in the middle of the road. We hooked several rings of the fruit over our fingers and walked toward captivity eating nonchalantly.

Two Japanese soldiers were standing on either side of the road in front of the first of the magazines. My initial impression of them was that they carried unusually long rifles and bayonets. A second glance revealed that the rifles were of ordinary size, but that the men holding them were very small. Both were wearing split-toed sneakers, which gave them a cloven-hoofed appearance. Round canvas-covered helmets came low over their heads and necks.

Beyond the sentries, a considerable group of nearly naked Americans were lying or sitting in the middle of the road. As we approached, the sentries grunted, making upward thrusts with their bayonets. We raised our hands over our heads. One of them stepped forward and pulled at my shirt, pointing at a heap of clothing by the side of the road. We stripped down, being allowed to retain only our under-shorts, socks, and shoes. Then we were herded in with the other prisoners, most of whom were trussed up with telephone wire cut from nearby communication lines. Their legs were tied together at the ankles. Their crossed wrists had been tied and drawn up between their shoulder blades, the lashings then looped around their throats in such a manner that any effort to release their wrists, or to relieve their arms from the twisted, cramped position, automatically resulted in cutting off their wind—an ingenious lash-up which rendered them perfectly inert. Many men wore dirty, blood-soaked bandages.

Japanese sentries with fixed bayonets stood guard over us. On top of a nearby high-explosive magazine, a sailor trained a light machine gun in our direction. The Japs were highly elated. Planes roared overhead. One of them—a biplane with pontoons—meandered over at an altitude of forty or fifty feet. The sailor on the magazine stood up, yelled "*banzai*," and waved his cap.

I looked out to sea. Hard by the reef, standing so close to each other that it seemed the bow of one overlapped the stern of the other, rising and falling with the ocean swells, Japanese men-of-war completely ringed the island. Not until years later, after V-J day, in fact, when I flew over Yokohama harbor en route to Guam, did I see so many ships assembled.

—June 1959

ONE WHO SURVIVED: SEAMAN HEYN'S STORY

Day after day, the sun, the sea, and the sharks cut down the men who clung to the doughnut raft.

*O*f all the men who have gone down to the sea in ships, none has clung to life with more tenacity, or lived to tell a more graphic story, than Allen Clifton Heyn, gunner's mate second class, one of the ten survivors of more than seven hundred men aboard the U.S. light cruiser Juneau. What follows is a transcript of a recorded wartime interview between Heyn and a naval interrogator. Save for a few cuts to remove repetition or digressions, and for a few alterations in wording in the interests of clarity, nothing has changed. This is a tale which loses nothing from the elementary English of the teller.

Heyn was a seaman aboard the Juneau when she took part in the complicated series of night and day actions which are lumped together as the Battle of Guadalcanal, from November 12 through 15, 1942. In this decisive struggle for the Solomon Islands, American surface and air forces succeeded in reinforcing their ground troops on Guadalcanal while largely preventing the Japanese from doing the same thing. But victory was accomplished at a terrific cost, littering the floor of the narrow seas between Guadalcanal, Savo, and Florida Islands with so many sunken U.S. ships that the Navy christened those waters "Ironbottom Sound."

The Juneau fought in the cruiser night surface action of Friday, November 13. A U.S. force of five cruisers and eight destroyers under Rear Admiral Daniel J. Callaghan was steaming northwest toward a larger Japanese bombardment group coming directly at them between Savo and Guadalcanal, hoping

*to shell our troops and airfield ashore. The American advantage
of surprise was lost before fire opened at 0145, and both forces
were soon intermingled in a bloody melee. Heyn's story starts as,
in the black of the midwatch, the* Juneau *finds herself picking her
way across a hopeless checkerboard of mingled friendly and
enemy ships.*

LT. PORTER: Heyn, you were on the *Juneau* in the
Guadalcanal action, that was 13 November 1942, wasn't it?

ALLAN HEYN: Yes.

LT. PORTER: What was your battle station?

HEYN: I was the 1.1 on the fantail.

LT. PORTER: What did you see of the action that night?

HEYN: We were in a column of ships and we went in, in
between these Japanese ships, and we got word down from the
bridge to stand by, that they would challenge the enemy. And
it wasn't but a few minutes when everything just broke loose,
flames and shots and gunfire all over. And they sent word all
around to all the minor batteries like 1.1's and 20 millimeters
not to fire because the tracers would given away our positions.

So, we held our fire until the enemy knew where we were
and the star shells lit us all up. Then we started firing and you
could see the Jap ships so close that you'd think you could
almost throw something and hit them. So we just fired our
smaller guns right into the topsides of their ships, trying to
knock off some of the guns on their decks. That went on for
quite a while and the ship maneuvered around a lot. It would
turn sharply and the water would splash all over where I was, in
the fantail. A lot of small bullets hit around me. I don't know
what caliber they were but you could see the shrapnel laying all
over the deck. And they sent word to take cover.

I don't know whether they knew there was a fish coming
or what, but all at once a fish hit. it must have hit up forward
because it just seemed like the fish jumped out of the water.
And when it did, all of us fellows that were on the main deck, it
stunned us like and knocked us down. The propellers didn't
seem to turn for a few minutes. Sounded like they were
jammed or something. The ship wouldn't steer, just seemed to
skid through the water like. I don't know whether it was a Jap
cruiser or what it was, but it was just on the other side of us
and it just seemed like we were going to run right into it and
ram it, but we didn't though.

They got control of the ship from the after battle station or something. And they pulled around just in time. Just then I saw another ship right after us in our wake. It must have been a Jap tin can because it was coming right at us. Our after guns fired on it and some other ships fired on it and it just blew up, just a bunch of oil and flame. There wasn't nothing left. And that was that.

Then we were in column again and I could see a Jap battleship, because it was awfully big and it was firing right at us. It seemed like everyone was giving it to us, you know. There was a big flash, and the salvos would hit the water on one side of the ship and splash all over and then they would hit on the other side. They didn't have it just right. Then something hit up forward. I don't know what it was because it hit again and the ship shook all over.

The ship seemed to be out of control kinda and someone says, they passed the word around to cut some of the life rafts loose. There were four or five of these doughnut rafts stacked on top of each other on the main deck aft and they were secured, so two or three guys from the battle station where I was went back up and cut them loose with a knife and come back.

You could see ships around us, Japanese ships, and we were still firing at them. And I don't know how it was but then the electrical power on the 5-inch mounts got out of whack, the juice was cut on them or something happened to the connections somewhere and they had to train them by hand.

After that things started to quiet down a little. We got out of position and didn't see any more ships around us. The forward part of the ship seemed to be way down in the water and the fantail way up high. And we couldn't make very good speed. You could hear things cracking underneath there—the propeller shafts and the rudder. They were bent or something.

We got off away from the rest of them. You could still see them firing. It looked just like the Jap ships were shooting at each other, that they didn't know that we weren't there. And they just kept firing and firing and we kept getting a little further away and they passed the word all over the ship to be sure to not have any lights or anything and to keep real quiet because we were going to try to get out of sight of the enemy somehow. We cruised around there, right next to the shore.

It was beginning to get daylight by then and we got out in the open sea again. The radars and things didn't work very good; they were all shot from the explosion. Then the look-outs picked up ships ahead. They signaled recognition signals and we found out then it was some of our own task force.

It was the *San Francisco*, the *Helena*, the *Buchanan*, and I don't know the name of the other can. The *Portland* or the *Atlanta* wasn't there, they'd been hit already and they were still in Guadalcanal. And we got together and it seemed like they were deciding what to do because we kept circling around off San Cristobal Island, just kept making a big circle.

The *San Francisco* sent over word to our ship asking for a doctor and some pharmacist's mates to come over and aid them. We only had two small motor launches on the davits and they were all torn away. So they sent a boat over, and a doctor and I don't know how many pharmacist's mates got in. After they got there, we were always having alerts. There were planes flying around. We were still at our battle stations and didn't know for sure what planes they were. They'd come in and then we'd find out they were our own and then they'd have submarine contacts and we'd go on Alert One.

Then it was kinda quiet and it was sort of a lull for a few minutes, and everybody was kinda talking and breathing a little easy—everybody was pretty well shook up from the night before. I remember I was just relieving another man on my gun on the phones. We took turns every once in a while so it would be easier. It was pretty hard on your ears and everything and I took over one phone. I was putting them on while he was taking the other ones off.

And I said to him, "Are you all ready?" And he didn't say anything, he just looked at me, kinda with his mouth open. I didn't know what it was, somebody was passing the word over the phone or what. It just seemed like everybody was just standing there and then an explosion. A torpedo struck or something. It struck about midship because the whole thing just blew up and it threw me against a gun mount and I had one of these steel helmets on and when I came to, everything was all torn apart and there was oil coming down the air and I thought it was rain but it was just the oil from the feed-tanks or something. The tanks had blew up in the air.

And there was smoke and there was fellows laying all around there and parts of their gun shields torn apart and the fantail where I was was sticking almost straight up in the air. It was so slippery that you couldn't walk up it and the guys that was still able to climb over the side couldn't walk up. They were crawling over the side and holding on the lifeline trying to pull themselves further aft and jump over. And they were jumping over and bumping into each other.

It was still so smoky and all, you couldn't quite see, and I was still hazy and I knew I had to get up and get off of there. I was afraid the suction would pull me down. When I went to get up, I felt this pain in my foot and I couldn't get my foot loose from the shield or something, it fell down on top of my right foot across the instep of it and I couldn't get loose. It was only a few seconds, and the water was closing in around the ship and there was just this little bit of it left. And I knew that I had to get off but I couldn't and there was a lot of kapok life jackets laying around deck.

I grabbed one of them in my arms and held it. I didn't even put it on and the water closed in around the ship and we went down. And I gave up, I just thought that there wasn't a chance at all, everything just run through my head. And you could see all objects in the water, all the fellows and everything and after we were under the surface I don't know how far but the sheet of iron or whatever it was, it was released and my foot came loose and the buoyancy from then the life jacket brought me back to the surface.

It was like a big whirlpool. There was oil very thick on the water, it was at least two inches thick—seemed that way, anyway—and there was all kinds of blueprints and drawings of the ship floating around. And then there was roll after roll of tissue paper and that's about all there was on top. I couldn't see anybody. I thought, gee, am I the only one here? My head was very hazy and I didn't think a thing about the other ships. I put the life jacket on when I came to the top, and I paddled around the water.

I don't know how long, it wasn't too long, when this doughnut life raft just popped up right in front of me. I don't know where it came from, it just seemed to come up there. I grabbed it and held on and then I heard a man cry. I looked around and it was this boatswain's mate second class. His name, I can't quite remember his name. If I could see it, I'd recognize it. He was in the post office on the ship and he was crying for help. I went over to help him.

He said he couldn't swim and he had his whole leg torn off, blew off. I helped him on the doughnut raft and then gradually one by one some more stragglers would come and we'd all get on.

Then we began to think about the other ships. When we were thinking about them, you could just see masts going over the horizon and it just seemed like they never scouted the area, they just kept right on going and we thought, well, they know we're here, they'll surely pick us up. So we all hung on this doughnut raft. There was so many of us that it was sinking way down in the water and there wasn't much room.

Everybody was kinda scared at first. Some of them couldn't swim, they were afraid they'd loose their grip and drown. So it went on that way and then these B-17 Flying Fortresses flew over the area. They just skimmed the water and they'd wave to us.*

Towards evening, the water was very calm and then it rained. You couldn't see anything at all and every couple of minutes someone would say, well, there's a ship and they were just thinking they saw it, it wasn't there at all. And the rain stopped, and there were other doughnuts nearby and we paddled and tried to get each other together.

Well, by nightfall we were about three doughnuts together. It just lays on the water and you try to lay on top of it. Well, there was a lot of fellows on them. I should say there was about 140 of us when we all got together. Some of them were in very bad shape. Their arms and legs were torn off. And one of them, I could see myself his skull. You could see the red part inside where his head had been split open, you might say torn open in places. They were all crying together and very down in the dumps and wondering if anybody was ever going to pick them up. And they thought, well, at least tomorrow there will be somebody out here.

And that night, it was a very hard night because most of the fellows who were wounded badly were crying and, you know, groaning about their pains and everything. They were all in agony. And in the morning this fellow that I said that had his head open, his hair turned gray just like as if he was an old man. It had turned gray right over night.

---

*The *Helena*, whose captain was now senior surviving officer present, asked a B-17 to signal naval headquarters that *Juneau* had been torpedoed and that survivors were in the water, but this message did not get through. Admiral Halsey later relieved the captain of his command for abandoning these survivors.

Everybody had so much oil on them, their ears and eyes would burn and the salt water would hurt so much that you couldn't hardly look around to see if anybody was there. You couldn't recognize each other unless you knew each other very well before the ship went down or unless it was somebody you'd recognize by his voice. So all these rolls of tissue paper were floating around there. If you unrolled them, in the middle they were dry and we'd take that and wipe our eyes out with them and ease the pain a lot and wipe our faces off a little.

Well, we all decided to stick together and try to secure the doughnuts so we wouldn't drift apart and help the wounded guys as much as we could. Those of us who wasn't so bad could float around and swim. The oil was so thick it sort of made everybody sick to their stomachs. So we decided to try to get out of the oil. Where the water was clear it didn't bother you so much, but then we worried because we knew there were sharks in those waters.

This Lieutenant Blodgett, he was gunnery officer, he was a full lieutenant on the *Juneau*, he took charge of the party and he decided that we ought to try to paddle for land because we could see land when we first went down. And what we done, we secured the doughnuts together, one behind another in a line and the fellows that were able would get up in the forward ones and straddle legs over it and paddle. And we done that all that day. We took turns. All that night we done the same thing. And the Lieutenant was supposed to be navigating by the stars in direction of land.

Well, we didn't seem to be getting anywhere at all because the doughnuts were too clumsy, and on the third day a B-17 Flying Fortress flew over very low and it dropped a rubber life raft. And we were all deciding what we should do about it—swim out and get it or what—because we were beginning to notice sharks. They were really sand sharks, the big sharks hadn't come yet. The rubber raft was quite a ways off but it was yellow and you could see it once in a while, as it could come up on top of a wave. So we decided two or three of us ought to paddle over on one of these doughnut rafts and pick it up. So that's what we done. We took this doughnut and we paddled over. There was a fellow named Hartney, and Fitzgerald, and there was a boy, a Mexican, I don't know what his name was, but I know he was of Mexican descent.

And we picked up this rubber boat. I'd never seen one

before and didn't know how to do it but it had tubes to blow it up, some kind of, I don't know what you call it, chemical or something, and we blew it up. One fellow paddled it back to the rest of the party. And we paddled our doughnut back.

In this rubber raft I noticed that there was little containers, I don't know whether it was water, food or what was in them. We decided a couple of guys ought to go in this raft and paddle it with the oars that came with it and secure it to the doughnuts and try to do like we did before.

When we all got back together we thought we ought to put the worst of the wounded fellows in the rubber raft because they would be free of the water and it would be better for them. They would rest more comfortable there. So, this Lieutenant Wang was hurt very bad. He asked Lieutenant Blodgett if he could go in this rubber raft and Lieutenant Blodgett said yes, he could.

It was toward evening now, and there were three men in this rubber raft. They hollered back to us that they had decided to go for land and send us some help. But all these fellows that was on the doughnuts who were very sick and wounded didn't want that. They wanted to be put in the rubber raft and all stay together. They felt, well, it was much easier there than on the doughnut. And why should those three go in that rubber raft and leave us here? It looked like we would be goners that way, that's what it looked like. Everybody figured that anyway.

Well, they said they were going anyway, so they unsecured this line and they paddled off. And all these fellows that was hurt bad was hollering for them to come back but they kept going.*

Well, after they went, we tried to get together again. The ones who were wounded that hadn't died already had narrowed down to about fifty men. The ones of us who were in the best shape, we tried to swim around and help out the other ones. And some of the fellows, there was some planks there, they decided they'd try to swim for land on these planks. Well, they tried to do it and I never did see a couple of them again

---

*The three made a small island safely, where friendly natives and a European trader nursed them back to life. A Catalina seaplane eventually brought them out.

but this one fellow came back, he found out he couldn't make it and he came back to our party on this big wooden plank.

Well, the sea began to get rough again. In the daytime the sun was very hot and I found out that the fellows who took their shirts off, or the ones that had them torn off by the explosion, their backs, their skin had all burned. They were in agony. And the ones of us who kept our clothes on were in the best shape because of the oil in the clothes. That protected us. At night it was very cold, you'd have to keep under the water to keep yourself warm. In the daytime the oil in the clothes would keep that sun off you, wouldn't penetrate your body so much.

But then on the fourth day the sea was very rough, the doughnuts began to separate. There were about twelve on mine.

There was a gunner's mate second, his name was—it's so long ago, I'm forgetting the names of all these fellows—well anyway, there was him, there was a boatswain's mate and myself and this George Sullivan, he was gunner's mate second. I think he was the oldest brother of the Sullivans, he was on the boat with me.* There was several others, there was a Polish fellow from somewhere in Pennsylvania. I remember him talking about he was a coal miner before the war. And then there was a fellow from Tennessee.

Well, anyway, after we were separated from the rest we thought maybe we'd better stick together again. We could see the others once in a while at a distance on the horizon. They'd be on top of a wave and we would too, and we'd see them. Well, we tried to get back to them but we never could and we didn't know what to do.†

We tried to paddle and we found it wasn't doing no good so we decided just to lay there and hope that someone would find us.

Airplanes did fly over and some of them would come down close to us and some of them wouldn't and after a while some of the fellows were getting very delirious and, if a few waved at a plane that went by, they'd get mad at you, say you were crazy for doing it, and not to pay any attention to the planes. They didn't want to save us and they were going to

---

*All five of these famous brothers were lost on the *Juneau* or in the water afterward; a destroyer, *The Sullivans*, was later named for this family that gave so much.

†Of these others, six were later rescued by another Catalina.

leave us there. Well, I always thought that probably there was still battles going on and they couldn't send a ship out there and if we just hung on, sometime somebody would some and get us.

They knew we were there, I knew that, so when they could send a ship they'd come. Some of the guys was kinda disappointed and pretty low in mind so they sorta gave up. There's one fellow, he was a gunner's mate from the *Juneau*, second class. Well, he kept swallowing salt water all the time and he'd let his head fall down in the water and swallow it and he'd begin to get very dopey and dreary. He couldn't help himself at all so I held him up. I held him in my arms, his head above the water as much as I could, and I held him that way all afternoon. Toward night he got stiff and I told the other fellows.

I said, "Well, how about holding him for a while? I can't hold him, I've got all to do to hold myself." And they wouldn't do it, they were arguing and fighting among themselves a lot. And I said, "I felt his heart and his wrists and I couldn't feel any beating." I figured he was dead and I said to them, "Well, I'm going to let him go."

And George Sullivan, the oldest brother of the Sullivans, he said to me, "You can't do that," he said. "It's against all regulations of the Navy. You can't bury a man at sea without having official orders from some captain or the Navy Department or something like that." And I knew he was delirious and there was something wrong with him and all, but they wouldn't let me let him go.

I said to them, "Well, you hold him," and they wouldn't hold him. So it went on that way for a little while. His legs were hanging down in the water a little way below mine when a shark bit his leg, bit his leg right off below the knee. He didn't move or say anything. That was enough for me. I figured, well, I'm going to drop him. There isn't any sense holding a dead man. So we took his dog tag off, this one fellow did, and said a prayer for him and let him float away.

At night it was so cold for the fellows who didn't have no clothes, we'd try and huddle them among us to keep them warm under the water. The sharks kept getting worse in the daytime, and you could see them around us all the time. We'd kick them with our feet and splash the water and they'd keep away. But at night you'd get drowsy and you'd kinda fall asleep and you wouldn't see them coming. As night went on they'd come and they'd grab a guy every once in a while and bite him. And once they did, they wouldn't eat him altogether, they'd just take a piece of him and drag him away and drown him. He'd scream and holler and everything but there wasn't anything we could do to help.

I had a small knife, about a four-inch blade on it, and we were handing that around to each other every once in a while, borrowing it. Some guy would want to cut a piece of line or something to try to tie this doughnut together because the water and the weather kept wearing it apart and the canvas around the sides had been tearing off and it was coming apart. And we thought, maybe, if it come apart, well then we wouldn't have nothing to hold on, so then we were trying to secure it together all the time.

All the time we were in the water up to about our shoulders. We couldn't get up on it because there were too many of us and it was too small for all to sit on. At night one of the fellows, he would all the time swim away. And he'd say he was going away and we'd drag him back and he'd go away again. And finally a shark got him about fifty yards away and that's the last we seen of him.

And then the fellows got kind of ideas that the ship was sunk under us, sitting on the bottom. You could swim down there at night and get something to eat and all them kinda things, and I was beginning to believe them. Then one night they said we were carrying ammunition from one of the forward mounts back aft and I don't know, they said they could see a light down there and this one fellow kept saying, "If it's down there what are we staying up here for, let's go down there and get something to eat then." So I said, "You show me the way down there." So he dives under water and I went after him and I never did find nothing there, no hatch or anything like he said was there. And then I got my sense again and I knew what I was doing and I didn't believe him anymore.

The fifth day was coming up then. There were only two or three guys gone but things were getting pretty bad. The guys were fighting among themselves. If you bumped into one of them, he'd get mad and holler at you. And they did talk a lot about home and what they were going to do, and a lot of them said if they could get on an island, they'd stay there, they'd never go back to the Navy. They didn't want to see it no more. And they were mad that they were left out there in the water. It wasn't fair they should be left like that! The ships went off and didn't pick them up.

Well, this day the water was calm and it was very hot. And the fellows that didn't have shirts on, the sun burned them something awful. It burned their skin all out and their back, it was just like as if you shaved them with a razor or something, all raw and some of them just decided they weren't going to try any more. They said they'd rather drown themselves than suffer like that. So that night after dark George Sullivan said he was going to take a bath. And he took off all his clothes and got away from the doughnut a little way and the white of his body must have flashed and showed up more because a shark came and grabbed him and that was the end of him. I never seen him again.

It went on that way, and that night they got two other guys, too. And towards morning, it was rough again and the waves were high and heavy. We were getting very hungry and it started drizzling rain. A sea gull flew around and it landed on our doughnut. We grabbed at him, and we missed. Then he come back and that time we caught him and wrung his neck. There was about three or four of us, I don't remember for sure, and we ate the sea gull. There wasn't much of it. We just floated in the water and talked together and the sharks kept bothering us all the time. We'd keep beating them off and try to keep away from them, and planes flew over all the time again. But they didn't pay any attention to us.

Well, another night went on and the next day, this gunner's mate second, his name was Stewart, he said that there was a hospital ship there and we were going over to it. There was three of us, him, me and another fellow, and he said that we should swim over to it and leave the doughnut. We didn't know whether to or not. You hated to leave it there because you knew if you got out in the water, you were gone. So he dove in the water and swam off and he just kept swimming out over the water and he wouldn't turn around. You could see the sharks going after him and he swam and kicked and swam. And he hollered to us to come and get him with the raft, to paddle towards him but he kept swimming the other way. We paddled towards him and finally he got tired. He turned around and come towards us and he got back before the sharks got him.

But that night it got cold again. He had thrown all his clothes away and he didn't have a thing and he wanted me to give him my clothes. I said no, there's no sense in that. And he said, "Well, then I'm going down to the ship and get a clean suit. I got a lot of them in my locker." He also said, "I got a case of peaches in my gun mount."

He was really thinking the ship was down there. I wouldn't let him go because I knew if he dove down into the water that something would happen to him. So I kept talking him out of it. And I kept him in between us to keep him warm. Well, that night he decided he wouldn't stand it no more. He just swam away and the sharks got him.

Well, then there was just the two of us left. And it was about, I guess it was about the seventh day or so; that's what I think it was anyway. We talked a lot that day and I remember I gave my knife to this Mexican boy. He was trying to secure the raft at his end. We were at each end with our feet kinda up in the water so we could fight the sharks off better. That night we got kinda sleepy and we dozed off I guess, because a shark grabbed him and tore his leg off below, just jaggedy like. And he complained, he said to me that somebody was stabbing him with a knife. I said how can anybody stab you out here? There's nobody but us two.

And he swore at me and called me all kinds of names and said I had to get him to a doctor. I guess I was delirious, because I was paddling and paddling in the water there. I didn't know where I was going, I was just paddling, trying to get him to a doctor. Well, finally he screamed and hollered and he came over to me and I held his arm and then I could see what it was. I knew that he had been bit by a shark and I held him and the shark came up and it just grabbed him underneath and kept eating him from the bottom and pulling on him. Well, I couldn't hold him anymore. The sharks just pulled him down under the water and he drowned. Well then, that's all that happened, it seemed the night would never end.

The next day I just floated around some more and it went on like that for the next couple of days and in the morning of the last day, which was the ninth day, I began to get delirious myself. I see these guys come up out of the water. It looked like to me that they had rifles on their backs and I'd holler to them and they said they were up there on guard duty. They'd come up from the hatch on the ship. Well, I asked them how it was. And they said the ship was all right, you could go down there and get something dry and eat. So I said to them, well, I'll come over there by you and go down with you. Well, I swam over to them and they just disappeared. I went back. I done that twice. Each time they disappeared when I got there. And then my head got clear and something told me to hang on a little longer.

And about noontime that day a PBY flew over and circled around and then it went away again. Well, I gave up. I figured, well, I guess it's just like all the other planes, they ain't gonna bother, they figure you ain't worth while coming for. Or maybe they didn't know what I was because I was all black. I might have been a Jap for all they knew. A couple of hours later they come back and they flew around me and they dropped smoke bombs all around me.

Well, that built up my hope a lot and I took off my shirt and I waved at them and they waved back at me and they went off and I could see them way off flying. And I figured, well, they must be guiding the ship to me. And that's what they were doing because it wasn't long before I saw the mast of a ship coming over the horizon and it was the U.S.S. *Ballard*. They lowered a small boat and came out and picked me up and took me aboard there and that's about all, for I went on there into sick bay.

LT. PORTER: What day was this they picked you up, do you remember?

HEYN: It was the 22nd.

LT. PORTER: And they took you where?

HEYN: They took me to Espiritu Santo.

LT. PORTER: When you got on the *Ballard* were you delirious?

HEYN: Yes, I was.

LT. PORTER: Suffer from anything else? Shock, of course?

HEYN: I had very bad headaches in my head where I had been hit on the ship. And I was sick all over and I don't know, I was sorta wore out.

LT. PORTER: Broken foot, too?

HEYN: Yes.

LT. PORTER: How long were you in the hospital ashore?

HEYN: I was in Espiritu Santo for about, I think it was about two weeks, I can't remember any more. Then I was transferred to the U.S.S. *Solace* and from there I went to Fiji to an Army hospital and stayed there until I got better. I wasn't really better but they needed the hospital so bad then that they transferred us out when we were able and I was sent to a naval dispensary there.

LT. PORTER: How long were you on Fiji?

HEYN: I think I was there about nine months.

LT. PORTER: Then you went to Australia?

HEYN: Yes sir. There was a letter came out asking for volunteers for submarines and I volunteered for it and they transferred me down to Australia.

LT. PORTER: Feel pretty good now again?

HEYN: Yes, I do.

LT. PORTER: Think you're fully recovered?

HEYN: I think I'm all right.

LT. PORTER: Good. Having fully recovered, you then asked for and were given submarine service. Is that right?

HEYN: Yes, that's right.

LT. PORTER: And you went out on war patrol?

HEYN: Yes sir.

LT. PORTER: And on that patrol, you're officially credited with sinking some five ships and damaging four?

HEYN: That's correct.

LT. PORTER: Your preference for future service would be in submarines?

HEYN: Yes sir, it would.

LT. PORTER: Back in the same hunting area?

HEYN: It wouldn't make a difference as long as it's out in the Pacific somewhere.

—June 1956

CULPABLE NEGLIGENCE

by EDWARD L. BEACH

A submarine commander tells why we almost lost the Pacific war.

My surreptitiously retained file of war-patrol reports of *Trigger*, *Tirante*, and *Piper* (submarine numbers 237, 420, and 409) still makes fascinating reading, to me at least. *Trigger* (SS 237), completed at Mare Island, California, early in 1942, started her career slowly, but as we learned our dreadful business her improvement was steady. Before she died, a tired old submarine at three years, she had been, for a time, the highest-ranking sub in the Pacific Fleet in terms of overall damage to the enemy.

I hold the honor of being the next-to-last "plank owner" (crew-member when first commissioned) to leave the *Trigger*, after rising from assistant engineer to executive officer during my twenty-nine months aboard. I had entertained ideas of just possibly becoming her skipper before it was all over, but it is just as well the Navy had different plans for me. Poor old *Trigger* came to the end of her allotted time in March, 1945, just as I arrived back in the war zone as "exec" of the brand-new and much more formidable *Tirante*. At war's end I was skipper of the *Piper*, in the Sea of Japan. By that time the coasts of Japan had become far more familiar to us than our own, and the waters offshore—and all over her "co-prosperity sphere" —were littered with sunken wrecks.

But it was not so at the beginning; and in those old patrol reports, starkly written nearly forty years ago, lie the details. In most cases we did not then even know what was happening. Our guesses were crude at best; we know much more today.

Today those reports tell how near I came to never having the chance to grow older, or be married, or have a family, or be promoted beyond the rank of lieutenant, or to write this article. All this was on the line for everyone in the combat branches during the war, of course. But for those serving in our submarines in 1941, 1942, and 1943, these risks were more often the fault of our own ordnance than that of the enemy.

On October 20, 1942, I heard the loudest noise I have ever heard. For a microsecond I thought I had been killed. A blinding flash enveloped me, and I thought, instantaneously, without articulating a single word in my mind: "This is how it feels. It's all over. So suddenly. I don't feel anything, and probably never will again." But it wasn't over. The blinding flash was from a light bulb, dangling on a short extension of wire to protect it from depth-charge shock, which had been extinguished by unscrewing it slightly on "darken ship." In our dimly lighted conning tower it hung, unnoticed, exactly in front of my nose. When the warhead went off, the bulb was shocked into searing brilliance, burst into the night-adapted retinas of my eyes. It was minutes before I could see again; but it was only seconds before I knew I was still alive. Such a feeling has to be experience to be savored.

We had been tracking an unescorted tanker at night, and judging the moon too bright for a surface attack, had submerged to close the range and fire our torpedoes. Sonar heard some of our fish detonate, presumably against the side or bottom of our target, and seconds later reported "high-speed screws" in her vicinity. Then came a distant explosion, which we thought might be a depth charge dropped by the tanker, and a moment later, with catastrophic suddenness, a violent detonation extremely close aboard which, in the words of our patrol report, was "absolutely not a depth charge." The report goes on: "After the explosion, Sound reported the tanker's screws were starting and stopping close aboard. Started for periscope depth. Sound reported high-speed screws near the target. . . ."

We sincerely believed we had sunk the target and that the high speed propellers came from a motor lifeboat. But the official endorsements of our report credited us only with "damage," and it now seems fairly likely that it got away, totally unhurt. The "violent explosion" was one of our torpedoes, running in a circle and coming back upon us. The magnetic or "influence" exploder, fitted to our torpedoes with great secrecy, was designed to set off the torpedo warhead at the highest reading of a target's magnetic field, directly under its keel. Thus, since we were at one hundred feet keel depth at the time, the fish must have gone off directly overhead. Venting most of its explosive force upward, in the direction of the least pressure, it had failed to sink us.

So ran the train of thought, but there were doubts which this theory could not explain. At one hundred feet depth to our keel, our conning tower was only about seventy feet below the surface. The torpedoes had been set to thirty feet, and we knew, even if Washington refused to admit it, that they ran up to twenty feet deeper than set. An explosion of eight hundred pounds of torpex only twenty feet away, even if directly above us, would have finished us. Could it be that it had detonated farther away, some distance off to the side upon entry into our magnetic field instead of at its strongest (and therefore nearest) point? Could our two "hits" on the tanker, heard and timed correctly, also have been upon entry into the target's field instead of passing under her keel? Could they have failed to damage her, just as that extraordinarily violent explosion had shaken, but not damaged, us?

It is today my conviction, bolstered by similar reports from other submarines and innumerable stories of unreported incidents told by friends serving in other subs—and at least one more such experience myself a few months later—that this was the case. That torpedo should have sunk us, as I thought it had for an instant, given that it did run in a circle, and did run deep. But it should not have run in a circle, and it should not have run deep, any more than it should have gone off on sensing the existence of our magnetism instead of waiting to detect its strongest point. I nearly died, with my shipmates, because our criminally defective torpedoes sometimes ran in circles and always ran too deep, and we survived because, in an entirely unrelated deficiency, they nearly always exploded before reaching their targets!

On this concatenation of circumstances so improbable that no novelist would have based a plot on them, hung my life and those of the seventy-five other men aboard.

On that same patrol I saw my first ship actually sink. It was a small, unescorted freighter which we had attacked on the surface at night, setting our torpedo data computer by "seaman's eye" and aiming through the target bearing transmitter on the bridge. As officer of the deck I was given the privilege of conning us into position and aiming the torpedoes. Two were fired and both hit, flinging highly satisfying columns of water, spume, and debris into the air. The freighter stopped, sank down by the bow, lowered boats into which the crew piled, and then stopped sinking. We decided on another torpedo to make sure of the now abandoned ship, lined up carefully. Our third torpedo took a sharp jog to the left, ran a quarter circle, then straightened out on the proper course. As a result, it missed aft. We fired again, and our fourth fish was a bull's-eye, like the first two. Its streak of white bubbles went unerringly to the center of the motionless target, passed under it, and kept going, visible in the distance for two miles beyond the stricken ship.

After a few more minutes it was evident the old freighter was going to sink. But in the post-mortems which began immediately we were back to the same question. What in the world was wrong with our torpedoes?

Our submarine force was one of the most professional branches of our navy, rivaled, in our estimate, only by the comparable professionalism required of those who flew aircraft off the pitching decks of our carriers. The law of nature, death to those unable to meet the challenge of constant alertness, operated in both. And yet, with excellent ships, well-trained crews, the highest possible motivation, our early submarine effort was an unmitigated failure, a debacle.

We could operate our submarines with safety and sureness and we could survive in waters controlled by the enemy. But we could hardly hurt the enemy at all. Try as we might, we could not interfere with Japan's advance into the Philippines and Southeast Asia. Our subs were present at the Battle of Midway but in total impotence.

Most inexcusable, those in ultimate authority refused to accept the continually renewed evidence that there was something wrong. All unsuccessful attacks, without exception, were blamed on the skippers, their fire-control parties, and their torpedo-overhaul personnel. We knew both British and German submarine torpedoes had had similar problems, which were solved by a few weeks of driven work (Admiral Doenitz is said to have refused to send any more U-boats on patrol until their torpedoes were fixed). Yet impassioned demands for similar investigation of ours were put aside. Our technical experts had produced a perfect weapon which, by the mechanical marvel of its design, could only function correctly and could never fail to function correctly. If our torpedoes did not function as designed, the fault could only be that they were not being used correctly, for there was no way that a perfectly designed torpedo like ours could fail to work. Any other explanations were merely self-serving excuses.

In 1941, when the war broke out in the Pacific, the United States had three completely autonomous submarine forces: the Atlantic and Pacific Fleet forces, and the Asiatic Fleet submarine force. The largest and most war-ready, based on Cavite Navy Yard in Manila Bay (the same from which an outclassed Spanish squadron fought George Dewey's some forty-three years before), consisted of twenty-nine submarines, twenty-three of them new, long-ranging "fleet" types. This Asiatic Fleet submarine force was under the direct command of Admiral Thomas C. Hart, himself an old submariner who clearly understood what his boats could accomplish. For the record, of all the top commanders in the Pacific on December 7, 1941 (west longitude time), Hart was the only one whose forces were not caught by surprise.

War was very much in the air. Hart was well aware of Japan's propensity for surprise attack. Formosa was the obvious base for an invasion by Japan, and the first thing to anticipate was an air raid to establish air supremacy. So ran Hart's analysis, and the event proved him right. His further evaluation, instantly and devastatingly substantiated by loss of H.M.S. *Prince of Wales* and *Repulse*, was that the surface units of the Asiatic Fleet were no match for the aircraft likely to be sent against them. He had, accordingly, sent his surface combatant ships to the south, beyond the range of Formosa-based bombers. His submarines he kept concentrated on Cavite, ready for instant deployment except for two under rapid overhaul. In the event of an air attack, all subs able to submerge were to do so in Manila Bay until it was over. When they surfaced, after nightfall as instructed, Hart planned to send them to designated positions to oppose the invasion fleet he believed would be Japan's next move.

The anticipated air raid came on Monday, the eighth, at about noon east longitude time, roughly ten hours after the treacherous Sunday-morning surprise at Pearl Harbor, and well after receipt of definite information about it. Incredibly, despite full awareness of the disaster at our most important Pacific base, the new attack caught Clark Field also by complete surprise. Clark Field was Douglas MacArthur's principal air base, the source of virtually all U.S. air power in the Far Eastern theater. When the enemy arrived overhead, our bombers and fighters were lined up almost as if on inspection parade. The Japanese attackers fully availed themselves of the opportunity, and most of MacArthur's air force, nearly all of it new planes, was wiped out.

Although one can legitimately fault Admiral Hart, as Clay Blair does in his monumental *Silent Victory*, for not having had submarines on patrol along probable invasion routes, in the main he had shown himself far more closely attuned to the problems that actually developed than had MacArthur. He rightly appreciated that his subs would be the only weapons he would have available to check Japan's invasion of the Philippines once the enemy had established air superiority. He was confident that the situation would produce a conclusive demonstration of the strategic and tactical importance of his twenty-nine submarines.

That twenty-nine submarines could, and indeed should, have made a significant impact on the invading Japanese forces which immediately began landing in Lingayen Gulf is fully substantiated by history. In 1914 Germany achieved impressive results against England with an initial force of only twenty-five U-boats, some of them very primitive. In 1939 the story was the same. With not many more U-boats than in 1914, Germany's underseas campaign very shortly began once more to appear potentially catastrophic to England.

And yet, two full years later, despite all the opportunity they had had to observe the Atlantic war, two years to prepare to render an equally good account of themselves if necessary, our submariners were found wanting.

The causes of this failure are well known today, though perhaps even yet not sufficiently studied. In brief, while German, British, Italian, and Japanese torpedoes functioned well, ours performed so poorly that had they been had the subject of deliberate sabotage they hardly could have been worse. There were, of course, other problems, among them excessive bureaucracy. Our navy's concentration on paper-

paper results overwhelmed reality. Torpedo firing tests, for example, *had* to be successful. All submarines regularly fired practice torpedoes (fitted with light exercise heads instead of TNT-loaded warheads), in which "hits" were assigned on the basis of passing under the target vessel. Occasional "warshot" firing tests were assigned, but these were very few in number because of the cost of the torpedoes. Each submarine taking part in these more realistic firings was expected to go to extraordinary lengths, far beyond what could possibly be done in war, to make the torpedo perform according to specifications. The exercises were considered not only tests of the torpedo but also of the submarine and her crew, and failure in so conspicuous an exercise was career-damaging.

In the barrage of required reports, there was neither time nor desire to study the firings objectively. In addition, a new top-secret exploder, which detonated the warhead by the target's own magnetism, was installed in all Mark XIV warheads (the latest and most numerous), but because of its secrecy its performance was required to be accepted on faith.

Our submarines were commanded by men who were products of a system that penalized those who questioned too hard the established order of things. None were fighters against illogical bureaucratic decisions. None were rebels, and none were warriors, although some of them clearly possessed the requisite potential. All were strong, sober, cautious, and jealous bureaucrats, although, again, some were less so than others. They were, in short, what they had been trained to be. When war came, the success many actually deserved would have brought out their latent potential for combat (and in a few celebrated cases such potential came out anyway). But when success was lacking, men schooled in bureaucratic caution became confirmed in their caution. Lack of success made them wanting in confidence; lack of confidence made them cautious; and fear of failure made them timid.

While there were a few fine, aggressive, combat-oriented skippers in our submarines during those early wartime months, most were wretched failures. It was not their fault but that of the mold in which they had been formed, and the fact that they had a criminally defective weapon.

Had the Germans been in our place in Lingayen Gulf, it is my opinion that the Japanese landing would have been frustrated. Of course this cannot be proved, but I will always believe the loss of the Philippines could have been prevented. As it was, the entire battle for the Philippines was not only a failure, it was a shameful failure. We lost control of the air on the first day, and our effort to control the sea with our submarines, or at least contest it, was pathetically inadequate. The root cause of the debacle at sea was almost complete failure of the submarine weapon, the torpedo.

The torpedoes, unfortunately, did not fail utterly. Sometimes they worked, though more often they did not; and sometimes they appeared to work when in fact they had not hurt anyone. This, of course, not only made the problems harder to isolate, it also made it much harder to convince Washington that there really was something wrong. In the denouement there were not one but four things wrong with the torpedoes, any one of which should have led to thorough investigation, fixing of blame, instant and urgently prosecuted correction, and disciplinary action against those who had failed in their duty. They were:

(1) Running deeper than set. Report after report told of torpedoes running harmlessly under targets whose draft clearly was greater than the depth settings of the fish. Such reports were largely ignored as being self-serving excuses, since the ingenious magnetic, or "influence," exploder should have functioned even if the torpedo underran the target. Therefore, they had not passed under; they had missed entirely. Proposals to fire torpedoes through nets with their heavy warheads (believed to be at least partial cause of deep running, since they were much heavier than the exercise heads) were dismissed as wasteful of precious torpedoes, a huge stack of which had been lost at Manila Bay. When such tests were finally made, the fish were found not only to travel much deeper than set but also to move up and down in a sine wave, sometimes at depths so great that the influence exploder would not have worked. The more successful skippers, by this time, had long been setting their torpedoes to artificially shallow depths, three feet against a big ship, zero feet against small ones. Or as in *Trigger,* they strove always to attain the same firing situation in each attack, since it produced good results. In our case, it was fifteen hundred yards with a six-foot depth setting (I think, now, that the combination caused the torpedoes to be on the "up" curve when they reached the target; naturally, we had no idea of all this at the time).

These became the secrets of our trade, exchanged over booze between patrols and confidential conversations with fellow torpedo officers and skippers. They were not officially reported in our patrol reports because such flagrant disobedience of specific orders would have brought censure, particularly since most torpedoes missed anyway.

(2) Premature explosions. Often the influence exploder functioned too soon, immediately upon entering the target's magnetic field—which, we finally discovered, was stronger in the Pacific than in the Atlantic, and therefore actually protected our targets. From the submarine these would look like sure hits, and we could not understand how some targets kept steaming unscathed—although, indeed, they usually began violent evasive measures. This was a particularly invidious problem, since the natural tendency was to claim a hit. Many times it was not possible for the submarine to play the spectator, and sounds in the water, from whatever cause, could be interpreted as "breaking up noises" confirming a sinking; or in the case of an attack at night, an excited lookout's report that he saw a ship sink after such an explosion might receive more credence than it deserved. Circumstances such as these caused inflated reports of success during the early years of the war and made enemy ships seem even better able to sustain damage than they were in truth. And later on, when intelligence or subsequent observations of the same ship showed that it had not been sunk, the sub skipper's veracity was thereby put in question.

(3) Impotent contact exploder. When cumulative evidence against the magnetic exploder finally became too much to be ignored, some force commanders ordered it deactivated. The startling result was that the backup contact exploder, designed to set off the torpedo warhead if it hit even the slightest glancing blow against an enemy hull, would function *only* if the contact were indeed slight and glancing. A direct, solid hit, ninety degrees to the target's course, a perfect shot, in other words, would cause the exploding mechanism to deform before it could fire. Many submarine skippers reported noises that sounded to the sonar like a hit, without accompanying explosion but coincident with abrupt cessation of the torpedo's own machinery noise. Finally, Dan Daspit, the scientifically inclined skipper of the *Tinosa*, having damaged and immobilized a large tanker in mid-ocean, fired one per-

fectly aimed torpedo after another with carefully recorded data. All torpedoes hit. All were duds. Some he saw bounce out of the water, damaged, after striking the tanker's side. He returned to Pearl Harbor in a towering rage, with one torpedo which he brought back for a full-scale examination. This at last broke the back of the torpedo bureaucracy, which was now willing to concede that expending a few extra torpedoes in laboratory tests was better than expending them impotently in combat.

And so, in late 1943, all known defects in the torpedo exploders had at last been discovered and eliminated. Or so we thought; three problems had been solved, but there was no one around to complain that he actually had experienced the fourth and final problem. No attention was paid to those who voiced suspicions before the war's end. So the fourth difficulty, which had been largely obscured by the others, remained hidden, a very real danger to our subs during the entire course of the war, very likely more dangerous at its end than at the beginning. For, after 1943, the torpedoes were lethal when they hit home.

(4) Circular-running torpedoes. Torpedoes whose rudders jammed ran in a circle and returned, with warheads fully armed and ready to explode, to the spot from which fired. Nearly every submarine experienced one or more of these. Three times during my service aboard, one of *Trigger's* torpedoes ran back toward us, and two of them exploded magnetically while we were desperately going deep to avoid them. Destroyer torpedoes had an "anti-circular run" device, but for some reason this had not been installed in submarine torpedoes. As Rear Admiral Dick O'Kane suggests in *Clear the Bridge* (his memorial to his lost submarine, the extraordinary *Tang*), someone may have thought a submerged sub, under depth-charge attack, might try to sink the enemy overhead by firing a torpedo set to run in circles. No one tried this, for one went deep if under threat of depth charges, and our torpedoes would flood and sink if fired at such depths. But at least two of our subs, the *Tang* and *Tullibee*, were lost because their own torpedoes, fired at the enemy while they were on the surface, turned back on them.

We know about the *Tang* and *Tullibee* because both submarines had survivors who were picked up by the Japanese and came back from prison camps after the war. But what of the others? Of the fifty-two submarines we lost in the war, one was bombed while under overhaul at Cavite when the war began, and nine were lost to various operational accidents. Forty-two were sunk on patrol, and of these we know exactly what happened to seven because survivors came back. The remaining thirty-five were lost with all hands. Correlation of all known circumstances and action reports from both sides causes us to feel fairly sure of what happened to fifteen of these (we believe my poor old *Trigger* was depth-charged to extinction on March 27, 1945). Lost to unknown causes, with all hands, were twenty-five fleet submarines, and the only thing we know for sure is that no agency of Japan can be given the credit. It is possible that some of our boats struck moored mines, and some, I suppose, may have suffered improbable internal or operational casualties. But if the same percentages hold as for the seven from whom we do have survivors, as many as six of the twenty unexplained losses could have been from circular-running torpedoes they themselves fired. Or figuring the statistics in another way, if the seven with survivors are added to the fifteen whose losses we can correlate, then, statistically, two of the uncorrelated twenty *must* have been lost because of circular runs. The known circumstances point this way, but of course it is something we shall never know for sure. It will always remain only a dark murmur in the shadows.

In *Silent Victory,* Clay Blair treats our torpedo fiasco at considerable length and with authority. In his summation he says, "The torpedo scandal of the U.S. submarine force in World War II was one of the worst in the history of any kind of warfare." With this, all submariners in our navy will wholly agree, and many of them still passionately feel all those responsible should have been court-martialed. Nothing, in fact, was ever done (except that the torpedo factory in Newport, Rhode Island, is still a silent monument to its disgrace). Blair's carefully researched tome fails in only one thing: it cannot reproduce the anguished uncertainties, the self-doubts, the lack of confidence, which were attendant upon the total reversal of all pre-war training results. Nothing can be more demoralizing to men who must risk their lives in combat than to be forced to use weapons which they know, from experience, are not dependable, and for which they have no substitute—unless it be stubborn, unrealistic opposition by "experts" who, in the face of evidence, refuse even to investigate it.

Thus, in the same time it took for an approximately equal number of German subs to have England hanging on the ropes, ours had sunk only a couple of Japanese ships. Our subs made not the slightest dent in the Japanese timetable for conquest of the Philippines. We succeeded only in evacuating some trapped personnel—and several million dollars in gold bullion—from Corregidor. These exploits were well publicized, for we had little else to be proud of.

But by the end of 1943, when our torpedoes became dependable, the damage to Japan mounted rapidly. What could have been accomplished in December 1941, and in the early days of 1942, with the right weapons and the resulting skill and self-confidence, became a reality our enemy could not cope with. Not only were weapons reliable in 1944 but also new equipment of other kinds began to come our way: new, tougher-hulled, deeper-diving boats; more powerful surface-search radar; a new periscope, with a radar inside; better sonar; a radar detector to warn against enemy radar; electric torpedoes which had no wake to betray their approach. We no longer felt like orphans fighting a war no one was interested in. And finally, many of the older skippers, conditioned by two years of futility, were being relieved by younger ones with many war patrols in junior billets and much frustration over missed opportunities.

The Germans had done their worst execution among Allied convoys by attacking at night on the surface, until radar and aircraft made this tactic too hazardous. Since we held the radar advantage, we felt we could do at least as well. Some of the new skippers spent virtually entire patrols on the surface; but this should not be misunderstood, for it was the ability to submerge that enabled us to remain, alone and unsupported, in enemy-controlled seas. In the old days, when a warship had to contend only with others of her own kind, superior skill or speed, usually a combination of the two, could allow her to survive in unfriendly waters and even carry out hostile military missions. Times had changed by World War II. The *Prince of Wales* and *Repulse* could not survive, but our submarines did, even though they could not accomplish much.

The airplane is a strike weapon; it can bring overwhelming destruction to anything it can see to aim at but it does not stay.

It seeks, strikes, and goes. Most of the time it is on land or on the decks of an aircraft carrier, but it can control the air nevertheless, and with that goes control of the surface of the land or sea under that air. Unless it takes to the air itself, with its own missiles and aircraft, the surface ship—or the installation on land—cannot continue to exist under enemy air dominance. Only the submarine, which can depart the surface at will, can function in such an environment without diversion of most of its capabilities to its own defense. This was true in 1944, and it is true today. In the wild sea, only the submarine is free.

In 1944 Japan began to discover that her own home waters were no longer friendly. She had entered on the World War II adventure to secure unto herself the resources of the Asian mainland, but military conquest proved to be not enough. The sea lay between; and despite strenuous efforts at air cover, entire convoys could be wiped out in only a few hours.

At night, radar coverage was at its best and enemy air surveillance at its poorest. We, in the submarine, could cover a swath of sea forty miles wide, and all ships picked up by our radar, with the exception of other U.S. submarines (whose locations we kept track of), were enemy. Usually they traveled in convoys under escort of destroyers or antisubmarine ships of some kind. When an enemy contact was made, the radar tracking party would be called and quick initial observations plotted to determine the direction of movement and some idea of the speed. Then the boat would be swung to the intercepting course, using if necessary the full power of her four diesels, twenty knots. From the bridge we could see only the dark gray of night, the dark sea, and the dark sky. With the wind whipping against our faces, spray thrown from our rushing bows spattering on deck and over us, larger seas sometimes coming entirely aboard and drenching us, we could tell, from the manner of its rotation, what the radar antenna was doing: taking a fix on the convoy for plotting, searching the area to guard against surprise from some other quarter, or taking a navigational fix on the nearest land. Down below, the two plotting parties, one in the dimly lighted control room and the other in the brightly lighted wardroom, would be working out the many-times-practiced solutions, vying with each other for speed and accuracy: enemy base course and speed; the zigzag plan; the interval between successive zigs;

formation of the convoy; location of the biggest ship or ships; locations of escorts; and their manner of patrolling station. In the conning tower, the radar operators with their circular, red-lighted dials, could see the pips representing vessels. From their size and configuration, they determined which were the most valuable and most accessible targets, and they also became intimately familiar with the appearance of the escorts as reproduced on the scope.

Depending on the various considerations—time to first light, the phase of the moon, time of moon-rise or -set, visibility, the proximity of land, probable enemy course changes, the zigzag plan, the number of escorts, where and how they were patrolling, what types they were (if we could deduce this), the number of torpedoes we had remaining and their locations, forward or aft, whether steam or electric—we would select the position from which to begin the attack. It was, of course, necessary to remain out of enemy sight or radar range, but within our own, during the entire tracking period. Often this was difficult, for an alert escort on the convoy's near bow would force us to stay farther out than desired. And the way this escort patrolled his post had a great deal to do with our choice of attack position. Ideally we would want to come in at a high speed fairly sharp on the convoy's bow, preferably beginning the run-in immediately after completion of a zig. This would give the fastest closing speed and the longest interval before another zig would be due.

If a convoy had two escorts, their normal placement would be one on either bow. If more, the extras would patrol the flanks and quarters. At the beginning stage, the one near the bow would be our greatest worry, for we would have to pass close aboard him during the run-in. Sometimes the zigzag plan would have him out of position during one of the legs, and if so, we would choose this leg for the attack. Otherwise, we might plan to run in under his stern, reasoning this would be his least alert sector. In this case the resulting approach might be on a much broader track than we would have desired and thereby cause us to fire from a point nearer than we'd like to the flanking or quarter escort. Once past the bow escort, we feared the flank or quarter escort most, for it would be heading directly toward us.

It was always with a sense of total commitment that the order would be given to put the rudder over, go to full or flank speed, and start the run-in. Previously we might have been cruising along at convoy speed, outwardly leisurely, making our final observations, checking convoy disposition, ensuring that the situation remained as predicted by the plotting parties, that we had not been detected during the last few minutes. Once the rudder was put over we would be closing at high speed, nearly the sum of our speed and the convoy's, and there would be little or no chance of changing our mind about anything. Everything now hinged on remaining undetected as long as possible. Even detection by the target ships themselves could put us into peril, for a simple rudder movement on their part could place us dead ahead of them, our fire-control spoiled and our boat herself in danger of being sunk by ramming.

All four main engines would naturally long since have been on the line, waiting the climactic order, muttering gently through their exhaust ports. With the order to the rudder would go another to them, and their deep, throaty response would bellow as our propellers dug in. White spray, mixed with dark engine exhaust, would spurt out of four huge water-cooled mufflers squeezed under the main deck aft of the bridge, two exhausting to each side, and the light steam vapor produced would rise gently in the still air, drift quickly aft and to port, the plume to starboard floating across our low-lying afterdeck, as hard left rudder caused our stern to scud across the roiled waters of our wake. To me this was always a scene of defiance and poetry combined, even though total destruction, for someone, lay at the other end of the fantasy. This was the instant which divided those who could, and would, from those who could not.

Depending on all the local factors, and what we had been told about enemy radar, we generally reconnoitered the convoy from eight to ten miles—sixteen to twenty thousand yards—away. Escorts usually patrolled stations about five thousand yards away. The run-in, therefore, always involved passing an escort at uncomfortably close range, with our broadside exposed to him, throwing spray high above our bows, frequently over the bridge as well, and blaring our intentions to him through the rocketing roar of four big locomotive diesels he hardly could fail to hear. If he was listening, that is. The whole idea was to remain undetected and then to make our move so swiftly that we'd be come and gone before he had a chance to react. If we had picked the right time to begin, the escort would be at the far limit of his station, with his stern more or less in our direction at our closest point of approach. At worst, he would still have to turn completely around; at best he wouldn't see us at all. . . .

Once past the escort, we would have a few precious minutes to get set. Optimum firing range, with the electric torpedoes, would be about one thousand yards, half a nautical mile. The silhouettes of the enemy ships, originally tiny or completely invisible, would now be big. Slow down. The fish cannot be fired at high speed. The angle on the bow of the lead ship in the convoy should have been slowly increasing. What should it be now, conn? The answer, instantly back from the torpedo data computer, the TDC, checks with the visual estimate. The lead enemy ship can now be seen clearly. Two columns, six ships. We know this from radar, but now we see them. Our eyes on the bridge are at their maximum night adaption. The nearest is a big ship, with a big superstructure, probably once a combined passenger-freighter type with white upper works and black hull. Now totally darkened, she is simply a black silhouette against a cloudy gray of night, clearly outlined in form but without depth: the shadowy substance of a ship.

Angle on the bow is now estimated at starboard forty-five degrees. That checks with TDC. Speed the same as before, twelve knots. Plot, where's the ahead escort we just passed? Starboard quarter, still going away. Good. He hasn't seen us. How about the other escort, the tin can coming up to port? Still patrolling on his station, range closing but no sign of having detected us yet. What's our speed, conn? Fourteen knots. Still too fast. All ahead one-third. Our speed drops perceptibly. We roll easily to the slight chop. Range to leading ship? Two thousand. Angle on the bow now starboard fifty-two.

She is doomed, if the torpedoes work right. So is the ship next astern, also in clear view. Three fish to each. Then we'll swing hard right, so as to maintain maximum distance from that astern tin can coming up to port, and let fly with stern tubes at the third ship. Radar is now reporting ranges steadily. Bearings have been going in from the bridge target bearing transmitter, the TBT. No indication anywhere that we've been spotted. *Open outer doors forward!* In the older subs these had to be cranked open by hand. With us, in our rugged, just-built death weapon, they're opened hydraulically, the work of an instant. Range is twelve-hundred, torpedo run a thousand. Angle on the bow, starboard sixty-five. Gyros five right, increasing. *Outer doors are open forward! Stand by forward!* Standing by, bridge! Final TBT bearing, *mark!* Set, bridge! *Shoot!*

Three electric fish are away, running unseen in the dark water. The target is bigger than ever, looming above us. It is unbelievable that he can't see us. He's gone now, but he doesn't know it yet. That is, if the fish work right. They'll work. Quit worrying about them. *Shift targets!* TBT bearing, *mark!* Mark the radar range to the second ship! Angle on the bow, starboard sixty. Set! Range, fifteen-twenty! Gyros eight left, decreasing! Final TBT bearing and—*mark! Shoot!*

All torpedoes away forward, bridge! *All ahead flank! Right full rudder!* Six fish in the water, but nothing has happened yet. We think we can hear the machinery of our targets, the swish of water under their bows. Our own engines are roaring again. Our bow is swinging right, and we're closer than ever to the convoy. It will take about a minute for the first torpedo to get there. *What's the astern tin can doing?* He's closer, bridge, but still no sign of speeding up—BLAM! A flash of light, stunning! A column of white water, right amidships! BLAM! Again! Another hit, aft. Must be the third fish; the second must have missed forward. Still a chance for it; it must have been spread forward to allow for last-minute maneuvers or errors in our solution and, running on, it may hit something in the second column. Our speed has begun to pick up, and we're approaching the stricken ship as we swing starboard. She's listing toward us—you can tell because her silhouette now shows the curve of her deck on the far side— clouds of smoke are pouring out of her stack. She's badly wounded. There's still the bustle of much movement about her decks, humanity, disorganized, seeking to save itself. The ship must have been crowded with people. Almost certainly a troop transport. Well, these particular troops won't be campaigning anywhere for a while . . . BLAM! A hit in the second ship! Forward, and she goes down immediately by the bow! There should be another hit in her, at least one more—there it is, well aft! Another troop transport, and she's done for, too! Our stern is sliding across the greedy waves, which will soon claim two more ships, lining up for the third. There has not been enough time for the convoy to disintegrate, or the ships to maneuver, but the third ship in the column will certainly throw his rudder one way or the other. A quick adjustment to TDC will take care of him.

Range to stern escort is closing fast! The yell from the conning tower means that the tin can on the convoy's starboard quarter, the one from whom we expected most trouble, has speeded up, and has probably stopped station patrolling. He's coming to investigate and no doubt calling his crew to general quarters at the same time. We are practically dead ahead of him. A quick look: will there be time to get off the fish aft as originally planned? He *is* close, lean and ugly, headed straight for us. No doubt he's seen us at last. Funny that I don't hate him for wanting to kill me. *Four thousand yards to astern escort, bridge!* A fast decision; our torpedoes in the four stern tubes may be needed for a desperate defensive shot. The boys in the forward torpedo room have not had time to reload—difficult anyway with the motion of the ship on the surface. If we have to dive they'll have to be given warning well in advance, so as not to be caught with a down angle and a two-thousand-pound torpedo in midair. *What's the ahead escort doing?* Swivel around to steady the TBT on him. This is the lad we passed at high speed only a few minutes ago. While radar and the plots are hurriedly evaluating the range and bearing, we can see clearly enough what he's doing. He's already broadside to us, obviously turning around. *Range to ahead escort, four five double oh! We think he's closing slightly!* Both of these destroyers will be on us soon. *Forward torpedo room, secure the reload! Rig for depth charge!* We have opened out slightly from the convoy, our rudder still at right full, our engines complaining somewhat less as our speed builds up. If there was time, now would be the moment to slow down again and shoot the four stern fish at the third ship. But he, too, has waked up, has evidently put his rudder right, and is sheering out of column toward us. Maybe he's trying to ram; more likely he is simply trying to avoid his sinking fellows.

There is shambles in the convoy. Two big ships are hit and sinking, their forward motion swiftly dragging to a halt, lights flashing around their decks (no need to worry about darken ship any longer), lifeboats and life rafts hastily being readied, men working madly, others seeking their abandon-ship stations on the sloping decks. No time to waste thinking about them, nor of the probability of wholesale destruction and death in broken engine rooms and scalding firerooms. This is what we came for! It's what they deserve! Let them die! It's what they did to our people at Pearl Harbor, on Bataan, and everywhere they touched! But I can't really hate them. I've killed them; I've done what had to be done, but I don't hate them. I'd do it over, but I feel sorry for them.

Both ships are listing badly now. How to avoid the convergence of three others, one of them a big transport, headed our way with unfriendly intent? The rudder is still hard over, our propellers at full thrust—well, not quite. *Shift the rudder! Put your rudder left full! All ahead emergency! Maneuvering, give her everything you've got!* Everyone below is fully awake to the perilous situation. Even the rudder mechanism seems to respond faster than usual. One can instantly feel the effect on the motion of the ship. The closest ships to us are still the two just torpedoed. There's room to slip between them, and it's what the enemy might least expect. Moreover, they'll not be able to do the same as easily, and they'll not be able to shoot at us with those others in the way.

Having had time to build up speed, throwing increased smoke from the exhaust ports as the last notch of power is demanded from her diesels, our boat swings rapidly left, toward the sinking ships. We steady her on the open space between them, let her lunge ahead. Our engines, so suddenly put on maximum emergency power, have left a large cloud of exhaust smoke at the spot where we did our fishtail maneuver. That will confuse the issue a bit more for our opponents. Passing between the two sinking ships, there is a moment to savor the full impact of the disaster we have wrought on them. The first one hit is now virtually on her beam ends and down by the stern. Everything on deck is in impossible confusion. Deck gear, hatch covers, loose barrels and lumber, lifeboats and life rafts—equipment of all sorts is sliding and falling down vertical decks into the water. The outlines of men can be seen everywhere, many of them apparently wearing their knapsacks, for their shoulders are bulky. Some are standing in clear silhouette on the now horizontal port side. Our engines are drowning out all other sound, but we can imagine the hoarse shouts, the screams, the sound of heavy objects falling into the water and the duller thuds of them falling inside the broken hull. The ship to port is a little farther away, but in equally bad shape. She was nearly as big as the lead ship, and she, too, is covered with agonized humanity.

Neither ship can last many minutes longer. Nearly everyone we see is doomed. For many, trapped inside in what is by now a topsy-turvy nightmare, the nightmare will be mercifully short. For some it is already over, in the stillness of a flooded compartment. Most important, here are two ships whose service to our enemy is now terminated. Their absence will bring the Empire of Japan that much closer to the end.

On the other side of the convoy, the port side, the situation is as chaotic as on the starboard. One of our torpedoes, running through the near column of ships, has struck a freighter in the far column. Her bow is completely gone, from halfway to the bridge. She'll be under inside of an hour. The two escorts on this side are not visible, yet, anyway. The two remaining ships of the port column have radically altered course and, so far as we can determine, are simply fleeing the scene. This is made to order. We are already going as fast as our diesels can drive us; we simply parallel the nearest ship, taking care to stay out of visual range, drive ahead and then slow way down, with diesels muttering softly again, keeping our stern toward him, barely maintaining steerageway, waiting for him to come on. He does not even zigzag; he maintains a steady course, no doubt wishing to put the maximum distance between himself and the mayhem he has just witnessed. In vain, for two torpedoes come out of the blackness, and he is finished.

We have, in the meantime, directed the reload forward to resume. *Radar! Search all around and report!* The thing of greatest interest is the escort locations, for on this will depend our own next movements. There are two undamaged ships left of the original convoy, and four destroyer types with whom we'd as soon not tangle except in situations of our own choosing. While plot is evaluating the radar reports, we maintain moderate speed and steady course to ease reload. Eventually—it seems an interminable time—all torpedo tubes are reloaded and ready. In the meantime, we have begun to hear depth charges, under the circumstances a delightful sound.

Plot announces that the two starboard escorts are milling around the spot where we made our first attack. Evidently they think we made all that smoke when we dived, and whatever they are depth-charging, it is not us.

Daybreak is not far away. The two port-side escorts have joined with the single remaining ship of the port column and are escorting her on the original course, now zigzagging more radically than ever, and the third ship of the starboard column, which had sheered out toward us, is going it alone, still in that direction, diverging from the convoy's initial base course. We will have to select one of the two potential targets, for we cannot reach a submerged attack position for both. In the instant case, there is no choice. Up goes the power of our engines again, and plot is directed to steer clear of all contact with the enemy until we can submerge unseen, just before first light, dead ahead of the track of the single ship.

It is dawn when our target comes over the hill. He is zigzagging, but he should have made a radical course change, too. Possibly he was on the point of doing so at daybreak, which was why we planned our diving spot so as to be shooting before sunrise. With no escort, the approach is simple, submarine-school textbook, despite the zigzag. To make sure, we fire three torpedoes in a standard spread and get one hit. It blows her guts out in a highly satisfactory manner, and we let everyone in the conning tower have a look as she goes down.

Five big ships on the bottom; an excellent night's work. One we could not by any stretch have accomplished in 1942. But this was in 1944, and the steady execution of her shipping had become a national disaster for Japan. Not nearly able to cope with the hemorrhage by building new ships to replace those being lost, she took to sending fewer vessels in short daylight dashes from anchorage to anchorage. Instead of sending ships across the Yellow Sea, she sent them around its perimeter, along the coast of Korea to Tsingtao or Shanghai behind outlying islands whenever practicable. Anything to make the night surface attack less likely. Statistics backed up Japan on this, for by far the greatest damage to her shipping during those climatic last two years of the war came from submarines attacking on the surface at night.

But now, finally, there was nothing Japan could do.

Still, Japan had nearly succeeded at the outset of the war

because we were unready, because we were materially deficient, and because some of our top people were culpably negligent. It was a very hard lesson, but it was one we must ponder very carefully, lest, in different ways to be sure, and over different details, we let it happen again.

—December 1980

THE JUMP INTO SICILY

by GENERAL JAMES M. GAVIN

"For this challenge, I had come three thousand miles and thirty-six years of my life."

In July, 1943, we, the 505th Parachute Regimental Combat Team of the 82nd Airborne Division, were to spearhead the Allied invasion of Sicily. The fateful day of July 9, 1943, seemed to rush upon us, so busy were we with last-minute preparations, and almost before we realized it, we were gathered in small groups under the wings of our C-47s ready for loading and take-off. Appearing from a distance every bit like Strasbourg geese, the airplanes were so loaded with parachute bundles suspended beneath them that they seemed to drag the ground. These bundles carried equipment that would be dropped when the paratroopers jumped, and would float to the ground, we hoped, where we could find them. Because of security restrictions, it had not been possible to inform every trooper of our destination until just before take-off. Then each was given a small slip of paper which read: "Soldiers of the 505th Combat Team: Tonight you embark upon a combat mission for which our people and the free people of the world have been waiting for two years.

"You will spearhead the landing of an American Force upon the island of SICILY. Every preparation has been made to eliminate the element of chance. You have been given the means to do the job and you are backed by the largest assemblage of air power in the world's history.

"The eyes of the world are upon you. The hopes and prayers of every American go with you. James M. Gavin."

The plan was simple. Taking off from Tunisia in a long column of aircraft, we were to fly via the island of Linosa to

Malta. There we were to dog-leg to the left, coming in on Sicily's southwestern shore. This was an important point—the island was to come into sight on the right side of the approaching aircraft. The orders were that every man would jump even though there might be some uncertainty in his mind as to his whereabouts. No one but the pilots and crews were to return to North Africa.

Individual equipment was given a final check, and loading began. The equipment consisted of a rifle or carbine, rations, water, knife, grenades, compass, and here and there a bazooka. The bazookas were most important, since they were the only weapons the troopers were carrying that would enable them to engage the German armor on reasonable terms. The pilots were revving up their engines, and we were ready to roll down the runway when an airman from the weather station ran up to the door of the plane yelling for me, "Colonel Gavin, is Colonel Gavin here?" "Here I am," I answered, and he yelled, "I was told to tell you that the wind is going to be thirty-five miles an hour, west to east." He added, "They thought you'd want to know."

Well, I did, but there was nothing I could do about it. Training jumps had normally been canceled when the wind reached about fifteen miles an hour, in order for us to minimize injuries. Few of us had jumped with winds of more than twenty-five miles an hour. But we couldn't change plans now. Besides, there were many other hazards of greater danger in prospect than the thirty-five-mile-an-hour wind.

At about this time in my troubled thinking another individual staggered to the door of the plane with a huge barracks bag on his shoulder. He heaved it through the door onto the floor of the plane, saying as he did so, "I was told to give this to you or your S-1." The S-1, or personnel officer, is responsible for the administrative handling of prisoners.

I asked, "What in the hell is it?"

He replied, "They are prisoner-of-war tags. You're supposed to put one on every prisoner you capture, and be sure to fill it out properly."

This was no time for argument, when we were within seconds of roaring down the runway, so I merely replied, "O.K."

About an hour after departure the personnel officer, Captain Alfred W. Ireland, threw them into the Mediterranean.

Due to the high winds, the entire air armada was blown far east of its intended landing zones. Some pilots made landfall along the eastern coast of Sicily and, having done so, turned back to find their way around to the southwest coast. Several planeloads actually jumped in front of the British army on the east coast. These troopers were from the 3rd Battalion and Regimental Headquarters. The first problem they encountered, to their surprise, was that the British had a different countersign. The American countersign was "George Marshall"—that is, when one met an unknown person that night, one was supposed to challenge by saying, "George." The response from a friend was expected to be "Marshall." Otherwise, a shooting engagement took place. To the dismay of the American paratroopers, they found that "George" was greeted by a fusillade of fire. One big, burly, redheaded Irishman, well over six feet tall, in the Regimental Demolitions Platoon, talked to me about his experiences afterward. When first challenged, he was shot at, so he decided to hide and grab any British soldier he could get close to and explain his predicament. Soon a British soldier came by. He jumped out and pinned his arms to his sides and told him who he was. Thus, he learned the British countersign and survived. That detachment fought side by side with the British for several days, but was finally put aboard a boat and sent to the American landing beaches near Gela.

The 2nd Battalion, commanded by Major Mark Alexander, was the next farthest to the east to land. It landed about fifteen miles east of Gela, near the town of S. Croce Camarina, an area that had figured prominently in Thucydides' account of the Peloponnesian Wars. As Major Alexander's plane was crossing the Mediterranean, he stood at the door and watched its progress, looking for familiar landmarks. The red warning light to be ready to jump came on, and his troopers stood up and readied themselves. Suddenly, while they were still over the ocean, the green light came on. The men tried to push him out the door, as they were trained to do when the lead man hesitated, but he succeeded in fighting them off. He then went forward to ask the pilot, "What in the hell are you doing?" The pilot replied, "The co-pilot was in too much of a hurry." They continued a bit farther, crossed the coast, receiving considerable tracer fire, and the battalion jumped.

Although they landed amid a number of huge pillboxes and areas organized for defense, they were quite successful in reorganizing the battalion. The Italian pillboxes were formidable affairs, several stories high, with apertures here and there, so sited as to overlook other pillboxes. The troopers quickly learned that the way to reduce them was to keep firing at the slits until a trooper could get close enough to throw a grenade into them. The battalion fought most of the night and by daylight had assembled a majority of its men. It then moved toward the coast near a village overlooking the town of Marina di Ragusa, and they organized an all-around defense for the night.

In the meantime they began to receive machine-gun and sniper fire from high ground near the area they had been in earlier. A British cruiser showed up off the coast, and Mark Alexander found that he had a lieutenant who could use a flashlight and communicate with the cruiser, using the Morse code. They requested fire support on the slope to the north of their positions. As Mark Alexander reported it later, "The cruiser immediately laid in two salvos. The first must have come in about seventy-five feet over our heads, and you can believe me when I say that the whole slope went up in flames. I called for a cease-fire and we received no more harassment from snipers the rest of the night." By daylight, July 11, his battalion turned north and moved in the direction of S. Croce Camarina, using donkeys, donkey carts, and wheelbarrows to help carry the weapons and ammunition. At noon his battalion captured S. Croce Camarina and later that afternoon captured Vittoria. They rejoined their division, the 82nd Airborne, on July 12. Meanwhile, those of us who had landed closer to the target areas had been having a busy time of it.

My own flight with the Regimental Headquarters group was uneventful until Linosa was due. It was not to be seen. Malta, which was to be well lighted to assist our navigators, could not be seen either. Suddenly, ships by the score became visible in the ocean below, all knifing their way toward Sicily. Obviously, we were off course, since our plan called for us to fly between the American fleet on the left and the British on the right. In fact, the Americans told us that we would probably be shot down if we flew over them. We continued on, finally dog-legging to the left on the basis of time calculation. Soon the flash of gunfire could be seen through the dust and haze caused by the preinvasion bombing, and finally the coast itself could be seen off to the right. Unfortunately, many of the planes overflew the Malta dog-leg, and the island first became visible on the left, thus causing confusion and widespread dispersion of the troopers.

We turned inland; the small-arms fire increased; the green light over the jump door went on, and out we went. The reception was mixed. Some of us met heavy fighting at once, others were unopposed for some time, but all were shaken up by the heavy landings on trees, buildings, and rocky hillsides.

I managed to get together a small group and start across country, searching for the combat-team objective. I had with me Captain Ireland, the combat-team personnel officer, and Captain Ben Vandervoort, the combat-team operations officer, and three other troopers. The cross-country going was rough, but we pressed on. Soon we came face to face with our first enemy.

It happened about an hour after we had landed. I was moving ahead with about twenty troopers who had joined us by then. I was leading, and Vandervoort was alongside. I moved along through the shadows in the olive groves, over stone walls, darting across moonlit roads, going in what I hoped was the direction of our objective. There had been occasional bursts of small-arms fire, sometimes quite close, but so far we had not seen an actual enemy. Suddenly, there were foreign voices, then the sound of a man whistling some distance away. As he got closer, it sounded like "O Sole Mio." I had my group stay down, and I moved up to a stone wall that paralleled the road he was coming along. It was a lone man, walking down the middle of the road, hands in the pockets of his baggy uniform pants. After twenty years of military service, I was about to meet The Enemy face to face. I stuck my head up over the stone wall. It seemed a long way up, but it was really about an inch, just to clear my carbine over the top of the wall.

I gave him my best Italian, "Alto!" He stopped in his tracks. Vandervoort rushed through an opening in the wall with a .45 in one hand and a knife in the other.

"I'll take care of him," Van said. I wasn't sure what he meant, but I said, "No, let's get the hell out of the middle of the road. Let's get over into the shadows and maybe we can get some information out of him."

There was still some doubt as to whether we were in Sicily, Italy, or the Balkans, although the odds strongly favored the first.

About half a dozen of us surrounded him, and I tried the few Italian words I knew.

"*Dove Palermo?*"

No reply. He seemed to be either too scared or too bewildered to answer.

"*Dove Siracusa?*"

I figured that if he would point in the general direction of either or both of these two cities, which were at opposite ends of the island, we could get our first fix on where we were. Since he acted as if he had never heard of either, for a moment it seemed that perhaps we were not even in Sicily. But he was obviously very scared. We had heard that the Germans had scared the wits out of the natives with their stories about the atrocities committed by American parachutists. They spread the news that we were long-term convicts who had been granted our freedom in exchange for becoming paratroopers. This was given credence by the practice in many parachute units of having all the men shave their heads. After the battle of Sicily was over, the Sicilians told us that shaved heads were one of the things that had convinced them that the Germans were right.

But to get back to Giuseppe, or whatever his name was, I hadn't been able to get anything out of him—not his name, where he was from, or where he thought we were. I reluctantly decided that we would have to take him along. Vandervoort had taken an intelligence course and knew how to handle a prisoner in a situation like this. The idea was to take the belt out of the prisoner's trousers and to cut the buttons off his fly so that he would have to hold up his trousers when he walked.

Van put his .45 in his holster, pressed his knife against the Italian's chest, and said, "I'll take care of the bastard."

The Italian was muttering, "Mamma mia, Mamma," over and over again. His concern was understandable. The moonlight was shining on the knife blade, and it looked as though it were a foot long. He took off his belt and dropped it. Then Van went into phase two of the operation and reached for the fly with one hand, bringing down the knife with the other.

A scream went up that could be heard all the way to Rome. The stories the Italians had heard about the atrocities of the paratroopers and Ethiopia must have flashed through his mind; he was being castrated. He screamed louder, grabbing the knife blade with his right hand. The blood ran down his hand as we fell in a kicking, yelling, fighting mass, and he got away. I do not know how he did it, but one second he was with us and the next he was gone. I was madder than hell. I asked Vandervoort, "What in the hell did you think you were doing?"

Vandervoort didn't answer. I decided that we had better get going. By now we had probably alerted any enemy for miles around.

We walked on into the night, crawling over the high stone walls. Although some men were suffering from jump injuries, they drove themselves toward the cascading flame and white phosphorus of bursting shells that could be seen on the distant horizon. The sight of the shellbursts was reassuring, since it meant that we were in Sicily. And we were "moving toward the sound of the guns," one of the first battle axioms I had learned as a cadet at West Point.

But human flesh could do only so much, and the night was demanding. By count at daylight, there were six of us. I approached two farmhouses, but at both of them the natives were terrified and hardly would talk. I continued on in a direction I figured would take us toward our objective. Suddenly, as we came over the crest of high ground, there was a burst of small-arms fire.

We hit the ground. There was a sickening thud of near misses kicking dirt into my face. I reacted instinctively as I had been taught in the infiltration course by hugging closely to the ground. In no time I realized that I would not continue to live doing that; I had to shoot back. I started firing with my carbine, and it jammed. I looked to Vandervoort about six feet to my left; he was having the same trouble. About fifty yards away an Italian officer stood looking at us through low-hanging branches of an olive tree. He was wearing leather puttees and reddish-brown breeches, both plainly visible beneath the branches. Captain Ireland gave him the first burst of his Tommy gun, and he went down like a rag doll. I began to fire my carbine single-shot. The leading trooper, who had gone down at the first fusillade, writhed and rolled over. He appeared to be dead, practically in the enemy position. Their fire increased, and there was a loud explosion like that of a small mortar shell. I decided that there was at least a platoon of enemy and that our best prospects were to try to work around it. I yelled to Vandervoort, Ireland, and the troopers to start moving back while I covered. It worked.

We had a close call and nothing to show for it but casualties, and our prospects were not very bright. I continued to move cross-country in a direction that would take me around the area where we had had the fire fight. We could hear intense firing from time to time, and we were never sure when we would walk into another fire fight or how we would get into the battle since we couldn't tell friend from foe. Then there was the problem of enemy armor. I decided to look for a place where tanks would be unlikely to travel and where we could get good cover to hole up until dark. I wanted to survive until dark and then strike across country again to the combat-team objective. It was the high ground east and north of Gela, and there, with the help of God, I hoped to find troopers, and an enemy to fight. For this challenge, I had come three thousand miles and thirty-six years of my life—for the moral and physical challenge of battle.

By mid-morning we came to some good cover. It was a shallow ravine crisscrossed by several irrigation ditches. Along one of them was a thicket of underbrush. The ditch was cut out of the side of a gently sloping hill, and from its edge there was a good view for about half a mile across cultivated land. The ditch I picked was almost dry; the others had a lot of water in them. It did not appear to be a place where a tank would travel by choice. I took stock of our situation, and it wasn't good. Among us we had two carbines that jammed, one Tommy gun, a pistol, and an M-1 rifle. We were holed up like hunted animals. Tired, wounded, hungry, but too sick at heart to eat, we apprehensively scanned the countryside for any sign of friend or foe. Occasional bursts of rifle and machine-gun fire could be heard in the distance.

It had been a long day. We waited and waited for dark. Soon the Sicilian sun was low in the sky and quickly disappeared like a ball of fire into a cauldron. We began to get things together so as to be able to move out. Water was a first need; it was almost gone. For food we had a few carton of K rations and some concentrated things in an escape kit. An escape kit was a small plastic box, about six inches square and an inch thick, that contained the essentials for escape and survival behind enemy lines, such as a map, water purification pills, and a rubber-coated file that could be hidden in the rectum. I felt I had been a failure on my first day in combat and had accomplished nothing. I was determined to find my regiment and engage the enemy, wherever he might be. We went into the Sicilian night, heading for what we hoped was Gela, somewhere to the west. It was a relief to be moving instead of sitting and worrying. Sitting and worrying had been the hardest of all, and I had done a lot of it.

After about an hour we were challenged by a small group of wounded and injured of the 505th under the command of Lieutenant Al Kronheim. We traded morphine Syrettes for their M-1 rifles and ammunition and continued to the west. About two-thirty we were challenged by a machine-gun post of the 45th Division, and at last we had re-entered our own lines. We learned that we were about five miles southwest of Vittoria. In about another mile we came to the main paved road from the beach to Vittoria, passing by a number of foxholes and dead Italian soldiers. By then I had about eight troopers with me. We heard the sound of armor coming and at once got off the road and concealed ourselves on both sides. I cautioned the troopers not to fire if it was a friendly tank. Everybody was so excited, however, that when the first tank appeared, there was a fusillade; it seemed as though everyone fired on it. It was an American tank, fortunately buttoned up, and no one was hurt.

We then went on to the edge of Vittoria, where I was able to borrow a jeep. I had heard rumors that there were more paratroopers a few miles away in the direction of Gela. I continued on to Gela and to my surprise came across the 3rd Battalion of the 505th, in foxholes in a tomato field, and just awakening. The battalion commander, whose nickname was "Cannonball," was sitting on the edge of a foxhole, dangling his feet. I asked him what his men were doing. He said that he had been reorganizing the battalion and that he had about 250 paratroopers present. He had landed nearby and had rounded everybody up. I asked him about his objective, several miles to the west near Gela, and he said that he had not done anything about it. I said we would move at once toward Gela and told him to get the battalion on its feet and going. In the meantime I took over a platoon of the 307th Engineers, commanded by Lieutenant Ben L. Wechsler. Lieutenant Colonel Edward Krause, commanding the 3rd Battalion of the 505th Parachute Infantry Regiment, said that there were supposed to be Germans between where he was and Gela and that the 45th Division had been having a difficult time.

Using the platoon of engineers as infantry, we moved at once on the road toward Gela. We had hardly started when, as we went around a bend in the road, a German motorcycle with an officer in the sidecar drove up in the midst of us. We put our guns on him. He threw up his hands, said he was a medical officer, pointed to his insignia, and told us he wanted to be released at once. We weren't about to release him. He was the first live German we had ever seen in combat, and we noticed that he had grenades in the sidecar. Reasoning that an armed medic should not be let loose, we took the motorcycle and sidecar from him and started him to the rear on foot, disarming the driver also. The medic said they had been moving down from Biscari toward Vittoria. We could hear a great deal of firing, so we continued.

By then it was broad daylight, about 8:30 A.M. In less than a mile we reached a point where a small railroad crossed the road. On the right was a house where the gatekeeper lived. There was a striped pole that could be lowered to signal the automotive and donkey-cart traffic when a train approached. Just ahead was a ridge, about a half a mile away and perhaps a hundred feet high. The slope to the top was gradual. On both sides of the road were olive trees and beneath them tall brown and yellow grass, burnt by the summer sun. I had no idea where we were at the time, but I later learned the place was called Biazza Ridge.

The firing from the ridge increased. I told Lieutenant Wechsler to deploy his platoon on the right and to move on to seize the ridge. Then I sent word to Cannonball to bring his battalion up as promptly as he could.

We moved forward. I was with Wechsler, and in a few hundred yards the fire became intense. As we neared the top of the ridge, there was a rain of leaves and branches as bullets tore through the trees, and there was a buzzing like the sound of swarms of bees. A few moments later, Wechsler was hit and fell. Some troopers were hit; others continued to crawl forward. Soon we were pinned down by heavy small-arms fire, but so far nothing else.

I made my way back to the railroad crossing, and in about twenty minutes Major William Hagen joined me. He was the battalion executive for the 3rd Battalion. He said the battalion was coming up. I asked where Cannonball was, and he said that he had gone back to the 45th Division to tell them what was going on. I ordered Hagen to have the troops drop their packs and get ready to attack the Germans on the ridge as soon as they came up. By that time we had picked up a platoon of the 45th Division that happened to be there, part of a company from the 180th Infantry. There was also a sailor or two who had come ashore in the amphibious landings. We grabbed them also.

The attack went off as planned, and the infantry reached the top of the ridge and continued to attack down the far side. As they went over the top of the ridge, the fire became intense. We were going to have a very serious situation on our hands. This was not a patrol or a platoon action. Mortar and artillery fire began to fall on the ridge, and there was considerable machine-gun fire. I was worried about being enveloped on the right; some of the 45th Infantry Division should have been down on the left toward the beaches, but the right was wide open, and so far I had no one I could send out to protect that flank. If the German column was coming from Biscari, the tactical logic would have suggested that they bypass me on the right and attack me from the rear. At that time I had a few engineers I kept in reserve, and two 81-mm. mortars. They were commanded by a young officer, Lieutenant Robert May, who had been my first sergeant almost a year earlier when I had commanded C Company of the 503rd Parachute Infantry. He sent two or three troopers off to the right as a security patrol. Later, men with Mountain Pack 75-mm. artillery pieces from the 456th Parachute Artillery joined me. These were artillery pieces that could be broken down into several parts and carried by paratroopers or mules. Occasionally, troopers, having heard where we were, would come in from the direction of Vittoria. I began to try to dig in on the back of the crest of the ridge. The ground was hard shale, and I made little headway. The entrenching shovel was too frail, so I used my helmet to dig; it wasn't much better. But we needed protection from the mortar fire that was becoming quite heavy, and I kept digging.

The first wounded began to crawl back over the ridge. They all told the same story. They fired their bazookas at the front plate of German tanks, and then the tanks swiveled their huge 88-mm. guns at them and fired at the individual infantrymen. By this time the tanks could be heard, although I could not see any because of the smoke and dust and the cover of vegetation. Hagen came in, walking and holding his thigh, which had been torn badly by fire. Cannonball had gone forward to command the attack. It did not seem to be getting anywhere, however, as the German fire increased in intensity and our wounded were coming back in greater numbers.

The first German prisoners also came back. They said they were from the Hermann Goering Parachute Panzer Division. I remember one of them asking if we had fought the Japanese in the Pacific; he said he asked because the paratroopers had fought so hard. Ahead of us, mixed with the olive trees, were low grapevines that covered men on the ground quite completely. I went back a few hundred yards to check the 81-mm. mortars and to see how many other troopers had joined us. A few had. Lieutenant May had been hit by mortar fragments. I talked to the crews of the two Pack 75-mm. artillery pieces and told them we were going to stay on the ridge no matter what happened. We agreed that they should stay concealed and engage the less heavily armored underbellies of the tanks when they first appeared at the top of the rise. It was a dangerous tactic, but the only thing we could do, and tanks are vulnerable in that position. I was determined that if the tanks overran us, we would stay and fight the infantry.

I went back to try to dig my foxhole. By then it had become evident that I would never get deep enough, so I decided to dig the front end about eighteen inches deep, and the back end about a foot deep; then if I sat down in it and put my head between my knees, a tank could roll over me without doing too much damage. So I continued from time to time, when circumstances permitted, to try and get farther into the ground.

At the height of the fighting the first German Messerschmitts appeared overhead. To my surprise, they ignored us and attacked the small railroad gatekeeper's house repeatedly. They must have thought that that was the command post; it was indeed a logical place for it to be. They did not attack any of us near the top of the ridge. A few more troopers were still coming in. Now added to the enemy small-arms fire was the tank fire.

Captain Al Ireland, who was still with me, suggested that he go back to the 45th Division and get help. It was the best idea I had heard all day. I had been so busy handling the tactical crisis that the possibility had never entered my mind. The mortar fire continued in intensity, and moving along the back of the ridge to check the security on the right and the position of a 75-mm. gun the troopers were dragging up, I found myself lying on the ground bouncing from the concussion. The best way to protect yourself was to place your palms flat on the ground as though you were about to start doing push-ups, and thus absorb the shock of the ground jolts.

In front of us, beyond the vineyard and about four hundred yards to the right, was a small group of buildings. Slowly, very slowly, a German tank became visible. We first saw the right track of the tank come around the corner of the stone house. Then we saw the muzzle of the gun. A Tiger tank is an awesome thing to encounter in combat. Weighing more than sixty tons, and armed with an 88-mm. gun and machine guns, it was far more formidable that anything we had ever seen, and we had nothing in our own armored forces to compare with it.

The artillery paratroopers decided that they would take a chance and engage it directly with a 75-mm. gun. The 75 was the only artillery piece the parachutists could get in 1943. No one had ever intended that the 75 would be an antitank gun, certainly not against the front of a Tiger. Nevertheless, the paratroopers snaked their gun up the ridge until they were plainly visible and could get a direct line of sight on the tank. Field artillery in the front lines, shades of gallant Pelham at Fredericksburg! The tank inched forward, the driver probably hoping that we did not see him. It was obvious that his problem was to get far enough out so he could swing the gun at us and then fire directly, but in order to do this he had to get at least half of the tank exposed. It continued to move out slowly, very slowly. The crew of our 75 mm. were on their knees and lying down, with the gun loaded and ready to fire.

Suddenly there was a tremendous explosion. The tank had fired and hit the ground just in front of the gun, knocking the troopers like tenpins in all directions. I was standing just at the left rear, watching the action, and I was knocked down too. Probably I hit the ground instinctively. The troopers got up and ran off like startled quail. A second later they realized, to their embarrassment, what they were doing, and they ran back to the gun. They fired one round that hit the tank or the corner of the building. In the smoke and dust the tank backed out of sight.

That was the last we saw of it. To my amazement, none of the gun crew were hurt. Tanks began to work their way forward off to our left, coming directly up through the vineyard. Although the tank we fired at had backed up, I got the impression that the tank activity was increasing and that we were facing a pretty heavy attack that would come over the ridge at any moment. Back to digging, with little progress.

Two troopers came from my left rear in an Italian tracked personnel carrier. They were equipped with rifles and wanted to go over the top of the ridge to engage the Germans. I suggested that they not do it, warning them that they would be knocked out, but they insisted they could take care of themselves. They added that they wanted to "scare the Krauts" into thinking that we too had armor.

They had hardly gotten over the top of the ridge when a direct hit exploded the vehicle into flames. All the next day it was still there, smoking, with two skeletons in the front seat. An ambulance that must have been from the 45th Division showed up, and a doctor from the 505th took it over. He drove it over the ridge—he was on the running board. It was engaged in fire, and he was knocked to the ground.

I had established an aid station with medics who were off to the left, a couple of hundred yards away. They were bandaging casualties and giving them morphine and sulfa. The fire continued in considerable volume into midafternoon. About this time Cannonball came over the ridge and said that all the men in his battalion were killed, wounded, or pinned down and ineffective. I told him we were going to stay at the top of the ridge with what we had and fight the German infantry that came with the tanks. He said that we didn't have a chance, that we'd be finished if we tried to stay there. He went to the rear. I could have relieved him of his command, but I knew how he felt and I let him go.

About four o'clock a young ensign, who had parachuted

with me the first night, came up with a radio and said he could call for naval gunfire. I was a bit nervous about it, because we didn't know precisely where we were, and to have the Navy shoot at us would only add to the danger and excitement of what was turning out to be quite a day. We tried to fix our position in terms of the railroad crossing over the road, and he called for a trial round. It came down precisely where the tank had disappeared. He then called for a concentration, and from then on the battle seemed to change. I kept thinking of Shiloh, bloody Shiloh. General Grant, sheltered under the riverbank, his command overrun, refused to leave the field, counterattacked, and the battle was won.

In about an hour I heard that more troopers were coming, and at six o'clock I heard that Lieutenant Harold H. Swingler and quite a few troopers from Regimental Headquarters Company were on the road. Swingler had been a former intercollegiate boxing champion; he was a tough combat soldier. He arrived about seven o'clock. In his wake appeared half a dozen of our own Sherman tanks. All the troopers cheered loud and long; it was a very dramatic moment. The Germans must have heard the cheering, too, although they did not know then what it was about. They soon found out.

By now no more wounded were coming back. A heavy pall of dust and acrid smoke covered the battlefield. I decided it was time to counterattack. I wanted to destroy the German force in front of us and to recover our dead and wounded. I felt that if I could do this and at the same time secure the ridge, I would be in good shape for whatever came next—probably a German attack against our defenses at daylight, with us having the advantage of holding the ridge. Our attack jumped off on schedule: regimental clerks, cooks, truck drivers, everyone who could carry a rifle or a carbine was in the attack. The Germans reacted, and their fire increased in intensity. Just about two hundred yards from the top of the ridge Swingler crawled up on a cut through which the paved road ran and saw a German Tiger tank with the crew standing outside looking at it. He dropped a grenade among them and killed them, and thus we captured our first Tiger. There were several bazooka hits on the front plate with holes about the size of one's little finger, but they went in only about an inch or so. The sloped armor on the Tiger was about four and a half inches thick.

Soon we overran German machine guns, a couple of trucks, and finally we captured twelve 120-mm. Russian mortars, all in position with their ammunition nearby and aiming stakes out. They were obviously all ready to fire. Apparently our men had either killed, captured, or driven off the German crews. The attack continued, and all German resistance disappeared, the Germans having fled from the battlefield.

That same night, learning that the Germans had completely withdrawn from the action at Biazza Ridge, I moved my command post from the top of the ridge back about a half mile under the olive trees. I deployed the troopers for the night, expecting an attack from the direction of Biscari to come into our right flank, probably at daylight.

It must have been about ten o'clock at night when all hell broke loose in the direction of the beaches. Antiaircraft fire was exploding like fireworks on the Fourth of July, tracers were whipping through the sky, and as we were observing the phenomena, the low, steady drone of airplanes could be heard. They seemed to be flying through the flak and coming in our direction. Everyone began to grasp his weapons to be ready to shoot at them. A few of us cautioned the troopers to take it easy until we understood what was going on. Suddenly, at about six hundred feet the silhouettes of American C-47s appeared against the sky—our own parachute transports! Some seemed to be burning, and they continued directly overhead in the direction of Gela. Some troopers jumped or fell from the damaged planes, and at daylight we found some of them dead in front of our positions.

Later we learned that it was the 504th Parachute Infantry that was being flown to a drop zone near Gela to reinforce the 1st Infantry Division. General Ridgway had been there to meet them. Unfortunately, the Germans had sent in parachute reinforcements on the British front to the east the same night. In addition, there had been German air attacks on our Navy, so when the parachute transports showed up, our ships fired at them, and twenty-three were shot down and many damaged.

Soon the battlefield was quiet. I dug a foxhole and lay down. The next thing I knew, the bright warm sun was shining in my face and it was broad daylight. Everybody around me was sleeping soundly in the foxholes. We had been so exhausted by the experience we had been through since our landing that we were all physically worn out. I started to get up and found that my left leg was stiff and sore. My trouser leg was slightly torn, and my shinbone was red, swollen, and cut a bit. I must have been nipped by a mortar fragment the day before. I went to the nearest aid station; they put on some sulfa powder and I was as good as new. They said they would put me in for a Purple Heart. I said nothing about it—I had already learned that among twenty-four-hour veterans, only goof-offs got Purple Hearts.

I then began to get the battalion organized for the move to our regimental objective near Gela. But the first order of business was to take care of our dead and wounded. We brought in fifty bodies and, using picks and shovels we had sent for, we buried them near the top of the ridge. We tried to use German POW's to dig the graves, but they were not very helpful. The regimental chaplain made wooden crosses out of K-ration boxes, and we gave the troopers an appropriate burial. It had been a sad experience: many of them had had pieces of bazookas ground up in them by tanks as they were crushed. We had also lost more than one hundred wounded.

As General Gavin learned years later, his hard, grim fight on Biazza Ridge was more important than he could have known at the time. The commander of the Hermann Goering Division, Major General Paul Conrath, had his troops perfectly positioned on the night of July 9. In fact, had he been aware of the Allied plans, he could not have been better situated. He was about twenty-five miles from the disembarkation beaches of the American 1st and 45th Divisions, ready to strike promptly when he learned where the invaders were coming ashore.

Many of the wind-scattered paratroopers of the 82nd Airborne, including Gavin's 505th Regiment, drifted down between the Germans and the Allied troops who were landing on the beaches. Thus, when Conrath tried to push the Allies back into the sea, he found his communication lines cut, and his troops harassed and pounced upon by American paratroopers.

While the battle of Biazza Ridge was taking place between Gavin's troopers and a tank-supported regiment of the Hermann Goering Division, another German column was attacking the 1st Infantry Division with more success near Gela. At this point, however, the German resistance at Biazza Ridge collapsed. As reported later in the official U.S. Army history of the war, "The paratroop stand on Biazza Ridge prompted

Conrath to change his plans," and pull out not only the mauled survivors of that battle, but also the other German column pushing toward Gela. This respite for the Americans, still struggling to hold a beachhead, contributed substantially to the capture of Sicily. The 82nd Airborne Division had passed its first test with honors.

—April 1978

PLOESTI: A PILOT'S DIARY

by LEWIS N. ELLIS

A thousand miles behind enemy lines, Liberator bombers struck Hitler's Rumanian oil refineries, then headed for home flying so low that some came back with cornstalks in their bomb bays.

*B*enghazi, Libya, July 23, 1943. Something new is in the air! This morning we were introduced to a Major Blank, an expert in low-level bombing, who lectured us on a new bombsight, which was a converted gunsight. He explained how A-20s had been making low-level attacks and that experiments were being made with B-24s. He said that he didn't know if the new sights would ever be used, but we assumed the Air Force wouldn't be running experiments that far out in the desert for nothing, so we decided to get interested in low-level bombing.

July 24, 1943. This afternoon several B-24s were rigged up with the new sights, and some of the lead crews ran demonstrations on wooden targets built much like billboards. The planes came in very low and released their bombs just before reaching the target. Bull's-eyes were scored almost every time.

July 25, 1943. Today all the ships on our field were suddenly equipped with the new low-altitude sight, and the bombardiers were given special bombing charts. Now we knew they weren't kidding! Rumors and tall stories began going around the camp about where the attacks would be made. Some guessed the Messina dockyards.

This afternoon we were briefed on low-altitude formation flying and also on security (which wasn't much of a problem in the desert; there was no one to talk to except ourselves).

July 26, 1943. Captain Packer called my crew in and explained that our group (the 389th) had more crews and ships than our quota and that the 98th Group was short, and since we had joined the group last, we were to fly the next mission with the 98th Group. We therefore packed and went the short distance over to the 98th and were assigned the airplane *Daisy Mae*, a veteran of some fifty-six missions but a good ship just the same. Little did we know what a difference this simple transfer was to make for us in the raid to come.

The next five days were busy ones. Every morning we flew low-altitude formation (from fifty feet down). It was really fun! All five groups (44th, 93rd, 98th, 376th, and 389th) were doing the same thing. I guess we frightened every Arab off every hay wagon and blew down half the tents for fifty miles around. Each morning we added something new. At first we flew in three- and six-ship formations, then squadron formation, then in our group, and finally in five waves with seven ships in each. I was assigned to fly on the left wing of the squadron leader (Maj. Herbert Shingler) of the fourth wave.

For days you could look around almost anywhere on the desert and see formations of B-24s skimming along the ground, just missing what few palm trees there were. In open spaces they swooped still lower until they barely missed the ground. The sheepherders on the desert really had a rough time! One lieutenant actually flew so low he scraped off his bomb-bay doors, kicked up a lot of dust, and blew down three tents. On the third day the British engineers erected the "target" on a clear space in the desert. It consisted of a large number of long, low, wooden buildings with an occasional circular building and a few towers. We always dropped a few one-hundred-pound practice bombs, but on the last day we put in some five-hundred-pounders with delayed fuses and blew the whole thing sky high.

In the afternoon and evenings we studied the target, for by now we knew we were making a low-level attack on the Ploesti oil fields in Rumania. I guess we received the most complete and detailed briefing of any air raid in history. Each of our five groups was assigned one of the thirteen oil refineries around Bucharest, and each of the five waves in our group had a certain area. Every airplane had a *specific* building or a part of a building on which the bombs were to be placed. Our target was the *left* end of a boiler house; the ship behind us was the *right* end. The briefing facilities, equipment, and assistance were unlimited. We had draftsmen to make drawings and sketches of every route, every target, every building. They constructed wooden models, to scale, of every building and every oil storage tank. We had pictures, maps, and drawings galore. Every pilot, navigator, and bombardier knew exactly what he was supposed to do. Group commanders Colonel Kane, Colonel Wood, Colonel Timberlake, and wing commander Brig. Gen. Ent knew all the targets better than the crews themselves. General Brereton and Air Chief Marshal Tedder talked with all the crews. In the evenings we were shown motion pictures of the target area and buildings, some borrowed from the files of American oil companies in the States, some smuggled out of occupied Rumania. One evening a group of engineers who had helped to build the refineries spoke to us and described many of the buildings, how they were constructed and how the plants could best be put out of action. For five days we talked only of Ploesti, trying to digest all the information the intelligence section had spent so long in preparing. On Sunday, August 1, we were ready.

August 1, 1943. At 3:30 A.M. the assistant operations officer came around to our tent and woke us up for the mission. We dressed, ate breakfast (powdered eggs, prunes, oatmeal, bacon, and coffee), and went over to the briefing hut. Not much additional briefing was necessary, so thorough had been our previous study of the target. Colonel Kane, from Shreveport, Louisiana, did most of the talking. (He reminded me a lot of Wallace Beery, only he was younger and undoubtedly tougher.) He reviewed the formation board and the briefed route (Benghazi to the island of Corfu, to the target, back to Corfu, and home—just as simple as that). It was a twenty-four-hundred-mile flight. We had an extra bomb-bay tank, which gave us a total of thirty-one hundred gallons of gasoline in addition to our bomb load of three 1,000-pound bombs with long-delay fuses, plus some incendiary clusters and an extra-large load of ammunition. We had the ten regular .50-caliber machine guns and two extras—double-waist guns, very formidable weapons. The weather officer, Captain Anderson, explained the situation. Pretty heavy clouds were expected along the coast in the Corfu area; otherwise it was OK. The intelligence officer, Major Exnicios, briefly reviewed the targets. Ours was *white* target (Austro-Rumania), *blue* route, building No. 6 (oil-refining plant). We already knew it perfectly. The question was raised whether we should carry our pistols. Colonel Kane explained that it was optional (that personally if he went down, he was going to shoot his way out of Rumania), and about half the crews decided to take them along. Our crew didn't. But everyone did take his water canteen (in addition to the huge thermos jug in the ship) and a good supply of K rations.

Altogether the briefing was comparatively short for so important a mission, but practically everything had already been covered many times in previous sessions. We went out to check over our ship. The mechanics had been working all night to get everything in shape, and it looked pretty good. The crew members reported their equipment as being in proper condition. Takeoff was scheduled for 6:30 A.M.

Father Beck came around in his jeep to give final blessings and to pick up any last-minute "just in case" mail (letters to be sent in case the crew didn't return). Almost everyone had already completed his letters home the day before. This was the first time we had written letters of this kind, and everyone knew this would be a tough assignment. Colonel Wood had said the mission was the reason for our trip to Africa, and Colonel Kane had explained that if the entire group was lost, the destruction of the target would be worth it. Not much consolation.

Pretty soon it was time to start the engines and taxi out. All of the fellows said good-bye to Peanuts, our mascot terrier, before turning him over to the crew chief for safekeeping. We had often discussed the possibility of taking him on a mission, but no one thought it was a good idea to take Peanuts to Ploesti for his first trip.

As we taxied out, everyone was surprisingly quiet and confident, at least outwardly. During our few missions in Africa we had learned something about fear and how to control it.

The ships were marshaled in long lines on both sides of the field, tails pointing slightly downwind to prevent columns of dust from covering the ships. Lt. Cal Fager and I ran up the engine and went through the checklist automatically. Then, trying to appear nonchalant, I smiled and said, "Here we go, boy." I gave it full throttle, and we began to gain speed across the dirt runway, then lifted slowly into the air. I had hardly relaxed after the takeoff (getting safely into the air with a heavily loaded ship is always a mental strain on pilots and quite often on other members of the crew as well) when Lieutenant Klinkbeil said over the Interphone, "Navigator to pilot, a plane has just crashed south of the field. You can see it if you look out your left side window." Something had gone wrong on the takeoff and the ship crashed and burned furiously. I wondered if this was a bad omen at the beginning of our trip and said half-aloud to myself, "Tough luck."

We circled over the field and formed the group above the black, billowing smoke of the burning ship and headed north, on course, across the blue Meditteranean. The other four groups were flying parallel courses, two up front and one on either side.

Sixty minutes slipped by without incident, and then suddenly the navigator (who always saw things first) called out that a ship up ahead was losing altitude and was going to crash and, sure enough, down it went, a long trail of blue smoke following it into the water. The radio operator reported that our leader had radioed a distress signal to Malta, but we could see no survivors. The waist gunner said that he had snapped a picture of the ship.

Another hour went by and we passed over the southern tip of the island of Corfu and headed northeast across Greece where it joins Albania. As we crossed the coast we expected some flak but saw none. We were flying low (six thousand feet) to avoid alerting the German radar stations, but now we had to climb to pass over the Pindus Mountains; so up we went to eleven thousand feet. We were over enemy territory and heading straight for Ploesti, still five hundred miles away.

The weather above the mountains was worse than we had expected; large cumulus clouds had developed and were towering high above the formation. Three planes began clipping the edges of the clouds, some losing the formation altogether for several minutes. It was difficult just to keep the groups together, impossible to keep them in their proper positions. The lead group became separated, and we did not see it again until we reached the target area.

Across the mountains the weather began to get a little better, and we started letting down to three thousand feet and finally to one thousand feet. We continued across Greece, southern Yugoslavia, Bulgaria, over the Danube, and straight into Rumania. One navigator noted in his log, "The Danube

River isn't blue but brown."

At this low altitude we had a good view of the country-side. Bombardier Gioana pointed out a Rumanian festival in full swing with girls in colorful dresses. They were unaccustomed to air raids and waved as we went by. Farmers were ploughing in the small, square fields. Some stopped to look upward, using their hands to shade the sun from their eyes; others ignored us completely. Some fields were green with wheat. In others sunflowers were growing between the rows of corn. Occasionally we passed yellow haystacks, which reflected the bright sunlight. It was a beautiful country and looked quite peaceful.

We had been briefed to expect fighters any time after making landfall, and this thought limited our enjoyment of the scenery. We flew for two and a half hours to a little town in Rumania called Pitesti. This was the place where the five groups would break up and proceed to their respective targets. Once we turned down the wrong valley but quickly turned back and were finally on our bomb run. We were at five hundred feet now and still going down. From Pitesti to Ploesti was only twelve miles, yet it was the longest twelve miles I ever hope to fly. The peaceful countryside wasn't peaceful anymore: the Germans had made good use of their two or three hours' advance warning. Haystacks opened up and turned into gun nests; machine guns and flak guns were on every hill. By now we were down to two hundred feet, but we knew instantly that we were still much too high. Down we went to one hundred feet, fifty feet, twenty-five feet, just clearing the bushes and shrubbery. At 2300 rpm and thirty-seven inches we were doing 230 mph in tight formation. As we got closer we were surprised to see B-24s from another group bombing our target. The ack-ack boys were already at work, and the oil tanks were smoking and burning furiously. Our route followed a railway line to the target. As we headed into the target area, dozens of machine guns from a flak train alongside opened up, and then all hell broke loose! Thousands of tracers criss-crossed through the sky making beautiful but terrifying patterns. I saw one heavy 88-mm gun fire point blank, and a long arm of orange flame spouted from the muzzle.

Our gunners were not idle. Twelve .50-caliber machine guns from each ship spouted continuous rounds of deadly fire concentrating on anything that moved. Many gun emplacements were put out of action; many ground gunners were mowed down. Our lead ships had several extra fixed guns in the nose section that fired continuously until the barrels burned out. One ship made a belly landing, and a couple of the crew members scrambled for cover. The storage tanks were exploding now, with burning oil flowing out, making towering, black smoke clouds. But we could still see the outline of the target, the buildings, and the chimneys. I was astonished to hear Gioana say calmly over the Interphone, "We're headed straight for our building; be sure you pull up in time." When the smoking target was almost in the windshield, Cal and I both hauled back on the wheel, held it a few seconds, and pushed it forward again, barely clearing the chimneys as we plunged through the smoke. I felt the bombs go and saw several balloon cables snap as they struck our wings. A ship on our left waited too long to pull up and flew directly into a storage tank. Burning pieces of it disintegrated into the air, and crewmen were thrown in every direction. Other ships, hopelessly damaged on the bomb run, plunged directly into the burning target.

Coming out of the smoke on the far side of the target seemed like a miracle, unbelievable! Sergeant Hunt, tail gunner, picked this time to say over the Interphone: "Look at all that oil burning. And to think this time last year I was working in a gas station." Quickly we looked around to assess the damage. Number three engine had been hit and was smoking. (I reduced the power and waited before feathering it.) The nosewheel was knocked out. The hydraulic system was inoperative, fluid pouring into the bomb bay. The top turret was out, and one gun in the tail turret was inoperative. Flak holes were all over the fuselage and several were in the wings and engine nacelles. But we were still flying, and no one was badly injured. Our chances looked pretty good.

Other ships had not been so lucky. *Boilermaker Number II* wasn't with us anymore. *The Cornhusker* had one down. *Lil Joe* wasn't there, nor *Semper Felix, Old Baldy, Air Lobe, Vulgar Virgin*, and others. Over on the right a B-24 suddenly started climbing, stalled, and spun in . Another, smoking badly, was forced to crash-land in a long field. A twin-engine fighter went down in flames. I was amazed at the capacity of my subconscious mind to record so many details at a glance.

Out of the target area the formation had loosened up, but

we closed in again quickly. I ended up on the right wing of Maj. Herbert Shingler, from Tennessee, our squadron commander, and flew the tightest formation I had ever flown. Junkers-88s and Me-109s were attacking stragglers and cripples and anyone above one hundred feet. We had been briefed to fly low to make fighter attacks more difficult, and for fifty miles after the target we skimmed the deck, cutting corn, wheat, and sunflowers with the propellers. The engineer, Sergeant Dillman, was posted between the seats as a safety measure, to observe any obstructions that Cal and I might miss. Lieutenant Gioana in the nose was very much concerned about a small wooden tower coming up ahead (which we had already seen), and he screamed over the Interphone until at the last instant we pulled up and just cleared it.

The navigator reported that Colonel Kane's ship, *Hail Columbia*, had slipped behind and turned off course with a feathered engine.

For fifty miles we flew low at 175 mph. Then someone called the leader over the command radio and complained that his rudder section had been damaged and fluttered if he flew above 160; so we slowed down. Before reaching the target, I had become very tired from flying, and Cal relieved me about every thirty minutes. Now I somehow felt fresh, almost completely rested, and in spite of all that had happened, I thoroughly enjoyed flying. We buzzed over small villages and, invariably, people waved. We passed so close over a two-wheeled hay wagon that three girls in brightly colored skirts jumped off, but nevertheless they smiled and waved. I wondered if they knew who we were.

A farmer ploughing in a cornfield saw us coming and left his horse and plow and lay flat between the rows, obviously frightened. He didn't wave.

Just past the Danube River we started a gradual climb. We flew north of Pleven, Bulgaria, and later passed south of Sofia. At about five thousand feet someone suddenly called out "fighters at three o'clock and a little high." Sergeant Coldiron in the top turret (our best man on aircraft recognition) looked them over and decided they were Italian fighters, and he was right. They made only a few passes and did not press the attack. I think we actually scared them away with our tracers, which showed up brilliantly in the rather dark sky. (There were many thunderheads in this area.)

We continued our climb to eleven thousand feet to clear the mountains. Some of the damaged ships were unable to climb and were forced to turn south and fly down the winding river valley. As we crossed the southern tip of Corfu we breathed a premature sigh of relief. The worst was yet to come! We had only nine B-24s left in the formation of thirty-five starting with our group, and again we heard the announcement, "Fighters, three o'clock, straight in the sun." We looked closely and there were fifteen Me-109s flying parallel to our course, looking us over. We tightened up the formation a bit and waited. I was on the right wing and dropped down a little to uncover the guns of the ship on my left. Pretty soon the 109s dropped their belly (gas) tanks, and five of them started in, flying abreast in a shallow V-shape formation. There was no surprise action. We recognized this as a cool, well-planned, German attack, and we knew the Jerries couldn't be frightened away. We either had to shoot them down, be shot down ourselves, or wait for them to run out of gas. At one thousand yards we started firing and at eight hundred yards everyone was firing. Tracers literally covered the sky, and 20-mm shells exploded all through the formation. Our gunners got the range, and the two Me-109s on the right were hit hard; one exploded immediately, and the other blew up just after passing the formation. The second Jerry bailed out in a yellow parachute.

But we didn't exactly win that round. One B-24 was burning furiously and the crew members were already bailing out. That left eight B-24s in formation for the second attack. The Jerries tried the same tactics, this time six abreast. Again they all fired together, and the lead Me-109 completely disintegrated in the air as it was caught in our deadly crossfire. Another was smoking, and again a B-24 went down in flames, this time we only counted five chutes out.

Then the Jerries changed their tactics and began coming in individually and from all directions. On the second pass we received several holes in the fuselage, and Lieutenant Gioana (who had exchanged places with Sergeant Alfredson) and Sergeant Ayers were injured by 20-mm explosions. Lieutenant Gioana smiled and said, "Guess we get the Purple Heart." A couple of seconds later an individual fighter ship slipped in from directly astern and planted a direct hit on the armored glass of the tail turret, knocking Sergeant Hunt into the fuselage and putting the turret out of action. Sergeant Hunt picked himself up and then manned a waist gun. We now had only our waist guns working and hurriedly transferred our spare ammunition to these positions.

Another 20-mm explosion knocked a large hole in the left rudder and still another tore away a large piece of elevator surface. And then suddenly two more shells exploded in the fuselage and seriously wounded Lieutenant Gioana. He had thirty-five cuts, mostly on the torso and legs. The explosions also severed the control surface cables. The nose dropped slightly, and the ship started into a shallow bank to the left, out of control. Cal, who was looking out the window at the time, turned and said, "Let's move back up into formation." I answered, "Can't do it, the controls are gone," as I pulled the control column completely back in my lap. I automatically reached for the elevator trim tab, but that too was loose and revolved freely without effect. I almost pushed the alarm button to prepare to bail out, but then I remembered the automatic pilot, which, fortunately, I always kept warmed up. I reached over and flipped it into the "on" position and, thank heaven, it was working. By this time we were down about five hundred feet below the formation. I adjusted the elevator and aileron knobs, and the nose came up slowly. We moved under the formation, where we stayed for about fifteen minutes until the fighters, out of gas, finally left us.

The trip home was one of sweating out the gas. Sergeant Dillman figured we had enough to last until 7:00 P.M. Lieutenant Klinkbeil said we would never make it by then. So we decided to stretch it as far as possible. We threw all the guns, except two, overboard and most of the ammunition and everything else we figured we wouldn't need if we were forced to ditch. I cut back the rpm to 1700 and the manifold pressure to twenty-five inches and indicated 155 mph. Oddly enough, the number three engine was running more smoothly now, although I could see several flak hits on the top cylinders and several spark-plug wires dangling in the air.

Sergeants Ayers and Alfredson and Coldiron were in the back bandaging both themselves and Lieutenant Gioana, who had passed out by this time from loss of blood. Sergeant Dillman was busy trying to splice the broken control cables, which were dangling all over the fuselage.

We waited and watched for the coastline and did a lot of

praying. Several times we thought we could see the coast, but it would always turn out to be a long string of clouds. Finally it began to get dark, and our spirits dropped even more. Gas was running low, and Sergeant Dillman, checking it for the twenty-seventh time, said he didn't see how it could last beyond 9:00 P.M. even with our low power settings.

I couldn't decide for sure what was best to do. I knew that ditching a B-24 at night was a very hazardous undertaking and should be done while we still had power. Bailing out into our individual dinghies would have been OK for everyone except Lieutenant Gioana, who was still unconscious. We decided to keep flying until we ran out of gas and then ditch without benefit of power from the engines. We reviewed the ditching procedure and did some more silent praying. Finally we saw some red flares straight ahead and knew we were approaching the field. Lieutenant Klinkbeil had kept us exactly on course. The engines were still going but couldn't last much longer; the gas gauges indicated zero. It was already 9:30 P.M. We only needed a few more minutes! Sergeant Dillman cranked down the main wheels as we crossed the coastline, saving what little hydraulic fluid we still had for the flaps. The nosewheel was useless, so we left it up. The radio was not working, but we could see other ships landing into the northwest, so I flew to the right of the field and started a gradual turn to the left. We were at about five hundred feet, and as we came in on the final approach, Cal started pumping down the flaps. I put the rpm up to 2100 but knew we could never go around if we missed the first time. Cal got the flaps halfway down and operated the ailerons and rudder. I manipulated the automatic-pilot elevator knob and handled the throttles. At two hundred feet Cal put on the landing lights. The ship was lightweight, so we slowed down to 100 mph as we flared out. The wheels touched, and she bounced several feet. I advanced the throttles, and she settled back to the ground as one engine cut out; she rolled halfway across the field, and as we lost speed, the nose began scraping the ground and we came to an abrupt stop. It was 9:54 P.M., fifteen hours after takeoff.

To say we were glad to be on the ground is a great understatement, but our first concern was Lieutenant Gioana. We had fired several red flares as we came in, and the ambulance met us as we came to a stop. The attendants put him on a stretcher and lifted him out of the plane. His clothes were torn, and he was bandaged up. He, and the inside of the ship were covered with blood. I thought sure he was dead or dying because he was so pale and white, but I was greatly relieved when he rallied and said, "Sure glad to be back." That night he spent four hours on the operating table, had a temperature of 105 and received two blood transfusions.

Sergeants Hunt, Ayers, and Waugh were taken to the hospital but were released after first-aid treatment. The rest of us went to interrogation where General Ent and General Brereton were very much interested in all the details of the mission. I was amazed to see Sergeant Alfredson in a huddle with both generals, telling them "just how it happened." After that we went over to the mess tent, where they were serving "fresh" eggs—all we could eat. Lieutenant Klinkbeil ate ten and regretted his inability to make it an even dozen. After eating all we possibly could and relaxing a bit, we began to realize just how tired we really were. Up to now we had been busy trying to learn what had happened to all the fellows, where and when they went down, and what damage had been received by the ones who got back.

August 12, 1943. At about six o'clock in the afternoon we woke up and decided to have a look around to check up on some more of the fellows.

We learned that Lt. William Nading, on the last ship in his group over the target, had followed his leader (Capt. Robert Mooney in *Blonds Away*) out of the target area, only to learn that Captain Mooney had been killed by machine-gun fire and the copilot was flying the badly damaged ship and trying to stay on course. Lieutenant Nading took over the lead, realized that the five damaged ships in the formation could never climb over the Carpathian Mountains, and decided to head for Cyprus. Lt. Charles Weinberg, his navigator, ran out of pilotage maps over Turkey but used a large Mercator map to pinpoint the tiny island in the middle of the Mediterranean. It had a small airdrome and short runway, but all the ships got down safely and were refueled. Colonel Kane, too, made it safely to Cyprus.

We heard that after Colonel Johnson's ship landed, the colonel noticed that his waist gunner, on his first mission, was looking a little sad, so the colonel explained to him that all his missions wouldn't be as rough as Ploesti. The gunner was greatly relieved.

Several ships from other fields had crash-landed at our base, and some of them looked like wrecks. Ours, *Daisy Mae*, didn't look so good herself. The crew chief and his men were already working on her. They had counted more than 150 holes all over the ship—flak, machine gun, and 20-mm. Number three engine was in bad shape. Flak had knocked several holes in the nacelle and cowling and penetrated the oil cooler in several places. The top was knocked off of the two top cylinders, and four spark-plug wires were severed. They were unable to measure any gas in the tanks at all and doubted if it would have flown five minutes longer.

The most ironic part of the whole thing was when Capt. Thomas Campbell, who had flown *Daisy Mae* on thirty-five missions, told me that he had never been able to get the automatic-pilot elevator control to work at all. The fact that it worked for us undoubtedly saved our lives.

We began to get some summary figures about the mission: "A total of 178 B-24s took off and 140 reached and bombed the target. Fifty-nine aircraft were shot down or crashed enroute, of which 20 were lost over the target. Eight landed in neutral Turkey and were interned. The casualties totaled 450 killed or missing and 79 interned. A total of 51 enemy fighters were shot down—Me-109s and -110s, FW-190s, Ju-88s, and some unidentified bi-planes."

Early reports indicated that great damage was done to the targets at Ploesti, so everyone felt pretty good except for our heavy losses. We stopped by to see Lieutenant Gioana as soon as he could have visitors.

August 13, 1943. It had been pretty quiet around the base for several days, but today the groups went to Wiener Neustadt, another long mission, and landed at Tunis. Our crew didn't go because our new ship, *Pistol Packin' Mama*, was having an engine changed.

August 26, 1943. Our African campaign was finally ended! We packed up, took off, circled over the field, and buzzed the place in formation as a farewell gesture. We flew over to Oran, landed, and stayed the night, and next day flew on to Marrakech. The following night we took off for dear old England and landed at our home base about noon.

September 15, 1943. Today we were presented with awards and medals for the Ploesti mission. It was a large gathering and there were Distinguished Service Crosses, Distinguished Flying Crosses, and air medals galore. A couple of Congressional Medals (for Colonel Johnson and Colonel Kane) had already been presented. Colonel Timberlake presented the awards to our group and said a lot of nice things about everybody. It's too bad that the many fellows who really earned the medals weren't there to receive them.

—October 1983

"NOT FORGETTING MAY BE THE ONLY HEROISM OF THE SURVIVOR"

by G.D. LILLIBRIDGE

Years after one of the bloodiest and most intense battles of the war in the Pacific, a Marine Corps veteran returns to Tarawa.

War is a country no traveler ever forgets. It haunts those who survive the journey as no other experience. The memories of war cling to the mind with astonishing tenacity, and sometimes in the dark of night when the glow of your cigarette is a distant fire on an island most people have never heard of, nothing seems to equal their demand for attention. Why? Possibly because the memories raise so many questions about oneself, particularly the unanswerable one: Why am I the one here to remember? Perhaps, however, that's the point—to remember. Indeed, the ordeal of not forgetting may well be the only heroism of the survivor.

Sometimes these memories assert themselves so strongly that you decide to have it out with them. One way to do that is to go back. In early 1968, after a quarter of a century, I returned to Tarawa in the Gilbert Islands in that vast stretch of the Pacific where islands hump their coral backs out of the ocean like so many whales at rest.

Here on little Betio, the last island in the Tarawa atoll, from November 20 to 24, 1943, there took place one of the bloodiest and most intense battles of the Second World War. The newspaper reports referred to the carnage as the most shattering experience in Marine Corps history. It may well have been. What is certain is that those who went through the ordeal and those who fell there remain bound together by unusual ties. Tarawa is the only battle I have ever heard of where so many who survived wished to have their ashes returned there.

For most of us Tarawa began in New Zealand at a little railway crossing about thirty miles out of Wellington called McKay's Crossing. And that's where my pilgrimage began. It is hard to imagine that this ordinary stretch of rolling land between the hills and the sea once felt the presence of several thousand men. In the intervening years the area had gradually taken on in my mind the tone of some tented encampment preserved for posterity by Matthew Brady. The last of the New Zealand winter was still with us then, and there was often a kind of damp blur in the air; we all scrounged wood and coal for the old Franklin-type stoves in our tents. Although there is always a certain impersonality about military camps, here there was an intimacy we never had again. The messes were small, and late at night if you had the duty, the cooks would fix you bacon and eggs, draw warm cake fresh from the oven, and pour hot coffee into large white mugs. There was no real sense of regiment or division. It was a village existence of companies and platoons.

We all got tired of maneuvers up and down those damned hills ringed with sheep paths, and the hills themselves naturally became higher and higher with every passing year after our departure. I was surprised in 1968 to discover that their summits were not perpetually hidden in clouds after all. The whole area is now a national park, with imposing gates and a bronze plaque. "Half the world distance from home they camped here," it reads. "They camped at this spot from June 1942 to November 1943 while helping to defend this country. Later they fought in the Pacific Islands where many of them made the supreme sacrifice and cemented everlasting friendship."

Now, beyond a few broken concrete slabs in the underbrush, there was nothing to indicate this was a wartime camp. Nothing to indicate it was a park, for that matter, except the sign.

This is not to say that New Zealanders have forgotten. Wellington of course was large enough to absorb a division of men, particularly when most of its own were far away. It would be hard to find a Marine who did not have a family he visited regularly on liberty and with whom the closest relationships developed. In 1968 the New Zealanders who had known Marines told me again and again that they seemed to be looking for a home. "The thing that struck me most," said one woman, "was that when you met them and you liked each other, then you sort of belonged to them and they belonged to you. They weren't interested in meeting other people and going around and that sort of thing."

Time has, to say the least, been kind to the Marines who have passed through the filtering process of New Zealand memory; everyone apparently was an Eagle Scout. Neat, clean, polite, generous, gentle with children. In 1968 when I asked a friend what her impression of me had been in those days, she said I was courteous, intelligent, lovable: "You recited poetry for my mother." My own image from those days was very different: gauche, confused, anxious, lost. Did I talk about the war? Never, she said. Yet it seems to me that it was always on my mind. How could I not have talked about it? But this, too, was a common observation. "No, they never talked about the war, where they had been, where they were going. They talked about New Zealand, what a lovely country it was, how they liked the people. Things like that. We were old-fashioned compared with America, I suppose. I think they liked that for some reason."

We did indeed. The homes in which we settled down and spent so much time on liberty were crowded with heavy, over-stuffed, old-fashioned furniture with lots of pillows and cush-ions, innumerable knickknacks, figurines, landscape paintings, and photographs. It was a little like visiting grandmother when a small boy in the Midwest.

There were of course girls in New Zealand, and they were made much of. Different fellows had different need of them. My own needs were not physical for reasons I am no longer able to fathom, if I ever was. Nevertheless there is a sort of law of spiritual logistics. The farther your supply line stretches from its source, the more you have to live off the land. Looking back on it much later, I often had the feeling that in those days I was trying to tap out a desperate message to my new wife thousands of miles away. To be occasionally with someone who wasn't fighting a war seemed absolutely essential.

In Wellington that someone was twenty-one-year-old Joan, a nursing student. She lived in a house perched on the side of a hill in Island Bay. You went out on the No.1 tram, and you had to walk up 137 steps to get there. Below were tennis courts where you could see young boys play in the late afternoon, and the garden was full of flowers.

We went walking, sat in the parlor and talked, dined out, or went to the movies. She and her parents and sister were extraordinarily kind to me, and I often had dinner with them. Once her mother asked me what my favorite dessert was, and I told her lemon pie. Since she was not familiar with this delight of my childhood, I described it as best I could, and the next time I came by, there was a fresh lemon pie. The family of course knew that I was married, and on one occasion her mother privately and with considerable delicacy asked me if my relationship with Joan was something she should be concerned about. I replied no, and she never mentioned it again. The pie, as I recall, came after that.

When I first met Joan, she was recovering from the news of the death in North Africa of a young New Zealander she had known well. In a sense, I suppose, she was having some difficulty facing the necessity of life and I the necessity of death, and without quite realizing what we were doing, each helped the other. The innocence of our relationship is likely to be received with skepticism by those whose image of the traditional Marine on his way from the halls of Montezuma to the shores of Tripoli included activities with women that went beyond conversation and dinner. In fact, today many would probably find it quaint that I struggled with the morality of the matter: Was I being unfaithful to the girl I had married and loved so much because I walked hand in hand with Joan, kissed her occasionally, and on the day of my departure stood out in the clear, open sunshine of their front steps and held her and wiped away the tears she was shedding—for whom? For me? For her friend lost in North Africa? Or simply for all of us?

I would have survived Tarawa without knowing Joan, but I think my capacity to deal with Tarawa might well have been different had I not known her.

In the fall of 1943 we sailed for Tarawa in the Gilbert Islands. None of us had ever heard of the place before.

Twenty-five years later I made the journey by air. The eight-hour plane flight from Fiji allows plenty of time to drift into the past, and as the plane circled high over the atoll for landing and I saw that dark streak across the water, I found my throat suddenly dry, chest tightening, that rising sensation of alertness in the stomach.

The view from the air was new to me. Twenty-five years earlier I had joined others on the deck of our naval transport long before dawn to watch the pre-invasion bombardment of the island. Naval shells arched in red streaks across the dark sky. At one point, before the big guns on the island had been silenced, a shell whistled overhead, and those of us who were new to this game ducked, to the amusement of the veterans.

This, however, was the lightest moment in a dark three days. Embarrassment was a feather compared with what hit me afterward. For Tarawa jarred my psyche with a blow so painful and long-lasting that in some ways that battle may have been the most dominant experience of my life. I was barely twenty-two years old, totally inexperienced, temperamentally unprepared for combat, by nature vaguely unsympathetic to things military, naive, and generally ignorant in the ways of command. A green second lieutenant responsible for thirty-nine men. It is with a sickening feeling at my own idiot innocence that I recall the little speech I gave the platoon just before we went down the nets into the landing craft. I told them there was no need to worry, no necessity for anyone to get killed, although possibly someone might get slightly wounded. No heroics, then, just do their jobs and what they were told. All would be well.

The platoon was to sustain twenty-six casualties—thirteen dead and thirteen wounded.

We had been told that, given the heavy naval and air bombardment, we would probably have little to do except walk across the island. We would be lucky, went the phrase, to fire a shot. On that score the high command was right: a great many Marines never had the chance to fire a shot.

The impact of the losses rendered me almost completely ineffective in any military sense. When the battle was over and we were taken off the island, my state of personal shock at what had happened is suggested by the fact that I sat in the wardroom on our naval transport and over and over again wrote down the names of the dead and wounded, as though somehow putting their names on paper made them alive and well. For years afterward I could order up the entire platoon before me, each man in his place, and call the roll. I was sure I would never forget. But of course I did. Most of the names gradually disappeared over the years. But the faces still remain.

All of this drifted uneasily through my mind as the plane circled and landed in the late afternoon on the airstrip about halfway up the atoll—just a cleared stretch of packed coral. The original airstrip built by the Japanese on Betio, and after the battle renamed Hawkins Field in honor of the young lieutenant posthumously awarded the Medal of Honor for his deeds, had long since disappeared.

My uneasiness dropped away after the landing. A large crowd of Gilbertese always gathers at the little airfield—Tarawa National—when a plane comes in or departs, and there are various government people on hand to greet new personnel or returning families. The terminal building was a small open shed with a low fence over which passengers passed luggage and goods—a process to which customs officials paid no attention at all. Informal, but still it was like coming into any airport: you end up being concerned about passports, baggage, transportation. The confusion was mild, however, and soon I caught a ride up the one narrow road that runs down the southern half of the atoll to the little six-room hotel on Bikenibeu.

In 1968 Tarawa was the administrative and commercial center for the Gilbert and Ellice Island Colony, one of the last fragments of the British Empire. It lies somewhat above the equator and across the international date line. With the exception of Betio, which has to be reached by motor launch, the small islands making up the atoll are linked by causeway. The highest point is about twelve feet above sea level. Betio is little more than two miles long, and eight hundred yards wide at its western end, tapering down to about three feet at its eastern end.

Tarawa is isolated by most modern standards. The then-fortnightly flight from Fiji existed primarily to handle government personnel and families on their way in or out for various reasons. I turned out to be the only Marine who had ever returned and one of the few genuine visitors in living memory. This made me something of a curiosity.

Since the war the British, in a concerted effort to bring the Gilbertese more or less into the twentieth century, had brought in various experts in education, agriculture, health, family life, and the like. The hospitality of these people was typical not only of the countries from which they came—England, New Zealand, and Australia—but also of what we associate in tale and myth with the Pacific Islands. I started to get invitations before I even reached the hotel, the first coming from the driver of the car that took me there.

Few of these expatriates, or the Gilbertese for that matter, knew much about the battle, although they were reminded of it all the time. For Betio, which is the most heavily populated island in the atoll, still carries on its narrow back the monuments of war. The Japanese had had about a year in which to turn the island into a defense bastion, and many of the fortifications that they built still stand, too massive to destroy. The naval guns still tilt in rusted anguish toward the sea or lie broken on the beach. Ammunition washes up with the tide. Shattered amtracs lie half-buried in the sand. Small children still dig up American grenades and bring them into the homes, and broken weapons are propped up here and there in front of houses, casual reminders of the past.

The morning after my arrival I hitched a ride down to Bonriki, where the government offices are located and from which I took the battered launch across to Betio, about a thirty-minute trip. As the launch eased alongside the pier, the sound of an explosion ripped the air—a startling but familiar greeting from the past. My stomach flipped. Ammunition and explosives uncovered during some construction were being destroyed—a common occurrence.

Twenty-five years earlier Betio had been shrouded in smoke and dust, most of its coconut palms blown to shreds, and the whole impression had been one of desolation, barrenness, and sand. Now it was green, quiet, and populous. I knew the island was small, but I had forgotten how small, less than half the size of Central Park in New York City. You can stand on one side with the lagoon at your back and view the ocean on the other. I went three times to Betio, motorbiked around it, bicycled, and walked. Once I tried to retrace my wartime course about the island and came across the small building housing one of the Japanese naval searchlights, where I had spent the fourth night lying in the midst of broken glass, rubble, and blasted equipment, while a single Japanese plane made a casual bombing run down the island. The twisted, rusted rim of the searchlight still lay on the sand. One wall of the building had disappeared, and the equipment and rubble inside had been cleared out; otherwise it was just as it had been. Later, when I paused in front of a bunker, its narrow rifle slits still surveying a long-forgotten field of fire in which I now stood uneasily, I found myself frozen for an instant, swept by the absurd sensation of being terribly exposed.

These blunt reminders of the past seemed unreal in their peaceful setting of village huts, expatriate homes, and low-slung government buildings. But then I remembered that battle, too, has its incongruous reminders of peace. On the morning of the second day of the fighting, with the first faint light of dawn just appearing, I stood up to have a look around. Coconut palms torn and shattered, broken equipment every-where, bodies all about in the awkward rigidity of death, Japanese pillboxes silent but menacing, the green dungarees of Marines now turned a dusty gray from the sand and salt spray, nothing moving, utter quiet. And then a rooster crowed. I was so startled by this sound from my childhood that I dropped to the ground as though I had been shot. And then with the crow of the rooster, the firing began again.

One of the things I tried to do in wandering about on my own was to find the place where Joe Sexton had been killed. He had been on my mind from the time I had undertaken this journey. In war few can make it psychologically without the buddy system. This is the basic unit of survival—one, two, or three comrades drawn together by factors quite beyond expla-nation and wholly unrelated to the common interests, ideas, and backgrounds that bring people together in peacetime. This comradeship does not often last when the war is over, but the memory of its deep, mysterious sense of identification is never lost or diminished.

Joe, Bill, Brownie, and I had been thrown together on the voyage out as replacements. On arrival in New Zealand the replacement officers were all crowded together in a hot, stuffy room for assignment to the various units of the division. In the confusion I became separated from the other three. When the captain in charge finished making the assignments, he discov-ered he had left me out. What am I going to do with you? his expression asked. I simply pointed across the room and, trembling inside with anxiety, told him, I want to go with them. He understood, and with them I went.

Joe was the only one of us to die at Tarawa. I hadn't seen it happen myself and only had Bill Howell's account vaguely in the back of my mind. I finally settled for what I thought ought to be the place and stood there for a long time, feeling curiously empty of emotion. Our reaction to his death had set in after we were sent to rest camp in Hawaii a few weeks later. Up to that time none of us had talked about it. Then, late one afternoon, our baggage from New Zealand caught up with us. Someone had two or three bottles of whiskey in his trunk, and in the midst of unpacking we began to drink. The binge, a collective rage really, lasted several hours and ended with our smashing what little furniture we had managed to scrounge or build, hurling books, clothing, and equipment all over the tent, and fighting one another with staves drawn from the ends of our cots, as though we were medieval ascetics scouring the devil from our bodies.

One of us was missing.

Joseph J. Sexton, 2d lieutenant, U.S. Marine Corps Reserves. Wife, Veronica. Three-year-old daughter, Tinker. He had died trying to get what was left of his platoon across the airstrip. I tried at least twenty times to write to his widow and had torn up every letter. His death didn't seem just unnecessary or wrong, but unreal. We staggered and crawled out into the night to get him back. It was raining heavily and very dark. We wept, we cried out, and there on our knees in the muck, we pleaded for him to come back.

And we never mentioned him again.

Thinking about Joe brought to mind again the slaughter that was Tarawa's principal distinction. Tarawa was not a very big battle, as battles go, and it was all over in seventy-two hours. But its briefness only sharpened its intensity and ferocity. Compared with many other fights, the number of casualties was not impressive—about thirty-three hundred Marines and somewhat over three thousand special Japanese soldiers plus about two thousand Japanese and Korean laborers. But the percentage of casualties was very high. Only seventeen Japanese, all wounded, were taken prisoner. The rest died in the fighting, some committing suicide in their bunkers near the end. The Marine assault units, whether platoons, companies, or battalions, suffered an appalling casualty rate, some as high as 70 or 80 percent. Bodies were everywhere—floating in the water, piled on the beaches, crumpled awkwardly on the sandy soil. The stench became overwhelming. The heavy, peculiarly sweet odor of death has been remarked upon in the literature of war a thousand times, but you have to experience it to understand its overpowering presence. It lingers in the nostrils and stays locked in the memory to be set loose by even the most innocent associations. I remember one afternoon later on when I was driving around the island of Hawaii for the first time and was suddenly hit a nauseating blow to the stomach by what turned out to be the fleeting scent of sugarcane on the breeze.

Death, of course, is what war and battle are all about. The idea is to inflict punishment, to destroy, to kill. General Patton allegedly remarked that patriotism is not dying for your country but getting the son of a bitch on the other side to die for his country. But it works both ways. Death is a part of life, as we know, the unavoidable fate of us all. But no one, especially the young, normally gives much thought to the matter, because it seems too distant, too unpredictable, too unreal. But in wartime death is very real indeed, and it is all around you.

Seeing a great many dead, when you have never even seen a single dead person before, is bound to have a disturbing influence on the nervous system. Not so much at the time, however. During a battle you are temporarily immunized against the shock of death. It is afterward that the shock hits. You know now what the dead in war look like, bodies ripped open, an arm or a leg gone, a head rolling gently at the water's edge, corpses bloated and split open from the heat. And death becomes very near and very predictable. Later, when we were in Hawaii to recuperate from Tarawa and to rebuild for the next invasion, I would lie awake in a literal sweat of terror in the middle of the night, hearing the sound of my own death rushing toward me.

Yet in actual battle I never experienced such a sensation. Uncomfortable, nervous, worried, confused on occasion, scared sometimes, but never terrified. Not even when I lay alone and badly wounded in Saipan, with the enemy a few feet away. The absence of fear under such circumstances doesn't imply the presence of courage; it's just that in battle there is little time for the imagination to work, only the adrenaline. The time for imagination comes later. Years after the war I would sometimes wake from an afternoon nap and have the frightening feeling that I was experiencing a kind of "Occurrence at Owl Creek Bridge," that if I opened my eyes I would find myself dying in that swampy reed field on Saipan.

Death may haunt the imagination with terrible images, but fear of death rarely determines behavior. What men tend to suffer the most intense private anguish about is their personal conduct when the guns begin to fire. How will I, how did I, measure up? You very much want others to think well of you, but even more you want to think well of yourself. Not many men come out of battle fully confident that they passed the test. In this, Tarawa was like any other battle.

Yet, at the same time, Tarawa was one of those rare battles in which every participant did his duty and became a hero in spite of himself. Just getting ashore, or trying to, was a major act of courage—one reason, I suppose, why the division received a Presidential Unit Citation. And there were four Congressional Medals of Honor, three of them awarded posthumously, as well as scores of other decorations. There are always men who meet the test so well that in comparison you have come in a distant second, at best. I knew three.

One of them was the commander of our battalion, Major Kyle. Only twenty-eight at the time of Tarawa, the major had already won his medal of heroism at Guadalcanal, but medals were the last thing on his mind. To the junior officers he was imperturbable, cool, always in command of the situation. Though so remote as to seem almost inaccessible, he had a poise and confidence that I greatly admired and wished I had. While it was possible to think of other people getting killed or wounded, it was impossible to think of anything happening to the major. He struck most of us, I think, as the sort of man who could saunter through a battlefield carrying only a swagger stick, urging men on by his very presence. All right now, on your feet, up the hill, that's a good chap—much like those nonchalant British officers on the Northwest Frontier whom we used to see in the movies in the 1930s. Little wonder that so many of us were in awe of him. He was, as far as I know, the first ranking officer to cross the island in the assault to split the Japanese forces, and in fact did so before most of the rest of us. I don't know whether he sauntered or ran.

My platoon sergeant was a very different kind of man, though no less effective. Far from being remote, Reich was menacingly close to the men of the platoon. He scared them, but they trusted him completely; in his military talents and instincts he seemed the classic warrior type. For him, combat was what life, not just war, was all about. He never worried; nothing bothered him. The company, the battalion, the division, meant nothing to him, only the platoon. On the beach at

Tarawa he casually ignored the enemy until after he had taken care of the wounded. No two men were less alike, in background and personality, than he and I, yet we became very close. Why this was so on his part I have never understood, but I do know that I might well not have made it as a platoon leader without him.

The third man was Japanese. By the end of the last day of the battle what was left of my company—I was then the only officer—was dug in on a line from the beach to the edge of the airstrip. Another outfit had moved through our battalion and would absorb the last suicide attack by the Japanese at the eastern tail of the island. Our line crossed over a huge sand-covered bunker. Late at night a group of Japanese burst from it and ran wildly toward the airstrip. Silhouetted by burning debris on the other side, they were instantly shot down. Dumbfounded, and assuming there might be more of the enemy within, I ordered the man dug in on top of the bunker to lean over and throw in a couple of grenades.

Then it began. There were two men left alive inside, and one of them clearly was badly wounded. He began to moan and cry out in agony and despair. His comrade first would try to reassure him, then to defy us. At the time I never really thought of this man except as a threat, that he too might make a run for it and someone would get hurt. Only much later, and not really until twenty-five years later when I stood on the spot where the bunker had been and where perhaps he still lay buried, did I think of him differently. I could imagine him there in the total darkness, on his knees, his voice raised against us in the raging pitch that comes from fear and anger and then lowered to a soothing tone as he sought to comfort his mortally wounded companion. How horrifying it must have been for him, trapped in that black world from which there was no escape. Yet he managed to keep terror under control—to let it out in shouts of obscene defiance to us (for though we could not understand, that is surely what they were), and then to siphon it off in quiet words to his dying friend. Doomed and knowing he was doomed, he never lost control of himself and remained in command of the situation until the end.

As the site of a battle unsurpassed in fury, Tarawa is probably unique in that it was almost untouched by the battle itself and indeed by the course of the Pacific conflict. The usual outriders of war were absent. No civilians killed, no architectural masterpieces leveled, no homes pulverized, no bridges or roads destroyed, no works of art vandalized, no health or food services disrupted. The Japanese occupation lasted only about eighteen months and was relatively mild. The Marine presence was brief. After the battle, nature and the British moved in on Betio, and the signs of war were soon gone, save for the battered fortifications, which in time came to be accepted as part of the natural landscape.

Returning, I felt like the last survivor of a distant catastrophe people knew had happened but which had not really affected their lives. No one ever asked me about the battle.

It was only natural, then, I suppose, that I became drawn into the Tarawa of today. I had long talks with officials about the problems of bringing the Gilbert Islands to independence (achieved in 1979); listened to British doubts about the future of the economy; talked at lunch with local merchants who weren't very sanguine either; spent a morning touring the little hospital, including its small leper section; lectured to the sixty students at the training school for Gilbertese elementary teachers; went out to dinner parties; struck up a lasting friendship with Derek Cudmore, the assistant resident commissioner, and his wife Vrai; went on a hunt with the agricultural expert for the dread rhinoceros beetle (we didn't find it); visited the Catholic bishop, who was in the throes of supervising the construction of a tropical cathedral, and who served me the coldest bottle of beer I had while on Tarawa. By the time I left I was beginning to feel at home and comfortable and somewhat reluctant to leave. A vivid contrast to twenty-five years earlier.

This involvement turned out to be an unforeseen benefit. For almost twenty-five years I had relived the battle so many times that I saw myself doomed to fight it over and over without end. But to see Tarawa now was to realize that even though the past does indeed influence and shape our lives, we cannot live there. Though I came to Tarawa bringing the battle with me, I left without it. There are those who flee the present to find relief in the past. I found that my journey had enabled me to escape the past back into the present. Tarawa, which had innocently placed so terrible burden on me, innocently lifted that burden a quarter of a century later.

When I first arrived, I was surprised to discover that there was no memorial to the battle. I casually mentioned this when I talked with the students at the training school, not realizing that such a remark, suggesting ingratitude, would cause great "shame" to a sensitive people like the Gilbertese. Several days later, to show they did care, the students put on a big outdoor feast one evening, making me a kind of guest of honor. As the meal progressed, one of the teachers whispered to me that at an appropriate moment I would be expected to rise and speak. I searched my mind frantically for something to say. Suddenly I was nudged. I got slowly to my feet, and that was the moment I realized what had been happening to me during those two weeks. After thanking the students for their invitation, I said, as much as to myself as to them: "When I left Tarawa twenty-five years ago, I took with me very bitter and unhappy memories, but I want you to know that when I leave Tarawa this time, I shall carry with me very happy and pleasant memories." Not eloquent, but the students cheered.

My peace with the battle I would never have to fight again was my own private memorial, but I still thought there should be some visible sign of honor for those who had died on this distant piece of coral. Then, quite unexpectedly, I found it. Not long before I left, I talked with an expatriate minister who told me the following story:

Visiting in the northern part of the atoll, he was being taken by an old Gilbertese to someone's hut. On the way they came to a place with a log and some piled stones, and the old man told him they would sit here. Puzzled, he sat down. Soon a couple of small boys came by, and they too stopped and sat. Then an old woman with a basket. After a couple of minutes, the old man got up. The minister asked why they had stopped there. After the battle on Betio, the old man said, a company of Marines had been sent in pursuit of several dozen Japanese soldiers who had managed to escape. During the chase up the atoll a Marine had been killed in a skirmish at that spot, and ever since then no one went by without sitting for a few minutes in silence. Later in 1968, on the formal anniversary of the battle, a concrete monument was unveiled in commemoration, but I think I prefer that silent ground in northern Tarawa. It doesn't matter that few remember why they stop there.

—October 1983

ROSIE THE RIVETER REMEMBERS

Interviews by MARK JONATHAN HARRIS,
FRANKLIN D. MITCHELL,
STEVEN J. SCHECHTER

For millions of women, consciousness raising didn't start in the 1960s. It started when they helped win World War II.

During the first three years of World War II, five million women covered their hair, put on "slacks," and at the government's urging went to work in defense plants. They did every kind of job, but the largest single need was for riveters. In song, story, and film, the female patriot, "Rosie the Riveter," was born. Many of the new recruits had worked in service trades—as maids, cooks, or waitresses. Many more had never worked at any paying job. Practically none of them had ever made as much money. How they felt about resentful male co-workers, race and sex prejudice, and their own self confidence is revealed in these interviews with ex-defense workers.

WINONA ESPINOSA:
RIVETER AND BUS DRIVER

In July 1942 I left Grand Junction, Colorado, where I grew up, and came to San Diego with my brother-in-law and my sister. I was nineteen and my boyfriend had joined the Army and was in Washington State. In my mind San Diego sounded closer to Washington than Colorado, and I thought that would make it easier for us to see each other. I also wanted to do something to help the country get the war over with and I knew there were a lot of defense jobs in San Diego.

I applied for a job at Rohr Aircraft, and they sent me to a

six-week training school. You learned how to use an electric drill, how to do precision drilling, how to rivet. I hadn't seen anything like a rivet gun or an electric drill motor before except in Buck Rogers funny books. That's the way they looked to me. But I was an eager learner, and I soon became an outstanding riveter.

At Rohr I worked riveting the boom doors on P-38s. They were big, long, huge doors that had three or four thicknesses of skins, and you had to rivet those skins together. Everything had to be precise. It all had to pass inspection. Each rivet had to be countersunk by hand, so you had to be very good.

I found the work very challenging but I hated the dress. We had to wear ugly-looking hairnets that made the girls look awful. The female guards were very strict about them too. Maybe you'd try to leave your bangs sticking out but they'd come and make you stick them back in. You looked just like a skinhead, very unfeminine. Then you had to wear pants—we called them slacks in those days—and you never wore them prior to the war. Finally, all the women had to wear those ugly scarves. They issued them so they were all the same. You couldn't wear a colorful scarf or bandana.

I worked at Rohr for almost a year, then, when I got married and pregnant, I went back to Grand Junction for a while.

When I came back, I went to work for the San Diego Transit driving buses and streetcars. I just saw a sign on a bus downtown one day that said, "I need you," and I went and applied. I hadn't even been driving very long. I only learned to drive a car after I got to San Diego, and I didn't know anything about driving a big vehicle like that. But the war really created opportunities for women. It was the first time we got a chance to show that we could do a lot of things that only men had done before.

The transit company had a three-month school. They had classroom lessons and training in the field. You had to learn the automotive aspects of the bus so that if it broke down you could call in to tell the mechanic what was wrong so he could come and fix it. You also had to learn all the bus routes.

I drove buses and streetcars for about two and a half years. In fact I was driving a bus the day the war ended. I let everybody ride my bus free that day.

INEZ SAUER:
CHIEF CLERK, TOOLROOM

I was thirty-one when the war started and I had never worked in my life before. I had a six-year-old daughter and two boys, twelve and thirteen. We were living in Norwalk, Ohio, in a huge home in which we could fit about two hundred people playing bridge, and once in a while we filled it.

I remember my first husband saying to me, "You've lived through a depression and you weren't even aware that it was here." It was true. I knew that people were without work and that lots of people were having a hard time, but it never seemed to affect us or our friends. They were all the same ilk—all college people and all golfing and bridge-playing companions. I suppose you'd call it a life of ease. We always kept a live-in maid, and we never had to go without anything. Before the war my life was bridge and golf and clubs and children. One group I belonged to was a children's improvement group. I sat one night at the meeting and looked around at the group of women—there must have been thirty of us sitting there-and each one of us had maids, and our children were all at home with the maids. We were discussing how to improve our children, and they would have been far better off if we'd been home taking care of them.

When the war broke out, my husband's rubber-matting business in Ohio had to close due to war restrictions on rubber. We also lost our live-in maid, and I could see there was no way I could possibly live the way I was accustomed to doing. So I took my children home to my parents in Seattle.

The Seattle papers were full of ads for women workers needed to help the war effort. "Do your part, free a man for service." Being a D.A.R., I really wanted to help the war effort. I could have worked for the Red Cross and rolled bandages, but I wanted to do something that I thought was really vital. Building bombers was, so I answered an ad for Boeing.

My mother was horrified. She said no one in our family had ever worked in a factory. "You don't know what kind of people you're going to be associated with." My father was horrified too, no matter how I tried to impress on him that this was a war effort on my part. He said, "You'll never get along with the people you'll meet there." My husband thought it was utterly ridiculous. I had never worked. I didn't know how to handle money, as he put it. I was nineteen when I was married. My husband was ten years older, and he always made me feel like a child, so he didn't think I would last very long at the job, but he was wrong.

They started me as a clerk in this huge toolroom. I had never handled a tool in my life outside of a hammer. Some man came in and asked for a bastard file. I said to him, "If you don't control your language, you won't get any service here." I went to my supervisor and said, "You'll have to correct this man. I won't tolerate that kind of language." He laughed and laughed and said, "Don't you know what a bastard file is? It's the name of a very coarse file." He went over and took one out and showed me.

So I said to him, "If I'm going to be part of this organization, I must have some books, something that shows me how I can learn to do what I'm supposed to do." This was an unheard-of request. It went through channels, and they finally brought me some large, classified material that showed all the tools and machinery needed to build the B-17s. So gradually I educated myself about the various tools and their uses, and I was allowed to go out and roam around the machine area and become acquainted with what they were doing. The results showed on my paycheck. Eventually I became chief clerk of the toolroom. I think I was the first woman chief clerk they had.

The first year, I worked seven days a week. We didn't have any time off. They did allow us Christmas off, but Thanksgiving we had to work. That was a hard thing to do. The children didn't understand. My mother and father didn't understand, but I worked. I think that put a little iron in my spine too. I did something that was against my grain, but I did it, and I'm glad.

Since I was the chief clerk, they gave me the privilege of coming to work a half-hour early in the morning and staying over thirty or forty minutes at night. Because I was working late one night I had the chance to see President Roosevelt. They said he was coming in on the swing shift, after four o'clock, so I waited to see him. They cleared out all the aisles of the main plant, and he went through in a big, open limousine. He smiled and he had his long cigarette holder, and he was very, very pleasant. "Hello there, how are you? Keep up the war effort. Oh, you women are doing a wonderful job." We were all thrilled to think the President could take time out of the war effort to visit us factory workers. It gave us a lift and I think we worked harder.

Boeing was a real education for me. It taught me a different way of life. I had never been around uneducated people before, people that worked with their hands. I was prudish and had never been with people that used coarse language. Since I hadn't worked before, I didn't know there was such a thing as the typical male ego. My contact with my first supervisor was one of animosity, in which he stated, "The happiest day of my life will be when I say good-bye to each one of you women as I usher you out the front door." I didn't understand that kind of resentment, but it was prevalent throughout the plant. Many of the men felt that no women could come in and run a lathe, but they did. I learned that just because you're a woman and have never worked is no reason you can't learn. The job really broadened me. I had led a very sheltered life. I had had no contact with Negroes except as maids or gardeners. My mother was a Virginian, and we were brought up to think that colored people were not on the same economic or social level. I learned differently at Boeing, I learned that because a girl is a Negro she's not necessarily a maid, and because a man is a Negro doesn't mean that all he can do is dig. In fact, I found that some of the black people I got to know there were very superior—and certainly equal to me—equal to anyone I ever knew.

Before I worked at Boeing I also had had no exposure to unions. After I was there awhile, I joined the machinists union. We had a contract dispute, and we had a one-day walkout to show Boeing our strength. We went on this march through the financial district in downtown Seattle.

My mother happened to be down there seeing the president of the Seattle First National Bank at the same time. Seeing this long stream of Boeing people, he interrupted her and said, "Mrs. Ely, they seem to be having a labor walkout. Let's go out and see what's going on." So my mother and a number of people from the bank walked outside to see what was happening. And we came down the middle of the street— I think there were probably five thousand of us. I saw my mother. I could recognize her—she was tall and stately—and I waved and said, "Hello, Mother." That night when I got home I thought she was never going to honor my name again. She said, "To think my daughter was marching in that labor demonstration. How could you do that to the family?" But I could see that it was a new, new world.

My mother warned me when I took the job that I would never be the same. She said, "You will never want to go back to being a housewife." At that time I didn't think it would change a thing. But she was right, it definitely did.

I had always been in a shell; I'd always been protected. But at Boeing I found a freedom and an independence I had never known. After the war I could never go back to playing bridge again, being a clubwoman and listening to a lot of inanities when I knew there were things you could use your mind for. The war changed my life completely. I guess you could say, at thirty-one, I finally grew up.

RACHEL WRAY:
HAND RIVETER, GROUP LEADER, MECHANIC

I grew up on a farm in northeastern Oklahoma, knowing nothing but the Depression. My father lost the farm, and we moved to town just when I was starting junior high school. I lived there until the eleventh grade, when I was forced to quit school to go to work.

When I was nineteen I fell in love with a boy from Oklahoma. George was also from a depressed area and joined the Navy to get ahead. He was stationed in California, and I decided to come and join him. I felt there would be more opportunity in California, and I was determined that I was going to have a different life.

I had twenty-five dollars when I left Oklahoma. I answered an ad in the paper looking for riders to California and paid twelve dollars for the trip. I arrived here with twelve dollars to my name and lived with friends until I could get work.

I got a job as a pastry cook at a restaurant in Whittier, a very exclusive place. I was making fifteen dollars (and board) a week and was very proud of myself. George and I were planning to marry. Then Pearl Harbor was attacked, and his ship was sent out to fight in the Pacific.

After he left I knew I had to make it on my own. I saw an

ad in the paper announcing the opening of a school for vocational training in aircraft. I was looking for the opportunity to learn something else, and I wanted to earn more money. I worked during the day cooking and went to school at night studying bench mechanics and riveting, how to read blueprints and use different aircraft tools.

After about three months the instructor said, "There's no use in you spending any more time here. You can go out and get a job." He gave me my graduation slip, and I went down to San Diego to look around, because George's mother lived there. I went to Convair, which was Consolidated Aircraft then, and they hired me.

I was one of the first women hired at Convair and I was determined that I wasn't going to lose the job and be sent back to working as a pastry cook. Convair had a motto on their plant which said that anything short of right is wrong, and that stuck with me. I went to work in the riveting group in metal-bench assembly. The mechanics would bring us the job they had put together, and we would take the blueprints and rivet what they brought us.

They would always put the new people with another person, a "leadman." The man I went to work for was really great. He saw my determination and would give me hard jobs to do. The other girls would say, "Joplin, don't give her that, I'll do it." But he would say, "I'm going to break her in right, I'm going to do it the hard way." He told me later that he had made a mistake and been too easy with the other girls.

I tackled everything. I had a daring mother who was afraid of nothing: horses, farm implements, anything, so maybe I inherited a little bit of that from her. I remember my brother, who was in the Air Corps at the time, and his friends laughed at me one day thinking I couldn't learn this mechanical stuff. I can still see them, but it only made me more determined. I think it probably hurt their pride a little bit that I was capable of doing this.

Pretty soon I was promoted to bench-mechanic work, which was detailed hand-riveting. Then I was given a bench with nothing to do but repair what other people had ruined. I visited a man recently who's seventy-four years old, and he said to my daughter, "All we had to do was foul up a job and take it to her and she'd fix it."

I loved working at Convair. I loved the challenge of

getting dirty and getting into the work. I did one special riveting job, hand riveting that could not be done by machine. I worked on that job for three months, ten hours a day, six days a week, and slapped three-eighth- or three-quarter-inch rivets by hand that no one else would do. I didn't have that kind of confidence as a kid growing up, because I didn't have that opportunity. Convair was the first time in my life that I had the chance to prove that I could do something, and I did. They finally made me a group leader, although they didn't pay me the wage that went with the job, because I was a woman.

Our department was a majority of women. Many of the women had no training at all, particularly the older women. We had women in our department who were ex-schoolteachers, -artists, -housewives, so when we could give them a job from the production line, the job would have to be set up for them. I'd sit them down and show them how to use the drill press, the size drill to use, the size of screws, the kind of rivets, whether it was an Army rivet or a Navy rivet—a Navy rivet was an icebox rivet, the Army rivet was not—and so on. Then I would go back and check to see if the riveting was okay, and if there were any bad rivets, they had to take them out. Most of the time I had to take them out myself. As a group leader that's what I did, and I did it at the same time I was doing my job as a bench mechanic. There were four male group leaders and myself. Theoretically we should have been classified as group leaders and paid for that type of work, but we were not. I felt that was discrimination and that we were being used by the company and fought against it.

Shortly after I went to work at Convair I was chosen by the people in our work group to sit on the wage-review board. The company had automatic wage reviews, and when I first started, those were the only raises that we received. The women were lucky, though, if we got a five-cent-an-hour increase on a review. Some of the women got three cents, some of the women even got two cents, and some of the women were passed over. To us it seemed that the men's pay automatically went up, and ours didn't. I was fortunate enough to get raises later, even a ten-cent raise, and I actually had an assistant foreman come up to me and say, "Don't say anything to the other girls about getting a raise." I told him, "I don't discuss my personal wages, but how about the other women who are deserving too?" So on the wage board I fought for the other women as much as I fought for myself. The highest-paid women at that time were making around $.80 an hour, but the men were probably making $1.15 to $1.50 an hour for identically the same work. In fact, there was a lot of feeling that the women were producing more work than the men on final assembly and on the bench because of their agility with their hands.

Some of the things we did change. For example, they were forced to classify you because of your work. And somewhere in the back of their minds they had the idea that they were not going to make a woman anything but a B-mechanic. As a B-mechanic you could only go to $1.00 an hour, and they were determined that no woman would ever become an A-mechanic or an A-riveter. But we really fought that and we proved to them by bringing them on the job that we were doing A-mechanic work and producing more than the men. So I got my A-mechanic classification and a raise to $1.15 an hour.

I also sat on the safety board the whole time I was at Convair, for the safety requirements they demanded of women were more unreasonable than what they demanded of men. In the beginning we had caps and uniforms we were supposed to wear, but the women rebelled at that. We felt that we could be safe and wear the clothes we wanted. Eventually the company did become a little more relaxed about dress, so we won some victories there too.

ADELE ERENBERG:
MACHINIST

When the war started, I was twenty-six, unmarried, and working as a cosmetics clerk in a drugstore in Los Angeles. I was running the whole department, handling the inventory and all that. It felt asinine, though, to be selling lipstick when the country was at war. I felt that I was capable of doing something more than that toward the war effort.

There was also a big difference between my salary and those in defense work. I was making something like twenty-two to twenty-four dollars a week in the drugstore. You could earn a much greater amount of money for your labor in defense plants. Also it interested me. I had a certain curiosity about meeting that kind of challenge, and here was an opportunity to do that, for there were more openings for women.

So I went to two or three plants and took their test. And they all told me I had absolutely no mechanical ability. I said, "I don't believe that." So I went to another, A.D.E.L. I was interviewed and got the job. This particular plant made the hydraulic valve systems for the B-17. And where did they put women? In the burr room. You sat at a workbench, which was essentially like a picnic table with a bunch of other women, and you worked grinding and sanding machine parts to make them smooth. That's what you did all day long. It was very mechanical and it was very boring. There were about thirty women in the burr room, and it was like being in a beauty shop every day. I couldn't stand the inane talk. So when they asked me if I would like to work someplace else in the shop, I said I very much would.

They started training me. I went to a blueprint class and learned how to use a micrometer and how to draw tools out of the tool crib and everything else. Then one day they said, "Okay, how would you like to go into the machine shop?"

I said, "Terrific."

And they said, "Now, Adele, it's going to be a real challenge because you'll be the only woman in the machine shop." I thought to myself, well, that's going to be fun, all those guys and Adele in the machine shop. So the foreman took me over there. It was a big room, with a high ceiling and fluorescent lights, and it was very noisy. I walked in there, in my overalls, and suddenly all the machines stopped and every guy in the shop just turned around and looked at me. It took, I think, two weeks before anyone else even talked to me. The discrimination was indescribable. They wanted to kill me.

My attitude was, "Okay, you bastards. I'm going to prove to you I can do anything you can do, and maybe better than some of you." And that's exactly the way it turned out. I used to do the rework on the pieces that the guy on the shift before me had screwed up. I finally got assigned nothing but rework.

Later they taught me to run an automatic screwing machine. It's a big mother, and it took a lot of strength just to throw that thing into gear. They probably thought I wasn't going to be able to do it. But I was determined to succeed. As a matter of fact I developed the most fantastic biceps from throwing that machine into gear. Even today I still have a little of that muscle left.

Anyway, eventually some of the men became very friendly, particularly the older ones, the ones in their late forties or fifties. They were journeymen tool and die makers and were so skilled they could work anywhere at very high salaries. They were sort of fatherly, protective. They weren't threatened by me. The younger men, I think, were.

Our plant was an open shop, and the International Association of Machinists was trying to unionize the workers. I joined and worked to try and get the union in the plant. I proselytized for the union during lunch hour and I had a big altercation with the management over that. The employers and my leadman and foreman called me into the office and said, "We have a right to fire you."

I said, "On what basis? I work as well or better than anybody else in the shop except the journeymen."

They said, "No, not because of that, because you're talking for the union on company property. You're not allowed to do that."

I said, "Well that's just too bad, because I can't get off the grounds here. You won't allow us to leave the grounds during lunch hour. And you don't pay me for my lunch hour, so that time doesn't belong to you, so you can't tell me what to do." And they backed down.

I had one experience at the plant that really made me work for the union. One day while I was burring, I had an accident and ripped some cartilage out of my hand. It wasn't serious, but it looked kind of messy.

They had to take me over to the industrial hospital to get my hand sutured. I came back and couldn't work for a day or two because my hand was all bandaged. It wasn't serious, but it was awkward. When I got my paycheck, I saw that they had docked me for time that I was in the industrial hospital. When I saw that I was really mad.

It's ironic that when the union finally got into the plant, they had me transferred out. They were anxious to get rid of me because, after we got them in, I went to a few meetings and complained about it being a Jim Crow union. So they arranged for me to have a higher rating instead of a worker's rating. This allowed me to make twenty-five cents an hour more, and I got transferred to another plant. By this time I was married. When I became pregnant I worked for about three months more, then I quit.

For me defense work was the beginning of my emancipation as a woman. For the first time in my life I found out that I could do something with my hands besides bake a pie.

SYBIL LEWIS:
RIVETER, ARC WELDER

When I first arrived in Los Angeles, I began to look for a job. I decided I didn't want to do maid work anymore, so I got a job as a waitress in a small black restaurant, I was making pretty good money, more than I had in Sapulpa, Oklahoma, but I didn't like the job that much; I didn't have the knack for getting good tips. Then I saw an ad in the newspaper offering to train women for defense work. I went to Lockheed Aircraft and applied. They said they'd call me; but I never got a response, so I went back and applied again. You had to be pretty persistent. Finally they accepted me. They gave me a short training program and taught me how to rivet. Then they put me to work in the plant riveting small airplane parts, mainly gasoline tanks.

The women worked in pairs. I was the riveter and this big, strong white girl from a cotton farm in Arkansas worked as the bucker. The riveter used a gun to shoot rivets through the metal and fasten it together. The bucker used a bucking bar on the other side of the metal to smooth out the rivets. Bucking was harder than shooting rivets; it required more muscle. Riveting required more skill.

I worked for a while as a riveter with this white girl when the boss came around one day and said, "We've decided to make some changes." At this point he assigned her to do the riveting and me to do the bucking. I wanted to know why. He said, "Well, we just interchange once in a while." But I was never given the riveting job back. This was the first encounter I had with segregation in California, and it didn't sit too well with me. It brought back some of my experiences in Sapulpa—you're a Negro, so you do the hard work. I wasn't failing as a riveter—in fact, the other girl learned to rivet from me—but I felt they gave me the job of bucker because I was black.

So I applied to Douglas Aircraft in Santa Monica and was hired as a riveter there. On that job I did not encounter the same prejudice.

I worked in aircraft for a few years, then in '43 I saw an ad in the paper for women trainees to learn arc welding. The salary sounded good, from $1.00 to $1.25 an hour. I wanted to learn that skill and I wanted to make more money, so I answered the ad and they sent me to a short course at welding school. After I passed the trainee course, they employed me at the shipyards. That was a little different than working in aircraft because in the shipyard you found mostly men. There I ran into another kind of discrimination; because I was a woman I was paid less than a man for doing the same job.

I was an arc welder, I'd passed both the Army and the Navy tests, and I knew I could do the job, but I found from talking with some of the men that they made more money. You'd ask about this but they'd say, "Well you don't have the experience," or, "The men have to lift some heavy pieces of steel and you don't have to." but I knew that I had to help lift steel too.

They started everyone off at $1.20 an hour. There were higher-paying jobs, though, like chippers and crane operators that were for men only. Once, the foreman told me I had to go on the skids—the long docks alongside the hull. I said, "That sounds pretty dangerous. Will I make more than $1.20 an hour?" And he said, "No, $1.20 is the top pay you will get."

But the men got more.

It was interesting that although they didn't pay women as much as men, the men treated you differently if you wore slacks. I noticed, for example, that when you'd get on the bus or the streetcar, you stood all the way, more than the lady who would get on with a dress. I never could understand why men wouldn't give women in slacks a seat. And at the shipyards the language wasn't the best. Nobody respected you enough to clean up the way they spoke. It didn't seem to bother the men that you were a woman. During the war years men began to say, you have a man's job and you're getting paid almost the same, so we don't have to give you a seat anymore or show the common courtesies that men show women, All those niceties were lost.

I enjoyed working at the shipyard—it was a unique job for a woman—and I liked the challenge. But it was a dangerous job. The safety measures were very poor. Many people were injured by falling steel. Finally I was assigned to a very hazardous area and I asked to be transferred into a safer area. I was not granted that. They said you have to work where they assign you at all times. I thought it was getting too dangerous, so I quit.

The war years had a tremendous impact on women. I know for myself it was the first time I had a chance to get out of the kitchen and work in industry and make a few bucks. This was something I had never dreamed would happen. In Sapulpa all that women had to look forward to was keeping house and raising families. The war years offered new possibilities. You came out to California, put on your pants, and took your lunch pail to a man's job. This was the beginning of women's feeling that they could do something more. We were trained to do this kind of work because of the war, but there was no question that this was just an interim period. We were all told that when the war was over, we would not be needed anymore.

FRANKIE COOPER:
CRANE OPERATOR

The first job I had lasted only a month. The foreman was sort of a frantic-type person and wanted me to start my machine at ten minutes to seven and I refused. I told him I've only been here a month and I'm already making my quota and I have no intention of starting my machine early. He said, "You know I can fire you," and I said, "You know I don't care." So he fired me.

Then I heard of an opening at American Steel for a crane operator, on a small ten-ton crane. I applied for it and got it. Then I had to learn it. The men said, "You won't learn it. Women can't do that job." But they were wrong. I think I was the fourth woman hired in the mill. It wasn't an important or dangerous job, just moving gun mounts and gun barrels around and cleaning up the floor in what they called the Navy building. The important work was inside the foundry, where they poured the steel. It was all men in the foundry. You had to have seniority to run one of those fifty-ton cranes because there was so much responsibility involved.

One day there was a terrible accident at the plant. One of the crane operators had lost a load of steel, poured it all over. It just streamed everywhere, put a lot of lives in danger. After the accident they took him to the doctor and he was examined carefully. They found that he was losing his eyesight, that he couldn't see that far away in the brightness to pour the steel.

They had to take him off the crane and needed an immediate replacement. They looked around and there wasn't anyone but women. The men they still had were on jobs where they couldn't be replaced.

By this time I had moved up to operating a fifty-ton crane and I had learned the language of the foundry, the sign language with which you communicate to your rigger or chainman. So they offered the job to me, and I took it. Pouring steel was the hardest job in the mill, and the men said, "It's too big a responsibility for a woman. She'll never last." But I did.

The hardest part for me was sanding the rails. The rails are what the wheels of the crane run on. They're way up in the air over the concrete floor and they have to be sanded every eight-hour shift, because if your rails get too slick, your hook will slide. That was the first time I had a crane with railings before, and when I found out that the operators had to sand them, I was almost scared to death. I thought, "I can't do it. I can't look down at that concrete and put this little bucket of sand up and down. I just can't do it." And one of the men said, "Well, that'll get her. She'll never sand them tracks." That's what made me sand them. After that I had to. I had to show them I could do it.

It took a while to be accepted. We had a big coke stove and we'd gather around it to get warm. On occasion, when I had time to come down and take my breaks, the men would stand so close together around the stove that there wasn't room for me. So I just leaned up against the wall. The wall was warmer than where they were standing anyway because it had absorbed the heat from all the hours the fire had been going. So I would lean up against the wall and laugh at their jokes. And I would offer them a doughnut if I had one and so forth. So actually I made the overtures. And after a while they began to accept me.

During the war the morale inside the plants was extremely high. Not just myself, but everybody, gave everything they had. They wanted to do it. Today you don't sit around and talk about patriotism while you're drinking a beer, but you did back then. I mean you had a neighbor next door—maybe he lived states and states away—and if you were like me, often you couldn't understand what he said, but you had this great thing in common. You were all pulling together for one great war effort.

I was never absent, and I wasn't unique in that. There was very little absenteeism where I worked. If I woke up in the morning and I didn't feel too good and I really didn't want to go to work, I could make myself go by thinking, "What about those boys who are getting up at five o'clock, maybe haven't even been to bed? Maybe they're leaning their chin on a bayonet just to stay awake on watch. I don't even know their names. They don't even have faces to me, but they're out there somewhere overseas. And I'm saying that I don't feel like going to work today because I've got a headache?" That would get me out of bed and into work. And by the time I'd stayed there a couple of hours it was okay. I was going to make it. So I never stayed at home.

There was only one really difficult problem with working. That was leaving my two-and-one-half-year-old daughter. When a mother goes away from home and starts to work for her first time, there is always a feeling of guilt. Any mother that has ever done this has had this feeling. I couldn't cope with it at first.

I relate so much with women who are trying to get into nontraditional jobs today, because during the war we had those jobs out of necessity, and then after the war they were no longer there. Women have actually had nontraditional jobs since the first wagon train went across the country. When they arrived at the place where they wanted to settle, they helped cut the logs, they helped put them together, they helped put the mud between the log cabins, and they made a home and had their babies inside. And every time a war comes along, women take up nontraditional work again. During the Civil War they worked in factories, they helped make musket balls, they made clothing for the troops, and they kept the home fires burning the way they always have. World War I came along and they did the same thing. After the war was over, they went back home. World War II, it was exactly the same thing, but the women were different in World War II: they didn't want to go back home, and many of them haven't. And if they did go back home, they never forgot, and they told their daughters, "You don't have to be just a homemaker. You can be anything you want to be." And so we've got this new generation of women.

—February 1984

"YES, BY DAMN, WE'RE GOING BACK TO BERLIN"

by LESTER F. RENTMEESTER

After two false starts, the B-17s got through. A pilot relives the 8th Air Force's first successful daylight raid on the German capital.

In March the nights were long and black over the airfield at Bassingbourn, which lies just north of London. Its latitude is about the same as that of Hudson Bay, and this proximity to the Arctic Circle means long summer days and long winter nights. During the cold months, the B-17s of the 91st Bombardment Group took off in the dark: a blackout was strictly enforced, all the windows had heavy curtains, and even the flashlights had recessed bulbs.

Our squadron, the 401st, was put on alert during the evening of March 5, 1944—a bombing mission was on for the next day. Designated crews were awakened by the assistant operations officer, stumbling through the dark barracks with torch in hand, and on this Monday morning it was a little earlier than usual—3:30 A.M. This early wake-up time always meant an especially long mission. We had been up at 3:30 on March 3 and 4 as well, and the mission had been announced as Berlin. On both days the clouds had been solid east of the Rhine, and targets of opportunity had been selected instead.

So when the operations officer declared, "Breakfast at 4:30, briefing at 5:30," to the sleepy crew members, we knew what lay ahead. Berlin again. This would be my fourth mission in six days.

The crews scheduled to fly missions were normally put on alert the night before so that they could get their rest and psych themselves up. If no missions were scheduled for the group for the next day, the announcement was made in the early evening that the group was on "stand-down"—news greeted by a collective sigh of relief and often by a visit to the bar or to the very infrequent movie on the base, or by a game of cards with the other officers, perhaps a basketball game, or a bicycle ride around the station. In my case many nights were spent writing to my wife, Jeanne, or reading. I had found Franz Werfel's book *The Forty Days of Musa Dagh* and was doggedly working my way through it. The feeling of impending doom generated by the story of the Armenian massacre was coupled with the gloomy atmosphere resulting from the heavy losses of B-17 crews and many friends during early 1944, so that it seems now that the sun didn't even shine during that period.

Some of the flight crews were difficult to awaken. Many took sleeping pills to get to sleep and pep pills to stay awake; after a mission they would visit the bar to dissolve the tension. This was not a problem with my crew; after the first few missions they adopted an attitude of taking things as they came.

When I was awakened on March 6, 1944, my movements were automatic and detached, a pattern developed from previous missions. Some fliers were very superstitious; they would try to do exactly the same things that worked for them on previous successful missions. The only obsession that I developed was to make sure that I had a bowel movement before takeoff. At high altitudes in unpressurized aircraft, the food in the bowels will expand, causing great pain. On my second mission, over France, I neglected this important physical function and was punished by six hours in purgatory. During the fighting that followed, my pain was so intense that I was hoping that I would be shot down to end it. Never again would I neglect my pre-mission ritual of a visit to the latrine.

The temperature at twenty-eight thousand feet over Germany in the winter sometimes goes down to minus sixty degrees Centigrade, so cold that our flying boots froze to any spilled oil or hydraulic fluid on the floor of the airplane. It was necessary to dress warmly but without bulkiness that would restrict movement. Each person had his own idea of what the well-dressed aviator should wear, but all started with the indispensable long johns. Over these I wore the dark Army shirt and trousers, very warm, and in the coldest days of winter, a flying suit along with the leather A-2 jacket. On my feet were a pair of silk socks, a pair of heavy socks, and the high-top combat shoes with the leather inside out. These were laced tightly, to prevent the common occurrence of shoes snapping off when the parachute opens. Later on, at the equipment hut, I would zip on a pair of fleece-lined winter flying boots over the shoes.

The crushed Army officer's cap was the final adornment, but it was exchanged at the equipment hut for tight-fitting leather and canvas headgear. The gloves never protected the hands adequately from the numbing cold, and I tried various combinations that would give me control over the numerous switches and levers and yet prevent my hands from freezing. After several missions I hit upon a pair of tight-fitting silk gloves underneath a pair of thin leather gloves.

Most crew members didn't carry a firearm, as we were told that the Germans could treat us as spies if they caught us with weapons. Instead we were issued a Swiss pocket knife with a blade under six inches to conform with the Geneva Convention rules. A silk scarf, on which a map of Europe was printed, also went into my pocket. Several compasses were concealed in buttons; a very small one was sewn into the seam of my shirt pocket.

When we first arrived at the base, we had our pictures taken in civilian dress with different combinations of clothing. If, once shot down, we were fortunate enough to contact the underground, these could be used for spurious identification cards. Our best bet, we were told, was to assume the identity of one of the many Poles deported to France as forced labor. At this stage in the war, many American fliers had made their way back out of German-occupied territory and provided invaluable data for escape and evasion tactics. It was my fantasy that, if shot down, I would work my way to a German airfield, steal a German plane, and fly back to England. These escape tactics were very real for us because we were told upon arrival at the 91st Bomb Group that only one person in eleven had finished his tour.

All dressed for the flight and ready to leave, I turned out the lights, and the room became pitch black. No use opening the blackout curtains, because by the time I returned it would be dark outside again. By virtue of the law of survival of the luckiest, I had moved up to be the fourth-ranking pilot in the squadron and had inherited a nice single room equipped with call buttons for orderlies, an overseas radio left by some luckless former occupant, and some foot lockers, which I never opened. One of the former occupants moved in one morning, then went out to fly a mission and was shot down.

I waited for Bill Behrend, my copilot, who came from Trenton, New Jersey. He soon appeared, and we went outside to where our bicycles were parked. Snapped to each bicycle frame was a torch, whose aperture could be controlled to furnish just a pinprick of light. Bill and I seldom used our torches while cycling on the base; we knew our way by heart. We pedaled to the officers mess, where good breakfast smells greeted us. Lucky Army units have a good scavenger who can find the unfindable. It was our good fortune to have a mess sergeant who scoured the countryside and cornered the local market in eggs. Each of us was guaranteed one fresh egg per day at sixpence each. We picked up our eggs at the door and turned them over to the waiter at the table.

Our navigator and bombardier were seated and had already begun to eat. Both were original members of the crew, which was formed at Moses Lake, Washington, in the spring of 1943. Bob Roberts, from Greenbelt, Maryland, was a likable, good-looking guy who didn't make many mistakes and learned quickly from the ones that he did make. He was one of the most skilled navigators in the squadron and had quickly made himself familiar with the ingenious navigation gear provided by the Royal Air Force. Joe Ashby was from Rolla, Missouri, and sometimes gave the impression that he was naive. If you were fooled into thinking that, he was good at taking advantage of the situation. He and another Missourian talked about returning there after the war and starting a stump farm. Joe was an A-1 bombardier.

When you eat breakfast at 4:30 A.M. and will not eat again until after 6:00 P.M., you choose your menu with care. Breakfasts were leisurely, with a choice of eggs prepared the way we wanted, pancakes, Spam, toast, orange marmalade (made from turnips), powdered milk, and coffee. There was little speculation about whether the forthcoming mission would be tough: instead we talked about the bomb load, gas load, how we could sneak some extra .50-caliber ammo aboard, the flying characteristics of our assigned aircraft, and so forth.

The theater where the mission briefing was held was always full fifteen minutes before the announced briefing time. From the doorway we spotted the six enlisted members of our crew; Bill and Joe went to the seats that they had reserved in the row ahead of them, Bob went to get his navigation materials, and I conferred with the operations officer.

He gave me a sheet of paper, which showed each plane's position in the group formation, the colors of the flares that would be used in given situations, the call sign, the recall sign, and the times that the 91st Bomb Group would use for takeoff, assembly, and departure from the coast. The operations officer also said that because of scheduling difficulties, three squadron leaders would be flying today, and that I, being the newest assigned, would fly a wing position. He looked like he expected me to say, "That's fine," so I said, "That's fine," and joined my crew.

The six airmen sitting in the row of theater seats greeted me as I found a seat in front of them. Two of them, Elmer Diethorn of Pittsburgh, Pennsylvania, and Ward Simonson of upstate New York, were technical sergeants; the other four were a step below at staff sergeant. They were so young; at age twenty-three I was the old man of the crew.

Elmer "Mickey" Diethorn was the flight engineer and chief honcho of the crew. His "office" during the flight was directly behind the pilot, from which point he could monitor all the engine instruments and furnish advice. During fighter attacks he manned the top machine-gun turret, which contained two .50-caliber guns and was power-driven. Although I don't recall his shooting down any aircraft (probably because they attacked from the front and dived down under his guns), his job was extremely important: he acted somewhat like a fire-control director, advising the other gunners where the attacking Jerries were, which way they were going, and which gunner should be ready to shoot at them next.

Mickey and I were worried about our ship, which had sustained major structural damage in the February 22 raid on Oschersleben. Although it had had a depot overhaul and had been flown since, it still had a few problems. I told him that Bill and I had cycled out to the ship after dinner and talked to the ground crew, who had promised to work through the night to clean up some maintenance problems.

Like Mickey, radio operator Ward Simonson was always

happy and cheerful. He had picked up his code information for the day, had been briefed on which frequencies to monitor, and said that there were no radio problems. We always kidded him about his Purple Heart: he had been hit by a truck the month before.

Bob Roberts joined us, carrying a packet of escape and evasion materials that the crew would use if shot down. The escape plan was to join up with Bob, who normally would leave the aircraft in the middle of the evacuation and should be in the center of the parachuting crew, and to make our plans from there. His kit, which then cost about twenty-three dollars, contained eight gold articles—three rings, two half-sovereign coins, one sovereign, one 20-franc coin, and one 10-franc coin. Mickey had a box of hard candies to carry, and Ward Simonson would bring the first-aid kit. After each mission Bob had to turn in the escape and evasion kit, but we usually ate up the candy, and Ward kept his medical supplies.

The noisy room suddenly became silent as the group commander and the briefing officers arrived. They mounted the stage, and a junior officer pulled the curtains to reveal a map of Europe on which our flight track was plotted from Bassingbourn to target and back to Bassingbourn. Three days earlier there had been a gasp and an explosion of noise from the aircrews when we spotted the flight track to Berlin. Today, when the opened curtains showed the same target, there was little reaction.

"Yes, by damn," said our group commander, "we're going back to Berlin and this time we're going to do it right. And I'm going to be right up there in the first plane, because the 91st Bomb Group is going to show them the way. We're going to lead the 1st Air Combat Wing of the 1st Air Division of the 8th Air Force. We're going to hit that ball-bearing works in Erkner, which is sixteen miles southeast of Berlin, and we're going to destroy it just like we did the ball-bearing works at Schweinfurt." This was not a highly motivating remark, because it was nip and tuck for a while which would be wiped out first—the 91st or Schweinfurt.

The group commander was followed by a series of briefing officers. The flak officer had put colored plastic along our flight route wherever there were concentrations of antiaircraft weapons. He showed us how our flight route was planned so that we would have minimum exposure to the 88-mm and

105-mm antiaircraft guns. This was reassuring. Once our group navigator had had our formation fly upwind over the Ruhr Valley, which had the greatest concentration of flak guns in the world. Weather, munitions, and maintenance came next. There was even a taxi-control officer who told us the direction and sequence for taxiing. Long before, in secret conclave at the bar, we pilots had all decided that this was the job we would grab during our next combat tour.

After the briefing the aircrew got together to decide if there was anything special that needed to be done before we picked up our equipment and went out to the aircraft. On two previous missions we had run out of .50-caliber ammunition and had to sit, helpless, while the Jerries attacked. After that we always took an extra fifteen hundred rounds per gun over the limit allowed by our munitions officer.

The crew split up to finish certain chores. In some of the rooms behind the theater stage, chaplains of various faiths were available to provide spiritual encouragement. Figuring that I needed all the help that I could get, I invariably received Holy Communion and the Last Rites of the Catholic Church before going on a mission.

It was a short stroll from the briefing room to 401st operations, where I chatted for a few minutes with the operations officer, James McPartlin, and his two assistants, Francis Porada and Neil Daniels. Sometimes they would have bits of information that might prove useful, and sometimes I would ask for help with equipment or aircraft problems. This was my fourth long mission in five days, each with nine hours of flying time and over seven and a half hours on oxygen. Such a stiff schedule was not normally expected, or asked, of an aircrew. But given all the discussions about the spring offensive to neutralize the *Luftwaffe* before D-Day, I would not have been surprised to be on the schedule again the following day.

Just behind operations was a medium-sized Quonset hut, which was filled with racks of personal equipment, parachutes, machine guns, and other paraphernalia of war. After each mission the machine guns were removed from the aircraft and returned to the flight line for inspection and maintenance. On the several occasions when we didn't make it back to the airfield, the guns were faithfully removed from the battered aircraft and laboriously trucked back with us.

Gordon A. Wiggett of Vermont, whose duty station was

at the right waist gun, was the armorer on our crew. It was his job to keep our thirteen machine guns in perfect working order and to beg or steal the extra ammo that we always carried after our embarrassing early shortages. From our first days of training as a crew, many missions were devoted entirely to gunnery and to the discipline necessary to prevent burning out the gun barrels, a common problem when so many rounds were fired.

Our guns were our protectors, and we took good care of them. With the bombs it was different; there was a feeling of guilt associated with them. In the States we spent countless hours on precision bombing until we could hit a "pickle barrel" from twenty-five thousand feet. Our generation was brought up with the belief that wars were fought under certain gentlemanly terms, involving only military targets and military men. Suddenly we were in a situation where we were bombing through clouds at targets surrounded by the civilian populace. When the Pathfinder aircraft, specially equipped for radar bombing through clouds, was brought to our group in December 1943, I registered a moral objection with my squadron commander. He listened but insisted that this was the only way to win the war. After a week of arguing with myself, I finally concluded that he was right. Fortunately there was a squadron stand-down during this last month of 1943 due to weather or I might have received some sort of punishment. However, every time the bombs dropped away and the aircraft leaped forward, relieved of its burden, I had ambivalent feelings: happy to have a more maneuverable plane to fly but troubled in my conscience.

Gordon Wiggett had commandeered a two-ton truck and driver to carry us and our equipment out to our aircraft. The guns went in first, then each aircrew member loaded his own equipment. I put on my fleece-lined flying boots, slipped a Mae West over my shoulders, fastening a strap from front to back between my legs, and checked both CO_2 cylinders to make sure they worked. A parachute harness went over the Mae West; it was the kind that had two snaps in front for a chest pack. The chest pack itself went into the back of the truck and during the mission was placed behind my seat.

We each had our personal leather helmet, which contained earphones and snaps for our oxygen mask, which had to be tightened constantly. Some had microphones built in, but these worked very poorly because the water condensing from the breath would freeze the instruments. Instead we used throat mikes, two hard, rubber, pill-shaped devices fitted against the larynx by a strap around the neck. There were three umbilical cords uniting the flier with the aircraft—oxygen mask, throat mike, and headset.

Back in the summer of 1943, somebody in the 91st Bomb Group had the idea that a suit of armor (later called flak jackets) for aircrew members would be useful. Wilkinson, the famous sword manufacturer, began producing a vest made up of overlapping steel plates wrapped in canvas. Right after they became available, one of the plates was torn out of mine by a 13-mm cannon shell, which then lodged in my seat without exploding. Some of the fellows who had to stand up a lot during flight found them too heavy. Bill always folded his up and sat on it. "First things first," he said, grinning.

We had to be stationed at our aircraft one and a half hours after briefing time. One hour after that was called engine time, when engines were started. Fifteen minutes later the planes would take off.

The driver made his way across the east side of the field to the circular hardstand in the dispersal area where our plane was parked. Little taxi strips branched out from the main one; at the end of each were three circular hardstands, like a cluster of cherries at the end of a twig. It was still dark, but we could just make out three ground-crew members waiting by the plane.

We unloaded our gear by the right fuselage door near the rear of the plane. Bill, Mickey, and I went to talk to the ground crew while our other aircrew members attended to their duties.

The first matter to be discussed was Redline, our squadron mascot. This friendly mongrel had wandered by the airdrome some time before and had promptly been adopted by Spam-carrying, ear-scratching, lonely airplane mechanics. In due course he was fitted with his own oxygen mask, checked out as an official B-17 passenger, and allowed his own place in chow line. His name came from a way of denoting aircraft status on the maintenance form: a red X for unflyable, a red line for flyable but with certain restrictions, or a blank indicating no restrictions. Redline was nowhere to be seen. Apparently he would have nothing to do with flying to Berlin. I heard that later in the war he flew to Paris after it was liberated, which showed that he not only had a lot of sense, but also a certain touch of class.

The men of the ground crew were devoted to their work and shared a special kinship with those who flew their plane. When we returned from a mission, they would be waiting on the flight line with other members of the group, anxious eyes scanning the aircraft for any sign of damage. They were accustomed to our questions by now: How many inches of manifold pressure did you get during maximum power at run-up? Was there excessive drop in rpm on any of the magnetos? Are all the engine instruments working? The question-and-answer session continued, with most of the discussion centered on the red-line items. There were always some items short in supply, so it was unusual to find an aircraft in perfect condition.

After finishing our discussion with the ground crew, Bill and I walked around the aircraft with the chief mechanic, examining the patches from the holes sustained during the previous three missions. In the main tanks and in the Tokyo (extra) tanks were eight tons of gasoline, based on weight for volume at current temperatures, and six tons of bombs hung in the bomb bays in the form of twelve 1,000-pounders. We agreed that we were operating above permissible limits because of the extra ammo, but from experience in flying other B-17s, I knew that this one had better flying characteristics than most. However, any B-17 drew great praise and trust from its aircrews because of its dependability and airworthiness.

We spent the final part of the hour before engine-starting time sitting in a circle on our parachutes at the rear of the plane. This was not a "get one for the Gipper" or "twenty centuries of history look down upon you" atmosphere; this was a circle of friends who had worked together for some time, getting last words said. We decided to pile all the movable weight into the radio room, just aft of the bomb bays, to have a better weight distribution for takeoff. Ward Simonson, as crew medic, offered Neo-Synephrine drops to anyone who needed to unplug his sinuses. Joe Ashby would normally notify us that he had activated the bombs, which would allow them to explode upon impact. Sometimes there was some joking about somebody forgetting his dog tags so he wouldn't be able to go or a lament about a missed pass to London because of the mission. About ten minutes before engine time,

Bill and I slid into our seats and started to get everything comfortable for the trip. It was now light enough to see the other aircraft clearly. We located our squadron leader and decided to taxi right behind him when he moved out; he was leading the low squadron (the one on the group's left flank), and I was flying on his right wing.

We checked our watches, and Bill reached for the starter switches. The aerodrome exploded with sound as Wright Cyclone engines roared into life. From the tower a white light arched upward, with two stars falling from it, a needless signal. We started all four of our engines and checked oil pressures. The plug to the auxiliary ground-power unit was pulled, and after a thumbs-up signal exchanged with the ground crew, the brakes were released and the plane rolled slowly forward.

When the leader reached the takeoff runway, he stopped, turned his tail so that his prop-wash would not blow a cloud of stones into another plane, and started his pre-takeoff check. One by one, all the B-17s followed his example. When we had turned our plane at an angle, Bill and I checked our engines, with Mickey overlooking the procedure from his perch on a jump seat suspended between the two pilot seats. Nothing about the engine performance appeared out of the ordinary. We prepared the aircraft for takeoff configuration—fuel booster pumps on, fuel/air mixture in automatic rich, propellers in full rpm, engine cowl flaps open, wing flaps up—and gave other aircraft systems a final check.

Fifteen minutes after we started the engines, the lead aircraft roared down the runway, followed by the others at thirty-second intervals. When our turn came, we taxied quickly so that our tail wheel was on the grass at the very end of the runway, locked the tail wheel, rolled forward to line up with the runway, made sure that the tail-wheel lock was engaged, and then stopped in takeoff position. When the squadron leader's aircraft left the runway ahead of me, I stood on the brakes, my left hand on the control-column yoke and my right hand advancing the four throttles. When they were advanced as far as possible, Mickey's "OK" confirmed my observation that we were getting full power, and I released the brakes. Immediately Bill's right hand closed the engine cowl flaps to reduce the extra drag; I could feel his left hand behind mine on the throttles to make sure that they wouldn't creep back. With his right hand he tightened a friction-control knob that helped to keep the engine controls in a set position. The knot of tension in my stomach tightened as the plane surged forward.

Gear up. Wing flaps up. Climb configuration. We are past a danger point in our mission. I had seen many aborted takeoffs, with at least two resulting in aircraft and bombs exploding at the end of the runway.

The sky was clear in all directions, with the gentle fields and green checkerboard of England spread below us. Rudyard Kipling's mansion, just to the south of the airfield, provided a familiar sight and always evoked memories of stories read during childhood about the British Empire in its glory. The royal highway, built by the Romans, points arrow-straight to London. People on the ground looked skyward, watching the growing air armada assemble. All during my tour in England, the people treated us like heroes, inviting us into their homes and telling us what a beautiful sight it was to see our planes fly toward Germany every day.

Within minutes after takeoff our plane was in loose formation on the squadron leader's right wing with the others gradually joining up. The low-squadron leader waited for the lead squadron to form, then found his position on the left side, slightly behind and below the group leader. The other squadron in the group, called the high squadron, would be to the right, slightly above and behind the group leader, who in this case was also the air-wing leader, division leader, and leader of the total force of some 660 four-engine bombers. The groups and the wings were stacked in the same way as the squadron building blocks, up and to the right. This is a formation that could make left turns more easily than right, so our turns today would be to the left at the initial point and also upon leaving the target. It was also a formation in which planes could be stacked very tightly to increase bombing efficiency and provide better defense against air attack. A B-17 group could put out eighteen tons of lead per minute with all machine guns firing, so a tight formation would have devastating effect against closely pressed attacks.

The group made its way to a selection of beacons (Splasher 1 through 8) in eastern England, gathering followers along the way. A series of turns built into the route allowed a delayed formation to find its place in the stream at a time and location of its choosing. The time from takeoff until we left the coast of England would be about one and a half hours.

Every fifteen minutes Bill and I changed off at the controls. Whoever takes over calls for an oxygen check; it is easy for a person in an isolated position to lose his oxygen supply and die. The disembodied voices came over the Interphone—tail/gunner OK, right waist OK, left waist OK, ball turret OK, radio OK, top turret OK, bombardier OK, navigator OK. It was good to hear the voices.

The voices changed during our time together, particularly that of Frank Topits, the ball-turret gunner from Chicago. After our first combat mission Frank was bubbling over describing his exploits. On our second trip he was credited with shooting down one of the Abbeville fighters. On our third mission we bombed a FW-190 factory sixty miles southwest of Berlin and met continuous fighter attack for two hours before getting to the target. At one point five FW-190s came directly at us. Topits got the first one, which exploded like a huge burst of flak, pieces flashing by our plane. The second and third went down smoking, and the fourth, out of control, smashed into a U.S. Fort ship on our right, hitting between the fuselage and the engine on its right wing. The ball-turret gunner of that ship was Topit's buddy. The fighter exploded and the Fort blew into pieces, with the ball turret dropping straight down. After that mission Topits was more and more reticent. He performed an outstanding job until the end, but he never claimed any more victories.

Over the Channel there was intermittent fire from the aircraft, as the crews test-fired their guns to make sure they were operable.

The formation had been climbing so as to penetrate the flak defenses at the best altitude. The view was beautiful—clear sky, boats in the Channel, the coast of Belgium and France. I checked the penetration time on my posted card against the little clock in the center front of the cockpit; we were exactly on time. The outside air temperature showed minus forty-eight degrees Centigrade, warmer than the minus sixty degrees that we had recorded three days before over Germany. The cold front must have been over Russia then, along with the innumerable decks of clouds that had confounded us; we now had clear and slightly turbulent weather and the shifted wind direction characteristically found behind a cold front. We could see a hundred miles in any direction, which meant that Jerry could see us as well. We wouldn't use chaff today—the strips of aluminum foil that showed up like aircraft on the enemy radar—because the antiaircraft guns would be using visual sightings.

A few puffs of flak appeared around the formation. It was like hunters shooting at high-flying geese back in my native Wisconsin. This is not to say that it didn't bother us, but what really put a person on the qui vive was to fly into a box barrage from guns directly below. The sound of steel fragments tearing into the fuselage was a little like large hailstones hitting the tin roof of my Dad's barn in Green Bay. The deep red-orange flash sometimes seemed to be actually in the cockpit, which would be filled with the bitter fumes of gunpowder. German gunpowder smelled different from American. Under-going a heavy flak barrage was much worse than the worst fighter attack. Sometimes the turbulence would throw a B-17 over on its back.

No enemy planes in sight. On the Interphone the crew started singing "The Beer Barrel Polka," a great favorite in England at the time. During our training days we had started telling jokes and singing songs when the action was dull, and we continued the practice during the first part of combat missions, Mickey Diethorn had a wonderful song, "Oh-o-oh, Aurora," which I have never heard since. Bob Roberts could do the whole performance of a very popular English comedian then appearing in London. Joe Ashby had some hoary stand-up-comic jokes:

"Hey, Joe, I hear that you bought a goat without a nose. How does he smell?"

"He doesn't smell, he stinks!"

Time did not pass swiftly over enemy territory. The singing and the jokes helped reduce the unpleasant sensation in the stomach. Still, the minutes on that little clock moved slowly. It was always best to think of immediate objectives, such as when the fifteen-minute stint at the controls was up, rather than when we would get to the target. Prayer helped. Brought up in a deeply religious household, it was natural for me to ask the Lord for help. I would ask for help in doing the proper thing when an emergency came—not to let my crew down and to meet death decently. I asked particularly that I not show fear in front of my crew members. My prayers were answered. While my adrenaline pumped at a furious rate during periods of danger, on only one mission did I experience the heart pounding, dry throat, and air gulping characteristic of sheer panic.

That fear was caused a few months earlier by our own B-17s. We came under attack by German fighters, and our squadron leader, who had experienced some very close calls, was extremely nervous and went into evasive action—so violent that the Fortress pilots found it impossible to maintain formation. I was pulling up with all my strength on the control yoke to keep a B-17 from crashing into us from below, while Bill was pushing with maximum pressure to keep clear of a B-17 on top of us, while a B-17 wing appeared inches from Bill's side window and German bullets crashed through the nose. Reason gradually replaced panic, and I called on the Interphone for a report on battle damage; Bob's calm voice replied that a small plexiglass window in the nose had been shot out and that the flying shards had stripped off his flying clothes on the left side without hurting him.

It was so clear over eastern France that I looked for the scars in the earth that are the reminders of trench warfare in the First World War. Often it was possible to spot several irregular lines where soldiers once lived under rain and gunfire; time must have passed much more slowly for them. They would have envied us, going home to comfortable quarters after a flight.

A twinkling light in the dark patches of woods directly ahead caught my eye. I looked instinctively at the clock and slid my plane into loose formation: four antiaircraft shells were on the way. I wished that the leader would turn and then I wished that he wouldn't, because the Germans may have made a mistake on our altitude, or wind speed aloft, or ground speed. From dead reckoning I placed the guns in the Maginot Line area. The shells exploded off to our right.

We were over Germany. Just north of Hanover, with visibility unlimited and scores of our fighter aircraft providing top cover, we were attacked by a group of He-219s and Me-410s. My diary records that the first wave got about four Forts and that three of my aircrew members each claimed a Jerry. The sleek, single-tail, twin-engine He-219 seldom rolled through the formation but delivered very effective firepower nonetheless. This was the first mission where we were told to expect Me-410 attacks. Willy Messerschmitt's latest creation was a black, twin-engine, single-tail aircraft that always looked menacing and was said to have more armament—two cannons and four machine guns.

From Hanover to Berlin we were under continuous attack from FW-190s, Ju-88s, and the Messerschmitts. Ordinarily the brunt of these attacks is borne by the low squadron of the low group, which we airmen dubbed "Purple Heart Corner." Either the low group had come apart or it fell behind; I have no recollection of any planes on our left flank as we swung into our bombing run southwest of Berlin. Once the leader got to the initial point, the formation had to fly straight and level in order for the bombardier to kill the wind drift and deliver the bombs accurately.

A dozen twin-engine Messerschmitts came straight at my squadron as we started the bombing run. These were experienced pilots; they throttled back when they came into range so that their cannons and machine guns would be more effective. We saw the dirty smoke from the cannons but tried to ignore it and get a good bombing pattern. Suddenly pieces of steel came ripping through the aircraft skin, something slammed me back in my seat, and everything went dark. The sound of Mickey's twin fifties firing inches above my head told me that I was conscious. I felt my body with my hands to find where I was bleeding.

I wasn't. A little window beside the windshield, which could be unlatched for the pilot to see through should the windshields lose their transparency, had sprung open and slammed into my helmet, knocking it over my eyes.

Fire was pouring from the squadron leader's plane, directly under my left wing; it was even coming out of the cockpit and from the radio-gunner hatch on top of the aircraft. A figure crawled out of this top hatch, with his parachute already half-open and on fire. He bounced off the horizontal stabilizer, where his chute briefly caught, ripped, and was torn free. The plane, losing speed rapidly, went out of sight with the copilot trying to get out of his small window on the right side of the aircraft.

On the radio I called for the deputy squadron leader to take over. No answer. Phil Lunt in the tail gunner's position reported that the deputy had been shot down. I called on the radio, "This is Mutter C Charlie, form on me," and waited for the rest of the squadron to regroup. No planes showed up. Later I learned that three of our planes were shot down on that fighter pass and the other two were so damaged that they fell behind.

I was angry and determined that at least one plane of the squadron would deliver its bombs on the target. A half-dozen Messerschmitts came around for another pass, and they all seemed to be aiming angry red flashes directly at us. When the smoke started to come out of the leader's wings, I put the aircraft into violent evasive action and kept it up throughout the attack. After the bomb run was completed, the group swung to the west, and I slid our B-17 into an opening in the lead squadron.

I always believed that a B-17 could shoot down any German aircraft in a one-on-one encounter, and this was one of just two times that my theory was put to a partial test. My plan, if I was caught in an isolated situation, was to drop the wing flaps and gear, slow the aircraft to 95 mph, and go into a steep turn, bringing as many of our thirteen guns as possible to bear on the target.

Lunt was an excellent gunner, but tail gunners in B-17s had only fleeting glimpses of the Jerries as they flashed by at a relative speed of over 600 mph. Lunt had an isolated post and the most unpleasant position, as far as motion sickness was concerned. It was not too pleasant as far as danger was concerned either; on one mission he had a rocket explode in the vertical stabilizer above his head, and on another mission a shell cut through his cheekbone. The aft section of a B-17 was far less comfortable than the cockpit or nose area, although the metal skin throughout was so bitterly cold that bare flesh would freeze to it. In the front of the aircraft most of the empty shell casings would eject outside the aircraft, raining on other planes and on the ground far below. In the rear of the aircraft the shells ejected onto the floor. On one occasion Rudy Malkin of Baltimore, the left-waist gunner, repaired his jammed machine gun in the ankle-deep shell casings, freezing his ungloved hands in the process. The Fourth of July gunpowder smell would be with us always under enemy attack.

As we made our turn away from the target, we could see part of the action behind us, falling planes, swinging parachutes, fighter planes wheeling in huge circles through the sky. Slender black columns of smoke on the ground indicated where a plane had crashed and was burning. We saw our target briefly but couldn't make out too much damage. Two days later, when we hit the same target, the flames leaped up thousands of feet, and Lunt could still see the smoke when we were 150 miles away.

Our fighter escort was effective from Berlin back to England, and we had only isolated attacks from German fighters and occasional bursts of flak. When we got down to fifteen thousand feet, we removed our oxygen masks. The cockpit glowed with Mickey's smile and Bill's happy face. For almost eight hours all we had seen of each other were pairs of eyes between helmet and oxygen mask; now there were three happy and relieved faces. Mickey found some rock candy in our emergency stores and spread it around the crew. The ball of tension that had been in our stomachs since early morning was replaced by a dead-tired but happy feeling—and hunger. We ate our last meal about twelve hours before; it would be a couple of hours before our next.

As always, the sight of green-quilted England brought the secure feeling of home.

The clouds had formed over Bassingbourn. With his Gee box Bob guided the plane to the runway for an instrument letdown and landing. The flight log showed the flying time for the mission as eight hours.

The loyal ground crew made us happy with their welcome. There were only two little holes for them to fix; Joe and Bob had heard the whisper of death again. The truck driver picked up the crew and the equipment and delivered us to the equipment hut, where he waited to take us to the Intelligence hut for debriefing.

There we learned that three planes were lost from our squadron and three more from the rest of the 91st Bomb Group. The *Stars and Stripes* announced the next day that we claimed 176 Jerries destroyed, with a loss of 68 U.S. bombers and 11 fighters. Later the *Luftwaffe War Diaries* called this flight one of the most bitterly contested air battles of the war. Nearly half the defending *Luftwaffe* force was destroyed.

Our ten aircrew members gathered around a table for the debriefing, dog-tired and withdrawn. One or two young Intelligence lieutenants asked questions, but they didn't ask the right questions and seemed somewhat in awe of us. We didn't help them and we didn't volunteer any information, except that three members—Lunt, Topits, Roberts—had each shot down a German plane.

It wasn't that way when we first went into combat. For the first five missions or so, everybody was excited and chattering after the flight, describing in detail the events of the past few hours. Then, with each mission, the crew became more reticent. Starting in mid-April an inch of whiskey in a water glass was given to each crew member at the table; it didn't help.

"Did you see any flak?"

"Yes."

"Where?"

"All over."

"Did you see any fighters?"

"Yes."

"How many?"

"Maybe two hundred."

"Where?"

"Between Hanover and Berlin."

"What kinds?"

"All kinds."

(In January they were skeptical about our reports of Stuka Ju-87 dive bombers and four-engine Dorniers mushing along at our altitude trying to shoot at us.)

"Did you see anybody go down?"

"Yes."

"Who?"

"Mason, Tibbetts, Coleman." (A crew was always identified by the first pilot.)

"Did you hit the target?"

"Don't know."

The frustrated Intelligence officer finally let us go.

—October 1983

ON OMAHA BEACH

by CHARLES CAWTHON

Along this narrow stretch of sand, all the painstaking plans for the Normandy invasion fell apart. One of the men who was lucky enough to make it past the beachhead recalls a day of fear, chaos, grief—and triumph.

I was a captain in the Stonewall Brigade when I first went into battle at Omaha Beach on June 6, 1944. Our outfit was directly descended from the famed command of Gen. Thomas J. (Stonewall) Jackson and proud of it, and D-day was for me much as the First Manassas had been in 1861 for a Capt. Randolph Barton, C.S.A., of the Stonewall Brigade, who wrote: "I think I went into that action with less trepidation than into any subsequent one. Inexperience doubtless had much to do with it, and discipline told on me from first to last."

For me, too, in those first twenty-four hours, innocence was lost, trepidation surfaced, and discipline and training somehow prevailed. In ways D-day seems more distant from today than from 1861 and, overall, like a particularly long and chaotic dream.

My command was Headquarters Company, 2d Battalion, 116th Regiment, 29th Infantry Division. The division, composed originally of National Guardsmen from Virginia, Maryland, and Pennsylvania, was in 1944, by reason of the draft, a cross section of American military manpower—the white part, that is; the army was still segregated. The commanding general, the three regimental commanders, and a few others, including our battalion commander, were professional soldiers; the rest of us were aggressively amateur in background and viewpoint.

For most of a year the 29th trained for this operation, first in general amphibious tactics, and finally in great secrecy all planning was focused upon a small stretch of Normandy coast at the base of the Cherbourg peninsula. No surprise assault, this. Apart from exact time and place, all the warring world knew it loomed and that its outcome would determine the course of the war in Europe.

The 2d Battalion began its preparation from a camp on the edge of the waterlogged expanse of Dartmoor, Devonshire, England, in the spring of 1943. Our commander at the time was a slightly built lieutenant colonel who addressed the battalion from a special stance—hands on hips, head tilted back and to the side. He had us formed in platoons of about thirty each, and then shouted that we were boat teams. From his posture, this cry appeared—not inappropriately—to be directed at Heaven.

Over the next few weeks, broad outlines of the plan emerged. We would cross the Channel in transports, transfer to landing craft near the coast, and storm into France, destroying all Germans and their works in the way. Practice of this grand design started off as vaguely as the first announcement of it. Outlines of landing craft were staked out between barrack huts, and cargo nets were swung from the eaves. We clambered up and down the nets and charged out of the mock-ups. Day and night tactical exercises were held on the soggy expanse of Dartmoor, where the rain was constant; uniforms, blankets, and food seemed always damp and cold.

About this time the 29th got a new commander, a demanding, uncompromising soldier. He was everywhere and into everything; his disapproval was forceful and usually final. We who were willing to make reasonable compromises with military perfection developed a marked wariness. He relieved two commanders of the 2d Battalion in turn; there was a similar shuffle throughout the division, and while deadwood was disposed of, some of his judgments were not borne out in battle; one of our deposed battalion commanders became a hero of the war in Normandy; a company commander who was relieved for not being forceful enough won the Distinguished Service Cross on the beach.

The tempo of preparation was constantly stepped up. New draftees, appearing very young, arrived to top the battalion off at full strength of nine hundred. Full-dress rehearsals were held on a Devonshire beach. We loaded into landing craft that pitched and rolled out into the Channel and then roared landward to drop ramps for us to flounder to the beach and go through assault drills.

We also practiced loading onto the U.S.S. *Thomas Jefferson*, a pre-war luxury liner that was to convey us to the offshore area for launching in landing craft for the beach. To foot soldiers the *Jefferson*, even stripped down for troop transport, confirmed exaggerated memories of the comfortable world before the war.

Another sign of the 29th's critical role was the interest in it shown by the high command. One day General Montgomery spoke to the division assembled in a huge meadow, but from my position all I could make out was a small figure gesticulating from the hood of a jeep. We were also addressed by General Bradley, who told us that we were select soldiers and assured us that casualties would not be as heavy as forecast. Few, I believe, really contemplated being a casualty.

All in all, something of a pre-big-game atmosphere developed, in which we, an enormous first team, were exhorted and examined for competence and spirit. On the whole I believe we were light of heart, caught up in the momentum of a mighty effort. I don't recall questioning a frontal assault on prepared defenses from the unstable base of the Channel, even though word had come through of the cost of such assaults in the Pacific, and at Dieppe and Salerno.

While rough winds were still shaking the darling buds of May, the battalion gave the Dartmoor camp a last policing and entrucked for the Stonewall Brigade's assembly area in Dorset. Watching the trucks roll out the camp gate, I thought that we were as ready as an outfit could be.

The next few days were rare, sunny ones that helped dry Dartmoor dampness from bones and bedrolls. In the evenings the 2d's lanky transportation officer and I found rides to Bournemouth, where we had made friends with an English dowager who organized parties on short notice. The south of England was sealed off, troops were everywhere and every leaf-roofed lane packed with supplies. The air was charged with restrained violence.

Parties ended as the 2d moved again to embarkation ports at Poole and Portland. Gradually the realization grew that no matter how many supplies were accumulated, or how brilliant the planning was, the job would come down heaviest upon the infantry. Rather than self-pity or resentment, this engendered in us what was probably an obnoxious arrogance.

Now came the final operations order, which we pounced on as the Book of Revelation. Here it was, on smudged, mimeographed sheets, with headings, subheadings, sub-subheadings, and annexes, stating that we would assault the Easy Green, Dog Red, and Dog White subsectors of the beach, which we learned was dubbed "Omaha." Our three rifle companies would go in abreast, preceded by tanks equipped with flotation devices enabling them to "swim" ashore. Directly behind the rifle companies would come combat engineers to clear beach obstacles, then our heavy weapons, battalion headquarters, and batteries of antiaircraft guns. All was on a split-second schedule, the rifle-company boats to touch down one minute after the tanks. Within thirty minutes the entire battalion was to be ashore, followed by wave after wave of artillery, engineers, medical units, and amphibious supply trucks. It is unlikely that even under training conditions such a schedule could have been followed; in the actuality, it proved fantasy.

The veteran 1st Infantry Division commanded the initial assault, and the 116th was attached to it for that phase. Attacking on our left would be 1st Division's 16th Regiment. The Stonewall Brigade's principal objectives were two roads that angle up from the beach to the crest of the bluffs, essential for moving heavy equipment inland. The 2d Battalion was to secure the road up to the village of Les Moulins.

The known difficulties were three separate bands of underwater obstacles, ranging from logs angled into the sand with mines attached to their tips, to steel gatelike structures, and giant iron jackstraws. The exit roads were guarded by concrete bunkers, barbed wire, and mines. The bluffs were zigzagged with fire trenches. An estimated eight hundred to one thousand troops manned this sector, some of them Polish or Russian defectors. Their willingness to fight to the death for the Third Reich was considered doubtful. The closest German counterattack force was believed to be an infantry division about twenty miles inland.

To destroy all this, the Allied command had assembled a force of awesome proportions; fleets of bombers and fighter bombers to saturate all known targets (and incidentally to crater the beach with ready-made foxholes), two battleships, three cruisers, eight destroyers, and rocket-launching craft.

In bare recital the defense was impregnable, the weight of our attack overwhelming. We believed the odds to favor the overwhelming. Some of our young greyhounds maintained that they were going to race across the beach so fast that if they hit any barbed wire, they might spring right back into the Channel. The operations officer, a steady and cheerful presence, vowed to keep up the spirits of his boat team by reciting "The Shooting of Dan McGrew" all the way to the beach, timing the final line with the fall of the ramp.

The last equipment arrived, and combat loads were found to be disastrously heavy. Some registered this by braying about the camp under their packs, saying that since they were loaded like jackasses, they might as well sound like them. There is a pang of pity looking back down the years to willing soldiers struggling into such a battle under the weight—in addition to weapons—of canvas assault jackets with large pockets in which were grenades, rations, mess gear, raincoat, a special first-aid kit, toilet articles, motion-sickness pills, water-purification tablets, DDT dusting powder, paste for boots in case of chemically contaminated areas, small blocks of TNT for blasting foxholes (never, I believe, used), and two hundred francs in invasion currency to start trade with the Normans. From a separate web belt swung an entrenching tool, another first-aid packet, and a canteen; from the shoulders were draped a gas mask and extra bandoliers of ammunition. Over sixty-eight pounds in all. All this worn over a heavy woolen uniform impregnated with a chemical to block blister gasses, giving the battalion the aroma of having been run through a sheep dip.

All of this was borne with ribald humor. But I recall one troublesome note during those last days. The evening before embarking, I returned to camp from a mission to find one of my men under arrest for refusing an order. I knew him as quiet and hardworking, and this was so out of character that I did not descend on him with the usual warnings of dire consequences. I tried to find out the reason for his refusal, which was not easy since he was not articulate. As we talked, it developed that his rebellion was not against what he termed "being pushed around" but against the insanity of the whole business. Perhaps I caught his feeling because—while never doubting that it had to be done—I, too, had a lurking sense of the insane. I could point out only that at this late date no replacement for his job was possible. He seemed relieved at having gotten his feelings across and said that he did not want to let his squad down and would do his best.

On the next day, June 3, we departed by truck for embarkation. The ride to the port was short. We stumbled out of the trucks, filed down a dockside street, were ferried out to the *Thomas Jefferson,* and against the pull of the heavy packs clambered up cargo nets to the deck. The closest to a send-off to war was a leathery old dock worker who croaked, " 'Ave a good go at it, mates!" It was like loading for a training exercise except for the mountains of equipment. Accommodations were spacious for a troopship, and I noted how the oppressive crowding, so much a part of a wartime army, thins out the closer the approach to battle. The initial assaults on the two American beaches—Omaha and Utah—was to be made by no more than three thousand of the million and a half troops then crowded into southern England.

The weather was that English, month-of-June type that simultaneously promises fair and threatens foul. The harbor was spaced with craft of all the sizes and shapes developed for landing tanks, troops, and cargo on beaches. Having stowed our packs, we lined the deck to look with tolerant curiosity over the busy scene. It was, after all, for the sole purpose of getting us onto the coast of Normandy.

D-day was to be June 5. We spent the night quietly, and also the next day, as worsening weather led to the decision to delay the landings. The new date was announced for dawn the next day—June 6. Ship's signal lamps set up a frenzy of blinking, and that afternoon the antisubmarine net across the harbor was towed open and the *Jefferson* churned out into the wind-rough Channel. Vessels of all shapes and sizes, towing barrage balloons as if in some gigantic dun-hued carnival procession, were all around us. My view of this mightiest of all armadas was limited: my only interest was to bring the battalion command post in near the Les Moulins beach exit exactly thirty minutes after the first wave. Then we were to follow the assault to the top of the bluffs—the battalion's first objective. All this was to be done within three hours, after which we were to await orders for further destruction of the German army, little of which, we innocently thought, would be left. I had selected on the map the command-post location and had in all confidence advised the regiment where it would be.

The last dinner on the *Jefferson* was quieter than usual; I recall no mention of the morrow. Afterward the chaplain tried to hold a service above the throb of the ship's engine. There were probably more than the usual number of private prayers launched that night. Friends gravitated together; an engineer officer played an accordion, but there was no singing. I talked with a British navy frogman who had several times gone to Omaha Beach from a submarine to examine its obstacles. He could tell us little that we did not already know, but it was curious to talk with a man who had already walked on the stretch of sand we were making such a titanic effort to reach.

Reveille was to be at 0200 with assault craft loading an hour later. The prospect did not induce sleep, but most of us turned in early. In our uncrowded state I had a cabin to myself. I lay on a bunk in that strangely lonely cabin and leafed through a copy of *Collier's* that was full of war stories—banal and bloody, as wartime writing tends to be. I put it down and dozed but was awake when strident gongs sounded reveille. The engines had quieted; we were twelve miles off the beach; even the big liner was registering the waves. I got into the dank, sour-smelling uniform and shaved for D-day. Breakfast in the ornate saloon was unreal: bacon and eggs on the edge of eternity. Conversation was perfunctory. Everything moved automatically, except for a brief discussion with the ship's mess officer, who demanded that troops going into battle should first clean up after the breakfast. The troops settled this by simply ignoring him. A message from General Eisenhower calling our effort a crusade to liberate Europe was read over the address system.

I struggled into my own gear, light compared with a rifleman's but heavy and awkward enough. The final item was a life belt of twin brown tubes to be inflated by triggering capsules of carbon dioxide. Thus clad for the crusade, I wedged out into the line of laden officers crowding down the corridor toward boat stations. There was handshaking and exchanges of good luck, all in a dreamlike atmosphere of Outward Bound. We filed out through heavy blackout curtains into the predawn dark of D-day; a cold, damp wind swept the deck and whistled through the rigging. The *Jefferson*'s rise and fall in the heaving sea was more noticeable than it had been below. Darkness was not complete; one of the requirements for the assault was a full moon, and some faint light from it penetrated the overcast and showed whitecaps breaking against the ship's sides.

Obviously chance had already elbowed onto the scene in one of its favored military roles: miserable weather. We had practiced landings in rough surf but had never risked seas such as were now rocking the huge *Jefferson*. The assault, however, was locked into conditions of moon and tide, perishable factors that had to be used at once or be lost. So strategically situated, chance had great sport with us all—not excepting the German commanders, who considered conditions too bad for invasion.

My boat team assembled on station. We counted off and helped each other into the open-topped, rectangular steel box that we were to ride to war. It had a motor and rudder at the stern and the bow was a hinged ramp; on a platform above the motor was the dark shape of the coxswain, hunchbacked in a bulky life vest. It occurred to me that this was the first time I had seen him. We had been told that he was in command from ship to shore, and I realized I had no idea of how well he knew his job or how determined he was to get us in at the right place. We sorted ourselves out to long-rehearsed places in the cramped, swaying confines. An awful seasickness was already immobilizing many. I was fortunate to be spared.

A stream of cryptic orders flowed from the ship's address system, and from a control launch in the Channel came unintelligible sounds amplified through a bullhorn. Suddenly, with a rattle of chains and screech of wire cable, the craft ground slowly down the *Jefferson*'s side to be met by a rising sea that slacked the cables and then dropped us with a crash as it rolled on. The next move brought us fully into the waves. By some miracle we were not slammed into the ship's side; the propeller caught, and we followed a shepherding launch out to join other craft circling as in some strange conga line, red and green riding lights appearing on the crests and disappearing in the troughs of waves four or five feet high.

Blowing spume had soaked us before we hit the Channel. It seemed we would surely swamp, and life belts were inflated. Not only our persons but also reels of telephone wire, radios, and demolition packs were girded with these in the hope that if they were lost in the surf, they would float ashore. The expansion of perhaps a hundred belts added to the bulk already crowding the craft, and so we rode, packed in an open can, feet awash in water and altogether cold, wet, and miserable. It seemed that we were slamming into waves with enough impact to start any rivet ever set.

After about an hour of circling, the control launch passed a signal, and the craft carrying us—the second wave of Stonewall Brigade—peeled off into line and began battering through heavy seas toward Normandy; thirty minutes ahead was the first wave; twenty minutes behind would come the third.

For the next two hours the line pitched and rolled toward Normandy and a gradually lighter horizon as we closed with the dawn of June 6. There was no attempt to talk above the roar of the engine, wind, slamming of the waves, and the laboring of the bilge pump that just managed to keep up with the water washing in. We stood packed together, encased in equipment, dumb with the noise and with the enormity toward which we were laboring. I recall offering no prayers and having no particular worries other than whether we were coming in on Dog Red sector.

The line roared past a great gray battleship, either the *Texas* or the *Arkansas,* that was by then to have obliterated the Les Moulins defenses. The ship's huge guns were silent. The naval fire-control party that was supposed to direct their fire had accompanied the first wave but had been killed or had had its radios knocked out by the curtain of German fire that had descended along the waterline.

We bore on toward this curtain still unaware that it existed. It was now as fully daylight as the overcast allowed. Signs that things were going amiss were all around us, had I been battlewise enough to read them: one was the silent battleship, indicating that it was out of touch with the assault and fearful of firing into it; another was a trickle instead of a stream of return traffic from the first wave, which told of craft either destroyed or landed badly off target. Still another ill omen was the vacant sky where we had expected to see fighter bombers diving and strafing. We were unaware that the overcast had moved air strikes inland.

A haze of smoke, barely darker than the gray morning, was the first sign of the shore, and then the line of bluffs emerged. Our craft shuddered to a halt on a sandbar two hundred or so yards offshore. We were in among the beach obstacles: big, ugly structures partially covered by the rising tide. The coxswain failed on a couple of attempts to buck over the bar and then dropped the ramp. This may have been fortunate for us as well as prudent for the coxswain—a landing closer in would probably have drawn the artillery, mortar, and machine-gun fire that was knocking the first wave apart. As it was, the German gunners had too many targets close by to bother with one more distant. So, as yet physically untouched by the battle, and in automatic response to the dropped ramp, we lumbered off in three files—center, right, left—into the cold, shoulder-deep surf. The life belt lifted me to the crest of a wave, and here, flailing around to keep right side up, I caught my first full glimpse of battle, the inner sanctum of war, toward which we had struggled so long and painfully. The sight was not inspiring. Where Channel and shore met was a wavering, undulating line of dark objects. Some of the larger ones, recognizable as tanks and landing craft, were erupting in black smoke. Higher up the beach was another line of smaller forms, straight as though drawn with a ruler, for they were aligned along a bank of shingle stone and seawall. Scattered black forms were detaching themselves from the surf and laboring toward this line. Looming up between beach and bluff through the smoke and mist was a three-story house. Such a structure was a landmark of the Dog Red sector, but I could not see the beach exit road. I believed that we had come in on target, but I ceased worrying greatly over whether we had or not. There is a definite calming effect to the casting of the die, and the die had been irrevocably cast on Omaha Beach.

The wave passed on, and in the trough I touched bottom, to be lifted again moments later and carried toward France. Such was the pattern of my advance in the greatest amphibious assault of history; up wave and down trough, propelled forward by an insweeping tide. By now the invasion had allied itself with gravity, and there was no escape from it for either the paratroopers of the airborne assault or we who came by sea. Our voluntary act was to step out of landing craft. From then on gravity—in the form of the tide—pulled us into battle. This alliance with natural force was not entirely harmonious. The tide tended strongly eastward and carried much of the 2d

Battalion far from its long-rehearsed objectives. Indifferent gravity had also brought paratroopers down in many unplanned places. All in all, the balance of natural force on D-day favored the enemy; fortunately, he took only limited advantage of it.

My alternative lift and fall with the waves gave me glimpses of the battle that were like the stopped frames of a motion picture. From the crests the beach was visible, in the troughs only green-black water. Thus, early in combat I developed what was to be a lasting regard for surface depressions. Omaha Beach coming into clearer focus made the successive walls of water between me and its exploding horror more and more welcome.

Others of the landing team were rising and falling with the waves around me like swimmers, unaccountably wearing steel helmets. Dirty red shellbursts were walking with rapid, short steps among the objects along the waterline. Off to the left a solitary landing craft skittered back out to sea, a sailor at its .50-caliber machine gun arching tracers toward Europe. Much farther down to the left one of our rocket ships loosed banks of missiles in gushes of white smoke. These, I learned later, fell innocuously into the Channel. Overhead to the right a single flight of the twin-tailed P-38 fighter bombers streaked inland, and close at hand a solitary destroyer ploughed along parallel to the shore. These were silent scenes; the wind was toward France and carried battle sounds away from us.

On his first day of battle the foot soldier probes new emotional depths, and his findings, I believe, are fairly universal. One is a conviction that he is abandoned, alone, and uncared for in the world. I looked into this depth on seeing the nearly empty sea and sky. The thought came that the crusade had been called off as a bad job, and that we few were left to struggle alone in the great, dark seascape. The first assault wave already on the beach did not resemble a battle line so much as it did heaps of refuse deposited there to burn and smolder unattended.

Abandoned or not, the tide and our own exertions brought us in through the obstructions to where the waves were breaking and rolling up the beach. There was no evidence that the engineers had succeeded in blasting the obstacles that now formed a barrier behind us. The water was waist deep, and we were moving faster. I would judge the time to be about 0730, and the first shots directed at us, however impersonally, keened above the sound of wind and surf. To my left a high cry in hurt surprise announced, "I'm hit!" I looked around. The white face, staring eyes, and open mouth of the first soldier I saw struck in battle remains with me. The image of no one—loved, admired, or disliked—is more vivid; his name I have lost. My first words in battle were not an exhortation to the troops but a useless shout to attend the wounded man. I think he was gone before the medic reached him.

With the burst of fire we all submerged neck deep in the surf. I lay flat out supporting my head above water by hands on the shifting sands and gave attention to the fact that a few more surges of the surf would eject me onto the beach where there were many dead things, both men and machines.

It was now apparent that we were coming ashore in one of the preregistered killing zones of German machine guns and mortars. The quick havoc they had wrought was all around in incredible chaos: bodies, weapons, boxes of demolitions, flamethrowers, reels of telephone wire, and personal equipment from socks to toilet articles. Discarded life belts writhed and twisted in the surf like brown sea slugs. The waves broke around the wrecked tanks, dozers, and landing craft, thick here in front of the heavily defended exit road.

From my prone position the beach rose like a steep, barren hillside. There was a stretch of sand, being narrowed by the minute by the tide, then a sharply rising shingle bank of small, smooth stones that ended at the seawall. Against the shingle bank and wall were the men of the first wave. Some were scooping out holes; a number were stretched out in the loose attitude of the wounded; others lay in ultimate stillness. I could see only the upper portion of the house, its mansard roof gaping with shell holes. I still could not make out the exit road, but we had come in not far off our appointed place. There were luckier sites but also unluckier ones.

While I was straining to see above the debris and still stay in the dubious protection of the water, one of the explosions that were rippling up and down the beach erupted close by. There was a hard jar to the side of my face, and blood started streaming off my chin. I don't recall any particular emotion on being hit for the first time, but I did realize that this was no place to linger; those along the embankment seemed much safer. My boat team had completely disappeared in the debris. Having decided that survival, never mind valor, lay forward, I tried to rise but seemed to be hoisting the English Channel with me. The assault jacket's pockets, the gas-mask case, boots, leggings, and uniform all held gallons of saltwater. I had long preached the maxim that a good soldier never abandons his equipment, but now I jettisoned the assault jacket and lumbered up the beach, streaming water.

Gasping for air and retching salt water, I reached the embankment. All around were familiar faces from F, G, H, and Headquarters companies. Those who had arrived with me were in about my condition; others were more recovered. All were quiet. The embankment was in the eye of the storm, and no one was inclined to leave it without some compelling reason. Minutes later a tall, very composed colonel knelt beside me and said calmly that we must get the assault started inland. My work at the moment was for breath and against nausea, and I must not have looked a very hopeful source of dynamic leadership. He departed, walking upright down the embankment. I have no idea who he was or what became of him. Incredible enough—and this may be a trick that memory has played—I recall his uniform as dry and clean, while the rest of us were soaking wet and sand encrusted.

Gradually my lungs and stomach stopped heaving. I took my .45 service automatic from its plastic bag and found it sticky with salt and gritty with sand. When I pulled the slide back to load a round into the chamber, it stuck halfway. The embankment was strewn with rifles, Browning automatics, and light machine guns all similarly fouled. Except for one tank that was blasting away from the sand toward the exit road, the crusade in Europe at this point was disarmed and naked before its enemies. The Germans clearly lost Omaha Beach by failing to assemble a single company of riflemen to descend and sweep us up. Looking down onto our obviously helpless condition, they still stuck to their bunkers. We may have sensed that this was all they would do. On no other basis can I account for the fact that I had no feeling of defeat and saw none exhibited around me.

About this time the battalion commander came over the embankment with some half-dozen soldiers in tow. He had been trying to get up the bluff at this point but was balked by weapons that wouldn't function. His first words, "This is a debacle," delivered in his volley fashion, remain with me; and *debacle* suited the scene as well as any word could. He told me to sort out the boat teams and round up some firepower, and then he left on the run down the embankment to find a way up the bluff. Those who could move were already drawing together into familiar squads. But to organize firepower was another matter, for not a functioning weapon could be found. Nor could anything of the enemy be seen from the embankment. I left some of the able-bodied trying to clean weapons and ran down to the waterline, taking cover behind a blown-over tank dozer. From here the face of the bluffs and the exit road were visible, and I expected to see flashes and smoke from German guns. The only smoke visible on the enemy side, however, was in separate areas far down to my right and to my left, where brush fires were rolling up the slopes. While I did not know it then, those common brush fires, started inadvertently by the naval cannonade, were the salvation of the assault on Omaha Beach. Under their smoke a few brave souls were climbing the bluff. Nothing else accomplished by naval guns could have exceeded the value of this act, which demonstrated that a few smoke shells would have served as well as all the weight of high explosive. This was chance's second intrusion, the invasion planners having ruled out deliberate smoking of the beach as a hindrance to naval fire direction.

We were not aware of it, but chance, with inexhaustible ingenuity, had made a third major entry onto the scene. The German counterattack division, which Intelligence reports placed twenty miles inland, was, in fact, in the coastal defenses. In addition to fortress troops, considered unreliable outside their bunkers, we were hitting first-class German infantry, than which there is none better. While we coped with the weather and took advantage of the smoke, the enemy, for his part, passed up the opportunity of wiping out the feeble beachhead with troops that happened to be at the right place at the right time.

Unaware of these workings of fate, I splashed down the waterline through the debris in the direction the battalion commander had taken and acquired a second bloodying. This time I didn't hear the shell, but there was another jar to the side of my face—opposite to the first one—and again I started leaking blood. My injuries, though much less serious than most, were spectacular by being so visible. Two soldiers advised me I'd been hit and guided me to a busy aid station. A medic looked over the wounds on both sides of my face and announced with professional authority that here was a rare case of a shot having gone cleanly through one cheek and out the other without damage to teeth or tongue. Most of those around the station were 2d Battalion men who knew me, and they seemed to look on this as extraordinary on a day of wounds. I didn't take the trouble to deny the diagnosis, and so, without intent, abetted one of the minor tales of Omaha Beach: that of the captain shot through the face while open-mouthed, suffering nothing more lasting than dimples. The story turned out to be harder to shed than the wounds. It gained wider currency through Ernie Pyle, who was on the beach later in that day and reported the "miracle" wound. When I tried to correct the story, people were reluctant to accept the more mundane truth.

Back to the beach: The aid man applied sulfanilamide powder to my face, and, having an excuse, I rested and worried over what to do in this nightmarish circumstance so different from any I had ever imagined. Out among the breakers two large infantry landing craft were broached sideways to the beach, gushing black smoke. And all the while, the clouds hung gray and low, and waves crashed with a slow-paced roar, reaching up the beach to roll the bone-white shingle stones. All around were dead and dying, and I wonder more and more at the amount of life borne so quickly away.

Reluctantly rousing myself, I ran down the beach, coming to a stretch vacant and quiet except for the wind, waves, and beach birds swooping and crying. Omaha Beach was of this pattern: violent swirls of death and destruction with areas of quiet in between. It was as if the funnels of multiple tornadoes were touching down at spots, whirling men and materiel into broken pieces and moving on to touch again.

I was about one thousand yards east of the Les Moulins exit road and in the area where the brush-fire smoke had concealed the first penetration. The face of the bluff was blackened, but the fire was largely burned out and little smoke lingered. I could see American uniforms slowly near the top. A barbed-wire entanglement between the shingle and bluff had been blasted open, and machine-gun fire from a distance was whining through it. To the left was a bigger gap in the wire, where a party of soldiers was starting up the slope. I joined them and found that they were from our 3d Battalion and had landed by good fortune in this smoke-covered area.

The trail, traced through the ash and soot, wound between small personnel mines with which the slope was sown. We came out on top onto a plateau of green fields, bounded by the embankments of earth and brush called hedgerows. There was no indication on this first encounter of the life and death role that these were to play in the battle over the next weeks. Here the hedgerows were not defended, the Germans being concentrated along the bluff line. But soon, pushing inland, we would encounter German reserves using them as ready-made field fortifications, and their deadly potential would become shockingly apparent.

Directly across the path at the top of the bluffs lay the first German soldier I had seen in two hours of battle. He was lying face downward, very dead, a stocky figure in complete uniform from boots to helmet. I recall no particular emotion on stepping over the body; in the brief course of that morning dead bodies had become commonplace; this one differed only in uniform and in title of "enemy." The time was about 0930. I had spent two unproductive hours on the beach. Ahead, small groups were moving inland, single file, along a hedgerow. I debated whether to return to the beach and bring up more of the battalion along this route or to find my commander to see if this was what he wanted. I certainly didn't want to return to the chaos below. I was a thousand yards off our appointed route, in the middle of another battalion, and in what I suspected was another regiment's sector. In training this would have raised serious questions about my leadership. Now it seemed trivial. Our plan did not provide for high waves, winds up to eighteen knots, and an extra German division in the defenses. The shock, inertia, and confusion of this was countered by the initiative and courage of a few (one study numbers them at no more than forty-seven) who rose above the circumstances. They are largely unknown; the republic is considerably in their debt.

I was following the path of some of these few, and I was not at all the happy warrior. Commissioned a leader, I was leading no one and was certainly not where I was supposed to be. Luck, however, continued with me. I came out onto a lane and here caught up with my enterprising commander, who was leading some mixed sections of F and G, and a few men of

Headquarters Company. The lane led to the village of St. Laurent, about one-half mile east of our designated route. Perhaps because of the spectacular appearance of my face, I was not taken to task for showing up alone. The commander told me to bring up whatever of the battalion I could find as he was to go for our objective from this direction.

Now that I knew what I was supposed to do, it was with considerable relief to the spirit that I began a search through the shallow beachhead for men of the 2d Battalion. And here it is that I can't remember clearly. Perhaps by this time my capacity for registering and storing sights and sounds in some order was saturated. Whatever the reason, the memory of that afternoon and night is a gray tapestry from which scenes emerge, then run together or change position, making it difficult to fix them in time and place.

I returned to the beach by the way I had left it. The burned-over area remained quiet, but toward the Les Moulins exit road the noise still mounted, and an even more distant rumbling was echoing from the Vierville exit far down to the west. The source of the noise, however, was shifting from German guns to our own. Destroyers cruising close inshore were methodically blasting the exit roads; a few surviving tanks were maneuvering in the limited space on the beach, adding the banshee screech of their high-velocity guns. The lighter debris was washed in enormous drifts along the high-water mark, and the receding tide was leaving windrows of it exposed. The seawall and shingle embankment were still lined with men, most of them wounded, others emotionally broken beyond use. I was not the only searcher for able bodies. Officers and noncommissioned officers from engineer outfits were trying to organize men and materiel for clearing the obstacles exposed by the receding tide. Fighters and workers were few; the abject watchers, many.

The aid station was still in operation and was a collecting point of disaster information on the killed and wounded, some of it wrong, much of it sadly correct. Our amiable and gentlemanly operations officer was dead, and I never learned how far he had gotten into "The Shooting of Dan McGrew." The commander of E Company was killed far down the beach; the commanders of H and F companies were badly wounded. Many others of all ranks had simply disappeared into the maw of the exit road. The next day we learned that fragments of F,

G, and H companies had climbed the bluff under concealment of the smoke west of Les Moulins. There they joined a surviving part of the 1st Battalion and the regimental commander near Vierville. This was only about a straight mile west of the 2d Battalion fragments outside St. Laurent, but the mile was German-occupied. Instead of being assembled on its objective, the battalion formed a giant letter *U,* with the points inland at St. Laurent and at Vierville and the base running along the beach. It was, moreover, a thin, wavering *U* with numerous gaps.

A few functioning soldiers came back with me to where the advance was stalled outside of St. Laurent. My search then turned eastward as I looked for sections of E Company, reported to have landed far down in the 16th Infantry area. I met the battalion supply officer on a road along which were modest holiday cottages. On this day of history we came across three soldiers ransacking the poor contents of a cottage. We sent them on, but it was probably a brief interruption to a wartime career of looting. Further along this road we crossed a long, straight mound of dirt that looked as though raised by a giant mole with a strong sense of direction. It was a covered trench, leading inland from the beach defenses. Some 2d Battalion men were there debating over whether to hunt for explosives to blow it up or try to smoke it out. The battalion commander's need being the more urgent, they were pointed in his direction and the tunnel left to others.

Continuing, I encountered my first liberated Norman: an elderly farmer in a faded blue smock, agitatedly pacing in front of a small cottage. My high school French didn't seem to reassure him that the battle had moved on, so I proffered some soggy notes of invasion currency as more universally soothing. This, too, had no effect, possibly because it did not resemble any currency he recognized; gold Napoleons might have calmed him. I left him still pacing.

This search through the short beachhead was at a run and half-run, canvassing stray groups of antiaircraft men without weapons, signalmen without equipment, and medics with waterlogged aid kits. None were armed effectively enough to be worth impressing into our ranks. Next I recall standing beside a small, rural hotel where the bodies of three dead Americans were sprawled. The corporal of a squad of the 16th Regiment deployed around the hotel told me that the dead had been there when he arrived. When asked if he had seen any of the 116th, he assumed that look of the soldier who is asked a question for which he doesn't have to know the answer. The look involves a trace of piety and also questions the sanity of the asker. It is acquired early in basic training.

He inquired of the squad, "Any of you seen anything of the—what was it, sir?—116th?" They all assumed the same look. "We ain't seen them," he summarized. In the meantime a lanky private started firing at, and missing, the insulators on a telephone pole. Everyone ducked, and in answer to the corporal's profane question about what he was doing, the private said that these might be lines that German observers were using. The corporal threatened to shoot him.

The corporal helped me arrange the lifeless young bodies in more decent postures and covered them with raincoats. I continued a search that, in retrospect, seems aimless.

The afternoon passed into the evening of a double-daylight-saving time by which the invasion planners provided for a long day of fighting in lieu of being unable to make the sun stand still. Sometime early in that evening I arrived at a crossing of lanes and realized that after many turnings I was thoroughly lost. Around me were only green fields and hedgerows; of war there was no evidence. The sodden mass that had been my map had been discarded. I turned by chance back toward St. Laurent instead of toward the encompassing German positions and out of the war. By that time I was far into the sector of the 16th Infantry. There were boat teams of E Company probably within shouting distance, but they might as well have been on another continent.

Back toward St. Laurent I crossed a new road that the engineers had opened from the beach. Trucks, jeeps, ambulances, and weapons carriers jammed this outlet and were turning into fields on either side. The Germans west of St. Laurent were still an effective stopper, but the pressure of men and materiel was building up in the beachhead. More helpful to the cause at the moment than these thin-skinned vehicles were guns of a decimated armored field-artillery battalion that had gone into action. For no reason that I can determine, I remember their red and white aiming stakes standing out brightly against the green field.

In the stream of men and material flowing in from the beach was the 115th Infantry, a sister regiment in the 29th

Division. The day hadn't killed deep regimental instincts, for I recall passing it with the feeling of superiority of a combat veteran of several hours' seniority. Near St. Laurent I met a squad of our 3d Battalion that was surprisingly knowledgeable of the situation. I was advised not to go into the village that had been shelled a short time before by either our warships or German artillery. The 2d Battalion was reported to be to the right along a farm road leading to Les Moulins, and to my amazement, that's where it was. I found the battalion, about ninety strong, deployed around farm buildings facing German positions that we should, according to the plan, have long since occupied. The battalion commander was in a barn across a cobblestone-paved yard from the farmhouse. I told him that aside from the few men retrieved from the beach, I had found nothing but the dead, wounded, and emotionally crippled. He exhibited no dismay; such news was standard that day.

One of my duties as battalion adjutant was to keep a journal of combat orders and actions. Early in the evening I remembered this but could find neither dry paper nor anything for writing other than a grease pencil used in marking maps. The entries would probably have been as inexact as much of the information of the moment. Perhaps I should have made a greater effort; instead, I posted the Headquarters Company men (about a dozen, I believe) for command-post security and then washed my automatic in the barn's horse trough. There was no gun oil and no certainty that it wouldn't jam again after the first round.

Word continued of death and disaster: the 111th Field Artillery Battalion, the longtime fire-support teammate of our regiment, had lost all its howitzers in the Channel, and its commander lay dead on the beach. The regimental commander and some of his staff were inland near Vierville—he and his adjutant wounded, his supply officer dead. There was a vague report that A Company of our 1st Battalion had lost all officers and most of its men in front of the Vierville exit road. This proved all too nearly true. (Many of the fragmented reports of that night are now verified by names on monuments across the United States. The memorial in Bedford, Virginia, the original home of A Company, bears twenty names under June 6, 1944.) Midnight found the Stonewall Brigade far-flung and hard used. First reports set losses at about one thousand men killed, wounded, or missing. This figure was scaled down, but not greatly, as some of the missing were gathered in. It had been one of the most costly days in the regiment's history since Chancellorsville and the wounding unto death of Old Stonewall himself.

Of all the capacities that the years diminish, none leaves a greater void than that of the youthful ability for easy friendships without the questioning and restraints that complicate those of later life. I feel a void now in looking back upon friends gone that day. Together we had been through months and years of wartime discomforts and strain; marched countless tedious miles; lived in mud and dust, heat and cold. The battalion dominated our time and efforts. Then it all came down to this brief first day of battle, and for them it all ended, and for the rest of us I believe that what has been since has not been exactly the same.

Sorrow had its beginnings that night, but it was still a dim presence. We were weary, for twenty-four hours of flat-out physical and emotional effort had elapsed since reveille on the *Jefferson.* But neither weariness nor sorrow was the dominant presence. Overriding both was a sense of life forced to a hard, bright flame to survive. It is this, and its illuminations, I believe, that burnishes the memory of battle. Soldiers who have experienced this have tried to describe it and at the same time the dread that accompanies it. Dread and exhilaration from the same source at the same moment are difficult to reconcile and impossible to convey convincingly. It is common for visitors to war to note the increasing cheerfulness encountered on approaching the front. I believe that they are witnessing this phenomenon of intensified, illuminated life.

Nothing was further from my mind that night than speculation upon whether the shade of Stonewall Jackson might be drawn from the shadows to this unlikely place where the current bearers of the name of his famed command were in deep travail. History indicates that he would have given his usual abrupt order: "Close up, press on." I cannot imagine disputing that awesome individual in person, but from this safe distance, I quote his less known pronouncement at the end of a hard and confused day at White Oak Swamp in the Seven Days' Battles before Richmond, when he told his commanders, "Now, gentlemen, let us at once to bed and see if tomorrow we cannot do something." I believe that the day on Omaha Beach was as hard and confused as at White Oak

Swamp, and rest from it was equally needed. In any event, in the early morning, I retired to a corner of the barn, cradled my swollen face, and slipped into a troubled sleep. The last sounds I recall were far-off artillery and machine-gun fire.

It was about two hours before dawn of the second day.

—October 1983

THE MARIANAS TURKEY SHOOT

by ADMIRAL J. J. CLARK

Japanese naval air power was wrecked at the Battle of the Philippine Sea, but, says Jocko Clark, the Navy missed a chance to destroy the enemy fleet and shorten the war.

Task Force 58, Marc A. Mitscher, sortied from its Marshall Islands bases on June 6, 1944, the landings on Saipan being scheduled for June 15. My Task Group 58.1 left Kwajalein to rendezvous with 58.2 (Rear Admiral A.E. Montgomery); 58.3 (Rear Admiral J. W. Reeves), and 58.4 (Rear Admiral W. K. Harrill), which came out of Majuro. Fueling took two days, June 8 and 9. On the night of the eighth, our radar registered several "bogies"—enemy search planes—but they never made contact with our force. "Snoopers" began to approach our combat air patrol on the tenth. Fighter director Charles D. Ridgway dispatched a group of Hellcats to destroy them before they could sight the force and radio back our position to their base. We shot down the first snooper forty-seven miles from the task group, and a few minutes later splashed another. Land-based Liberators from Eniwetok preceded the carriers; one of them shot down a Betty, but not before we overheard the pilot reporting our position. This incident prompted me to ask permission from Mitscher to station picket destroyers equipped with radar and fighter directors ahead of the group, with their own combat air patrol to detect enemy snoopers before they sighted the carriers. With Mitscher's approval, on the morning of June 11 I sent two destroyers fifty miles ahead of the force and a third one twenty-five miles. This precaution became standard procedure for the fast carriers and was greatly expanded later in the war.

Making excellent time from the Marshalls to the target area, Task Force 58 was attacked by long-range enemy patrol bombers on the morning of June 11. When the shooting started, I sent out a final word of encouragement to the men of my task group: "Message to all hands. We need no special incentive, but Guam belongs to us. Deliver every bomb and bullet where it will do the most good. . . . God be with you and good luck. S/S Admiral Clark." Our combat air patrol Hellcat pilots were the first to see action. During the morning and early afternoon, our new picket destroyers directed *Yorktown* fighters about forty miles beyond the force to shoot down six enemy patrol bombers, one of which yielded two survivors. I could not resist sending a signal to my old ship: "Your combat air patrol has turned in the usual and expected top-notch *Yorktown* performance. Congratulations."

Since Task Force 58 was already under attack from enemy air units based on the target islands, Admiral Mitscher realized that if we waited until the next day for our customary predawn fighter sweep, the force would be under constant attack during the night. To avoid that, and to catch the Japanese by surprise, we launched the fighter sweep on that very afternoon. At 1 P.M. we began launching from a position 192 miles east of Guam. *Hornet* and *Yorktown* each sent off sixteen Hellcats, while *Belleau Wood* and *Bataan* each launched twelve. In all, from Task Force 58, 212 F6F's and ten life-raft-laden bombers were included in the sweep.

The afternoon fighter sweep had indeed caught the Japanese unaware. Reeves and Harrill worked over Saipan and Pagan. Montgomery hit Tinian, and I took Guam and Rota. Lieutenant Commander William A. Dean, skipper of Fighting 2 from the flagship, led the Hellcats into their strafing and bombing runs, which pitted the airstrips and destroyed several parked planes. The thirty Zeros that appeared were quickly engaged and shot down. Though antiaircraft fire was heavy, our planes easily carried the day. I signalled the ships in the task group: "Damn well done. Upwards of thirty airborne aircraft destroyed against one of ours shot down." In all, about 150 Japanese planes were destroyed by Task Force 58 at the cost of eleven Hellcats; three of our pilots were rescued. The total score for my task group on that day was forty-one enemy planes shot down. That night and the next morning no planes molested Task Force 58.

The customary pre-invasion destruction of enemy positions and equipment on the target islands began on June 12. Japanese antiaircraft gunners, lying in wait for our bombers and fighters, threw up a fire so withering that Fighting 24 from *Belleau Wood* reported it as "the heaviest encountered by this squadron in its nine months of combat experience." At dawn I sent out search planes 325 miles to the southwest to look for enemy warships; they sighted a convoy of six small Japanese vessels, destroyers and transports, about 270 miles west of Guam, heading south at eight knots. We launched a special strike against this convoy, but our planes failed to relocate it. I had the bombers drop their bombs on Guam as they returned. To conclude the day's operations, *Hornet*'s planes dropped leaflets to the Chamorro natives on Guam announcing our intention to free them from Japanese domination.

Before daylight next morning, we launched another search-strike to look for that convoy. Two radar-equipped night fighters led twenty Hellcats from *Hornet* and *Yorktown*, followed by two rescue-equipped SB2C dive bombers. Each fighter carried one five-hundred-pound bomb. Finally the convoy was sighted and the planes attacked it, but the fighter pilots were inexperienced in the art of bombing warships and succeeded in damaging only one. Also, the 350-mile range was the longest carrier air strike of record at that time. Our other planes pounded Guam and were joined by the surface ships. By the end of that day, no aircraft remained on Guam that could possibly assist the defenders of Saipan when that island was assaulted two days later.

During the morning of June 13, Captain W. K. "Sol" Phillips, my screen commander and the skipper of the cruiser *Oakland*, had sent me a signal regarding Tokyo Rose, the infamous American-born Japanese woman broadcaster: "Tokyo Rose has just announced on the radio that all our ships are sunk."

I signalled back: "Do not believe Tokyo Rose. When the rising sun goes down she will sing a different song." This message began an exchange between Phillips and me referring to Tokyo Rose; thereafter, signalmen in my task group kept on the lookout for the Tokyo Rose messages to pass along to their friends.

During the attacks on Guam, Lieutenant (j.g.) Beath and his radio interceptors had been picking up Japanese radio transmissions and decoding messages relating to aircraft movements. We learned that the Japanese were sending great numbers of planes from the home islands to Chichi Jima and Iwo Jima, about seven hundred miles to the north, for attacks on our shipping off Saipan. Mitscher had the same messages confirmed by our submarines in the area. He wanted these planes destroyed.

Mitscher sent Harrill and me north to stop this buildup and to knock out the airfields in the "Jimas." On June 14, as our two groups rendezvoused, I received a message from Harrill saying that he did not want to go north to hit the Jimas. I could not believe he meant it, so I had Douglas "Tex" McCrary, my air operations officer, fly me over to Harrill's flagship, *Essex,* for a talk. Harrill was firm in his desire not to go north at all. He said heavy weather was going to cover the Jimas and that the Japanese fleet might come out from the Philippines to attack the shipping off Saipan. His reluctance to carry out orders surprised me. Formerly a topflight officer, he seemed to have lost his zip.

Mitscher's order to Harrill and me was unusual. It was a multiple-address dispatch giving the two task groups the mission of striking the Jimas while remaining "tactically concentrated." Ordinarily the senior officer would lead such an assignment, but neither of us was in tactical command. Later I learned that Mitscher had purposely written the order that way to give me freedom of action. Harrill's chief of staff, Captain H. E. "Blackie" Regan, and I spent hours trying to convince Harrill of the importance of stopping the Japanese air threat from the north. Exasperated, I finally said, "If you do not join me in this job, I will do it all myself." After that remark he agreed to participate, but he provided only token assistance. Nevertheless, seven carriers were better than four, and though concerned about Harrill, I returned to my flagship satisfied.

Our plans were to hit the Jimas for two days, June 16 and 17, and then to rejoin Mitscher off Saipan. That night, June 14, Spruance sent to Task Force 58 an important dispatch announcing that the Japanese fleet had left its anchorage at Tawi Tawi in the southern Philippines, presumably to prevent us from capturing the Marianas, and therefore we should shorten our strikes to just one day and hasten back to rejoin Mitscher for a possible fleet engagement. I calculated that two days were needed to destroy the enemy air strength at Chichi and Iwo Jima, so I speeded up my group to twenty-five knots to get us within aircraft range of the target one day early. This still gave us the two days of air strikes against the enemy.

When my task group reached a position 135 miles from Iwo Jima on the afternoon of the next day, we launched planes from my four carriers. They shot down about twenty-four Zeros over the islands, destroying more on the fields at Iwo and Chichi. Off Chichi Jima my planes intercepted the 1,900-ton transport *Tatsutakawa Maru*. Over four hundred Japanese went over the side as the steamer burned. The destroyers *Boyd* and *Charrette* finally sunk her, then proceeded to rescue all Japanese sailors who were willing to be picked up. The two ships rescued 118 people in all, but two of these changed their minds and jumped off the destroyers later. The 116 prisoners were delivered on board *Hornet*. Another sixteen picked up later made a total of 132 Japanese aboard my flagship, a record for the carriers.

While the Marines were landing on Saipan to the south, we attacked Chichi and Iwo. Our planes destroyed many of the choice targets—oil dumps, buildings, aircraft, and small vessels; we did not need Harrill, as it turned out, but he did assist by maintaining a combat air patrol. My planes also worked over the smaller island of Haha Jima.

Heavy weather developed by late afternoon, making recovery of our planes difficult. One crashed on the badly pitching *Belleau Wood*. It started a fire that looked serious, but Captain Jack Perry and his heroic crew put it out. The sea became so rough that I cancelled the remaining strikes, but I kept two night fighters over Chichi Jima during the night in order to heckle the Japanese and prevent their planes from taking off at dawn. Both task groups had retired to the south during the night, but we could not avoid the weather. The carriers were pitching too badly to launch any planes.

In the afternoon, as the wind abated somewhat, I launched a fighter sweep and two bombing strikes against Iwo Jima. They added to the destruction done on the previous day. After the recovery of my planes, both task groups headed south. The mission had been a great success; we had destroyed for the time being the Japanese air threat from the north staged through the Bonin Islands, thereby protecting the invasion forces.

Meanwhile, bigger game was approaching the Marianas—the Japanese First Mobile Fleet, which according to our intelligence estimates included nine carriers with about 450 aircraft. During the next afternoon, June 17, Mitscher ordered us to send searches to the southwest. The position of the enemy fleet was known by our trailing submarines; possibly it could be hit later from two sides, if our planes spotted it. I sent twelve search planes 350 miles to the southwest, then steamed in that direction to recover them and be that much closer to the enemy. The result of the search was negative, because the Japanese fleet was still seven hundred miles away.

That night I faced an important decision; an opportunity was presented that seldom comes in the lifetime of a naval officer. Had I steamed to the southwestward all night, by the next morning I could place myself between the Japanese fleet and its homeland, thereby blocking off its retreat and boxing in the enemy between our four task groups. I called Harrill on the TBS voice radio and explained the situation to him. I also called Rear Admiral Ralph Davison, who was riding in "makee learn," or training, status on board *Yorktown*. Davison strongly endorsed my idea, but Harrill would have nothing to do with it, maintaining that his orders were to rendezvous with Mitscher the next morning west of Saipan. He told me he had had enough of independent operations and was now going to make his rendezvous. Without further ado, he changed course and headed off to the south, leaving me all alone. I dared not break radio silence to consult Mitscher, for this would have disclosed my position to the Japanese fleet.

My staff and I discussed the alternatives. Conceivably, the Japanese might have concentrated on me before the trap was set and possibly sunk some of my ships. With Harrill, our two task groups had three hundred fighters and two hundred attack planes, which I considered more than a match for the entire enemy carrier force. But when Harrill sailed away, he took some ninety fighters and seventy bombers with him. I did not wish to find myself on a windy corner with so many Japanese airplanes that I could not shoot them all down. In addition, embarking on my own course might have embarrassed Mitscher in front of Ray Spruance; I admired both men, but it was obvious to me that Spruance did not understand the full capabilities of the fast carriers. Together, Mitscher's fifteen carriers made a virtually invincible force. If Mitscher had been in command of the Fifth Fleet, I would have continued to the southwest. But Mitscher was subordinate to Spruance, and I did not want to disturb their good working relationship. Finally, I asked myself if I were not about to take the whole world on my shoulders.

In many ways, my situation recalled the Battle of Jutland in 1916. Vice Admiral David Beatty made a similar decision in the opening stages of that celebrated fleet action of World War I. Beatty had been racing toward the enemy fleet with his fast battle cruisers, trying to get behind the German battle force to prohibit its retreat and box it in between his force and the British Grand Fleet under Admiral John R. Jellicoe. Beatty was out of touch with Jellicoe and made his dash without keeping Jellicoe adequately informed. His boldness made him the hero of that war, but he lost two of his ships and was almost caught by the German High Seas Fleet. He could have lost the battle. In 1925, Admiral J. M. "Billy Goat" Reeves, who was a great student of Jutland, gave a four-hour lecture on the battle at his headquarters in San Diego. Reeves's conclusion was that Beatty made a mistake in trying to trap the Germans without keeping Jellicoe informed. My friend Lieutenant Al Buehler, who had listened with me, summarized Reeves's lecture in three words, "Beatty bitches battle!" Now I applied Buehler's remark to my own situation.

After debating the pros and cons, my staff and I decided against striking off on our own, so I turned, following Harrill, to carry out my orders. Later, after the Marianas were captured, Mitscher told me he thought I should have continued to the southwest to get behind the Japanese fleet. He uttered practically the same words Admiral Ernest J. King had said to me when I had wanted to attack Rabaul very early in the war, "I almost ordered you to do it." So I missed the chance of becoming the Beatty of World War II. But the enemy had not yet closed, and there was still an opportunity to deal a crushing blow to the Japanese fleet. I rejoined the other three task groups off Guam on the morning of June 18, fully expecting Admiral Spruance to assume tactical command and head west to attack the Japanese fleet. But he did not. Conflicting or vague submarine reports suggested that two Japanese forces were approaching, as had been the case during the Midway campaign. One force was known to be due west of Guam, the other possibly southwest; consequently, Spruance kept the carriers off Guam as a shield for the exposed southern flank of our landing forces at Saipan, awaiting better reports of enemy movements. The Japanese fleet was still about seven hundred miles away from the Fifth Fleet, which meant no battle could be joined that day.

In the morning, the destroyer *Cowell* picked up sixteen survivors from the Japanese transport *Shinjiki Maru,* which had been sunk six days before by Harrill's planes. Later, my combat air patrol shot down a snooper 250 miles northwest of the formation, probably from the Jimas. We spent the day cruising back and forth near Guam, sending aircraft searches to the southwest.

During the night, Spruance was faced with the decision of whether or not to go west. It became evident that the Japanese held a theoretical advantage. They could launch their carrier planes from six hundred miles out, attack the Fifth Fleet, land and refuel on Guam, attack us again, and fly back to their carriers. We could not reach their carriers if we remained near the Marianas. The maximum operating radius of our planes was 350 miles, which meant we had to continue westward during the night to get within combat range of the Japanese for strikes the next morning. Spruance's great concern was the protection of the invasion forces. He was afraid of an "end run." The transports could have been protected just as well from 250 miles farther west, with our radar, our search planes, and our submarines keeping us informed of the movements of the enemy fleet.

At 8 P.M. Spruance ordered the fleet to head eastward, which we had to do anyway in order to operate aircraft, since the wind was from the east. This was definitely not closing the Japanese fleet. In my judgment, we should have steamed west at every opportunity. At midnight, Admiral Mitscher recommended that the fleet turn west to meet the enemy because at 10 P.M. a radio-direction-finder report had placed the Japanese fleet 355 miles to the west. Spruance, however, persisted in remaining near the invasion forces and sent a message at 12:30 A.M., June 19, to Mitscher: "End run by other fast ones remains a possibility and must not be overlooked."

At first light, Mitscher ordered me to launch a special 325-mile search to the southwest, which I did, with negative results. *Hornet* was on the eastern end of Task Force 58, and at daylight I could actually see Guam on the horizon. At 6:19 Spruance ordered all carrier task groups to change course westward in the general direction of the Japanese fleet.

A few snoopers had been splashed by the other groups, but not until 7:05 did my group get into the act. Lieutenant Charlie Ridgway detected many airplanes over Guam on his radar screen and dispatched four night fighters to investigate. Finding a number of Japanese planes in a landing circle over Guam, these Hellcats immediately went to work. I ordered twenty-four more fighters sent to Guam, then reported to Mitscher. Mitscher radioed all task groups: "Send fighter assistance to Guam immediately." My acknowledgement was: "Help is on the way." These Japanese planes were unquestionably from the approaching fleet. Lieutenant Russell Reiserer, leading the night fighters, tore into the Japanese planes at Guam. Other Hellcats, mostly from my task group, assisted. Enemy planes that were not destroyed in the air were shot up on the ground after landing. Reiserer himself scored five kills, which he modestly reported to me on the flag bridge upon his return. On my recommendation, Mitscher gave him the Navy Cross for becoming an ace.

At 9 A.M. Owen Sowerwine, my communications officer, intercepted a corrected contact report from a PBM Mariner search plane whose previous message, several hours earlier, had been garbled. The report pinpointed the Japanese fleet over 360 miles away, still beyond the range of our aircraft. We relayed the message to Mitscher, who sent it on to Spruance.

Task Force 58 was steaming west but getting nowhere, since the carriers had to swing around to the east to launch planes. At 9:37 Ridgway and the other task group combat intelligence officers began to pick up aircraft on their radars 130 miles to the westward. Mitscher recalled all his fighters from Guam to defend the carriers, ordering all dive bombers and torpedo planes to take off and orbit east of Guam. This expedient kept the carrier decks free to land, service, and launch fighters. At 10:04 general quarters was sounded, and all hands in the force went to their battle stations. Meanwhile, 450 Hellcats and a few night F4U Corsairs took off to intercept the attacking Japanese.

The melee that followed was aptly described by one pilot as "the Marianas Turkey Shoot." Our pilots and planes were so superior to those of Japan that only a handful of enemy planes reached our ships, and these were promptly shot down by antiaircraft fire. Throughout the day, the Japanese repeatedly tried to launch air strikes against our ships, but each time our pilots shot the enemy out of the sky.

Our operations took Task Force 58 even closer to Guam. Mitscher knew the Japanese were trying to land there, so he ordered the bombers that were orbiting east of Guam to drop their charges on the airfield, and the bomb craters they produced caused a number of Japanese planes to crash. The desperate enemy pilots fought savagely to defend the integrity of Guam as their one refuge. We lost several pilots there toward evening, but by nightfall Guam was quiet; the last snoopers had turned away before eight o'clock.

Reports of the battle were impressive. My pilots claimed 109 enemy planes shot down, while the total for Task Force 58 turned out to be 385. It was the greatest aerial victory in the Pacific war. Forty Hellcats were lost, but many of the pilots were rescued. The Japanese lost about eleven aviators to every one of ours, a ratio that continued throughout the war. Admiral Mitscher sent a message to all hands: "The aviators and gun ships of this task force have done a job today which will make their country proud of them. Their skillful defense of this task force enabled the force to escape a vicious, well-coordinated aircraft attack carried out with determination."

Admiral Spruance was not convinced that the Japanese air attack was spent until 10 P.M., when Task Force 58 took its last plane aboard. Then, at last, he headed toward the enemy fleet. At that stage we were forty miles from Guam, so closing the enemy became a long stern chase, but since the backbone of enemy air strength was expended, we possessed an over-whelming advantage once we got within aircraft range. As a precaution, I topped off my destroyers. Just then I heard Admiral Harrill ask Mitscher if his task group could stay behind, because it was low on fuel. My big ships had the same amount of fuel as Harrill's, but he had not topped off his destroyers, so Mitscher left him behind. I immediately signalled Mitscher: "Would greatly appreciate remaining with you. We have plenty of fuel." He replied that my task group would remain with him until the battle ended. To me this was a compliment, but it also indicated Mitscher's growing impatience with Harrill. Task Group 58.4 had broken away at 1 P.M. and continued to hit Guam, and then refueled the next day. "Harrill fought this group well through the Marianas 'Turkey Shoot,' " historian Samuel Eliot Morison later wrote, "but came down with appendicitis 28 June and was then relieved. . . ."

Task Force 58 steamed west at twenty-three knots during the night. While the pilots of Task Force 58 slept, the plane mechanics prepared the aircraft for the battle expected the next day. As we passed over the waters of the afternoon air battles, one of my destroyers picked up three of our airmen floating in a life raft. At first light we launched a long-range search flight 325 miles to the west, but these planes found nothing to report. Around 9 A.M. our combat air patrol shot down three snoopers. We pressed on, but sighted no enemy ships.

The quiet of this Sunday afternoon at sea was suddenly broken at 3:40 by excited chatter over the radio. The Japanese fleet had been sighted 275 miles due west of Saipan, steaming northwest at twenty knots. Eight minutes later Mitscher told all task groups to report to him any other radio messages they heard. At 3:53 he gave us the word: "Expect to launch everything we have, probably have to recover at night." The pilots, who had been in their ready rooms since dawn, now copied down the latest target information from the ticker-tape screens onto their navigation charts. Mitscher gave them a parting thought: "The primary mission is to get the carriers." At 4:10 the pilots manned their planes, and at 4:21 we turned into the wind to execute a record ten-minute launch.

The flight consisted of 216 planes—eighty-five Hellcats, fifty-four Avengers, fifty-one SB2C Helldivers, and twenty-six SBD Dauntlesses. But no sooner was the strike on its way than the search planes sent in a corrected position report placing the Japanese fleet sixty miles farther west. This meant that our planes had to fly 335 miles to the target, attack the enemy fleet before darkness, and fly back to the carriers in the dark. The trip and attack would amount to over seven hundred miles of flying, which was about the limit of fuel. Some planes would surely have to land in the water at night. Those pilots whose fuel lasted could land aboard, but unfortunately none of them had qualified for night carrier landings. This was a sample of Mitscher's indomitable leadership. He gambled despite the expected losses, knowing full well that this was our one and only chance to hit the Japanese fleet.

At this point in the battle I realized bitterly what a great opportunity I had missed on June 18 by not getting behind the Japanese fleet. Retreat would have been impossible, for my carriers would have stood between it and the homeland, making this precarious flight unnecessary. In the game of war an advantage unpressed may have tragic consequences. To me this seemed to be a case in point.

Around 7 P.M., as a half-hour air attack on the Japanese warships was ending in approaching darkness, we began to get reports from our planes. Antiaircraft fire was thick; the battleships and cruisers in desperation fired their heavy guns at our planes. About seventy-five Japanese fighters took off from the carriers, and our Hellcats attacked them immediately. By Japanese records, only ten of their planes survived. Racing against the sudden tropical darkness, our pilots executed hastily co-ordinated attacks on the flaming ships. Planes from *Belleau Wood* in my task group succeeded in sinking one carrier, *Hiyo*. Lieutenant (j.g.) George P. Brown flew down along the flight deck to draw away antiaircraft fire, thus allowing Lieutenant (j.g.) Warren R. Omark to drop his torpedo into the ship's side. Unfortunately, the courageous Brown went into the sea on the return flight and was never found. Some bombs hit and damaged the carriers *Zuikaku* and *Junyo*, but they managed to limp back to the homeland.

Pitch-black darkness had already descended as the running lights of the first of our returning planes appeared over the horizon. With understandable anxiety, for I had flown at night from carriers myself, I made a drastic decision. I ordered all my ships to turn on all their lights. Of course, this was taking a chance that no enemy submarines were lurking nearby. To identify my task group I ordered *Hornet* to display in addition a vertical searchlight beam. I notified Admiral Mitscher of my action at once, and he promptly signified his approval by ordering all the ships of the entire task force to turn on their lights. This was indeed one of the war's supreme moments—a multitude of ships emblazed the skies for many miles in a calculated risk to provide greater safety for the return of battle-worn airmen.

The assistant air officer of *Yorktown*, Lieutenant Commander Verne W. Harshman, rigged a cargo light to shine down on the flight deck to facilitate landings. Other ships then used this innovation to advantage.

Flown by Commander Bill Dean, skipper of Fighting 2, the first Hellcat landed aboard *Hornet*. Dean rushed up to the bridge to report the results of the attack and expressed great fear that he was going to lose many of his fine pilots in the recovery operation. I tried to allay his apprehension, and, as it turned out, he did not lose a single man.

Recovery of the returning planes, however, was a wild scramble, as the exhausted pilots rushed to get on board before their fuel gave out. We ordered them to land on any carrier they could find. Some deck crashes fouled flight decks for a few minutes, but very few flight personnel were injured. Many planes landed in the water, but destroyers picked up the pilots and crews. Everyone concentrated on rescue operations. During all this activity, Sol Phillips radioed that a Japanese Zero was circling *Oakland*. Thinking it was one of our carrier planes trying to land, I asked him: "How do you know it's Japanese?"

He signalled back: "I can tell by the red balls on its wings!"

Lieutenant Michael S. Alexatos, returning in a Hellcat, heard over the plane's radio circuit: "Hey, that was a Jap Zero!" Since it was not seen again, it must have ditched in the sea.

Knowing he was low on fuel, Alexatos asked for the location of his ship, *Yorktown*. The reply was: "We are the one with the searchlight turned straight up."

He headed for the first searchlight he saw, because his gasoline gauge read zero. He made a perfect landing, taxiing clear of the barrier. The engine of his plane sputtered and stopped. As he was climbing out of his cockpit, someone said, "Welcome aboard *Hornet*."

The mistake was understandable, since *Hornet* and *Yorktown* each had a searchlight turned straight up.

Task Force 58 steamed over the path of the returning flight during the night picking up more downed pilots. The final count of our task force losses on June 19 and 20 was one hundred airplanes, sixteen pilots, thirty-three aircrewmen, and, due to deck crashes, two ship's officers and four enlisted men. Postwar investigation revealed that Japan, in contrast, lost three carriers, including two sunk by submarines before June 19, and 445 aircraft, including twelve catapult planes from battleships and cruisers, along with about fifty land-based planes destroyed at Guam. The Japanese fleet still had aircraft carriers left, but only about ten planes aboard them, so if we had come within striking distance we would have encountered negligible air opposition. As we tried to chase the fleet through the next night and throughout the following day, June 21, our extreme-range scouting planes sighted the fleeing ships intermittently, but they were always beyond our combat radius. We did not have fuel in our ships to pursue the enemy farther west.

The two-day engagement that was fought west of Guam, in the direction of the Philippine Islands, became known as the Battle of the Philippine Sea and thus gave a name to the area. The first day, in the Marianas Turkey Shoot, we broke the backbone of the Japanese carrier air strength. The second day we inflicted damage on seventeen of their ships, including the sinking of *Hiyo*. Because it was Mitscher's one and only opportunity to strike the Japanese, it was called "Mitscher's Sunday Punch."

On my track charts I wrote the words made famous by Horace Greeley: "Go West, young man, go West," which in my opinion is what Admiral Spruance should have done on the night of June 18.

The naval analyst must examine dispassionately all aspects of a naval engagement. Through the pages of history, major wars have often been decided by the outcome of a single battle, as in the case of Salamis or Actium. The naval commander is at his best when he takes full advantage of every chance to destroy his enemy. The bigger the battle, the better the naval officer. It is a fair statement to say that had we sunk every Japanese ship the war might have ended in days instead of fifteen months. Spruance could still have provided maximum protection for the invasion forces even if his carriers had been farther west on the morning of June 19, and the airfields at Guam and Rota could have been kept inoperative just as well from that position. It was not possible for the approaching Japanese fleet to make "end runs" around our aircraft carriers. Had we been two hundred miles farther west that morning, we could have scored a decisive naval victory.

My high admiration for Spruance has been maintained ever since he was my first destroyer skipper aboard the *Aaron Ward* in 1919. He won the crucial Battle of Midway, he blazed a trail across the Pacific from Tarawa to Saipan, and now in the Battle of the Philippine Sea he had turned back the Japanese fleet with staggering losses, without losing a single ship of his own. The tactical decisions he made as commander of the Fifth Fleet during this battle have been supported by historian Morison and by Admiral King, and I hesitate to align myself against such stalwarts. Yet the inescapable fact remains that our lost opportunity allowed the Japanese fleet to sail away, to fight again at the Battle for Leyte Gulf.

—October 1967

AT WAR WITH THE STARS AND STRIPES

by HERBERT MITGANG

Army newspapers in World War II were unofficial, informal, and more than the top brass could handle.

In the summer of the year 1944, in a time of world war that is already history to my children's generation but remains vividly personal to mine as a moment of (in retrospect) astonishing simplicity and idealism, I found myself pointing a jeep in the direction of Pisa and Florence. On the so-called forgotten front in Italy, the *Wehrmacht* held the northern side of these cities; the line dividing their riflemen and ours was the river Arno.

The big show of the European war was being played out on the newly opened second front in Normandy. Along the French Riviera a diversionary side show became popularly known as the champagne war. Since the German 88's had not been informed that our Mediterranean theater had lessened in strategic importance, they were still to be reckoned with.

My windshield was down and covered with tarpaulin—any fool knew that glass reflected and could draw artillery fire or even a *Luftwaffe* fighter seeking a target of opportunity. I was driving along happily and singing to myself because all I needed was in that jeep: a Springfield rifle, a scrounged .25-caliber Italian automatic, two large cans of gasoline, one helmet (I wore the liner as a sunshade and the heavy steel pot, useful for shaving and washing, rattled around in the back), several days' worth of C and K rations, five gallons of water and two canteens of vino, and—most important of all—one portable typewriter.

That little Remington was the telltale of my military

trade: I was an Army correspondent for *Stars and Stripes,* Mediterranean. Below the masthead of two enfolded flags its only mission was inscribed: "Daily Newspaper of the U.S. Armed Forces published Monday through Saturday for troops in Italy." Although we were occasionally enjoined to do so, we were not supposed to propagandize, publicize generals, or even inform and educate. Our job was to put out a newspaper as professionally as we could. Although armed, the soldier-correspondent was not necessarily expected to go looking for the enemy but instead to report about the soldiers, sailors, and airmen who did.

As I drove along the seacoast road, noticing the island of Elba at one point but without worrying about Napoleon or anyone else's war, the parting words of one of the correspondents came to mind. "Don't forget," he said, "your job is to get back stories, not get yourself killed." Two of my colleagues, Sergeants Gregor Duncan and Al Kohn, had died covering the front, and all of us were shaken up when what was an everyday occurrence in combat outfits struck home.

There were stories everywhere. My immediate problem was not to be distracted before reaching the Fifth Army's pyramidal tents. Ernie Pyle, whose influence as the most important single reporter at home and abroad of the Second World War cannot be exaggerated, had dignified the GI and the "little picture" in his syndicated newspaper column. I recalled having a drink with Pyle near the end of the Tunisian campaign in North Africa and could see part of his strength as an ingratiating reporter. He was skinny, wet, and shivering—a civilian version of the rifleman without rank, and therefore to be trusted.

None of us on *Stars and Stripes* deviated very much, or cared to, from his kind of reporting. Most of our seasoned front-line reporters, such as Jack Foisie, Ralph Martin, Stan Swinton, and Paul Green, roamed the field as Pyle did, covering not only battles but the "mess-kit repair battalions" (as the stray outfits were jokingly called) that supported the infantry. When I saw a sign that intrigued me—an outfit running a GI laundry somewhere near Leghorn—I stopped briefly, made a few notes for "flashes," chiselled some gasoline for my half-empty tank, and remembered to keep going.

After getting a tent assignment and a briefing at Fifth Army headquarters, which was located in a forest near a village somewhere between Pisa and Florence (whose name I cannot recall, though I vividly remember a long evening's talk with the parish priest about the art of the carillonneur and how his bell ringing regulated life and death), I decided to look in on something called an "armored group." It consisted of a self-sufficient group of tanks, artillery, engineers, and riflemen—a forerunner of the integrated, brigade-size units several chiefs of staff assumed would work for the brush-fire wars of the future.

The artillerymen appeared to be most active that afternoon. They were maintaining their franchise by firing harassing shells across the Arno. I took my names and hometown addresses, listened to the battery commander explain his "mission" in stiff Army lingo, and then accepted the captain's invitation to try out the armored group's mess for dinner. What happened next sticks with me as an example of the confusion that existed right in our own theater about *Stars and Stripes* correspondents. I immediately noticed that the two long tables were divided between field-grade officers (colonels, lieutenant colonels, and majors) and company-grade officers (captains and lieutenants). The colonel directed me to sit with him and motioned the captain to sit with his ignoble kind.

There was only one slight error in seating rank here: I, like most correspondents on *Stars and Stripes,* was a lowly sergeant. By the rules of the Army game I was not supposed to be waited upon at either of these tables, but instead to be somewhere out in the field with a mess kit in which the Spam floated around in the brown gravy and peach juice. One lieutenant colonel—to be on the safe side—kept sirring me. I waited for the inevitable to happen, trying to postpone it at least until the dessert. Finally, after a series of questions, the colonel nearest me asked pointblank: "Are you fellows on *Stars and Stripes* civilians or soldiers?" I mumbled something to the effect that we were soldiers but operated in the same manner as the civilian correspondents. He pursued: "Then what's your rank?" Swallowing, I said: "Staff sergeant." Nothing, of course, happened, the embarrassment being all on my side.

The reason for the confusion was that we carried a patch on our left sleeve saying, "Stars and Stripes," without any mark of rank. This was by design. I recall a meeting of the *Stars and Stripes* staff in the Red Cross building on the Boulevard Baudin, Algiers, where we lived and worked. Several of the correspondents had just returned from the Tunisian front. An opportunity existed for some members of *Stars and Stripes* to be commissioned. One already had been—James Burchard, a former sportswriter for the New York *World-Telegram,* who was in his late thirties (most of us were in our twenties).

Lieutenant Burchard and two sergeants described their reporting experiences. The lieutenant said that in order to get GI's to speak to him freely he had to take his bars off and put them in his pocket; he did find the bars useful for eating and pulling rank for transportation.

As a result we decided to avoid commissions because correspondents could perform better as enlisted men. Most of us did not wear our sergeant's stripes precisely because we wanted to foster the impression that we were—or at least until discovered—as privileged and possibly as talented as the regular civilian correspondents (whose pay greatly exceeded ours). I always liked to think of it this way: a *Stars and Stripes* reporter could honestly interview himself and, without fear of contradiction, say he had talked to a GI.

Although *Stars and Stripes* did have commissioned officers on the staff, they were mainly engaged in administrative duties. A specific difficulty arose when I was managing editor of the combined Oran-Casablanca edition of *Stars and Stripes.* A cast-off first lieutenant was assigned to us to censor the mail, requisition food, sign pay vouchers, and so on. He had been pressured by a base-section colonel to run that bane of all military newspapers, "The Chaplain's Corner." I refused his demand to run it. Several days later our own *Stars and Stripes* commanding officer in North Africa, Colonel Egbert White, came down to Oran from Algiers and, rather bluntly in my presence, told the lieutenant that the sergeant who was managing editor had final say over the contents of the paper.

In nearly every other case involving this delicate issue of officer-and-enlisted-men relationships on *Stars and Stripes,* there was no awkwardness. Nearly everyone was on a first-name basis, regardless of rank. All of us were so pleased to be out of regular outfits that we gladly abandoned the normal military way.

Whenever another Mediterranean invasion was in the wind, everyone on the staff hoped to get a piece of the action.

Stars and Stripes reporters were poised with different units before the invasion of Sicily, for example. Sergeant Ralph Martin went in with the Rangers; Sergeant Phil Stern, an ex-Ranger himself, took three hundred pictures with the Seventh Army; Sergeant Paul Green swept over the island in a B-25; Sergeant Jack Foisie started out with the airborne infantry and, in the middle of the Sicilian campaign, was the only correspondent to accompany a small American force that made an amphibious attack seven miles behind the enemy lines along the coast of northern Sicily.

By the time the Mediterranean edition of *Stars and Stripes* had followed the troops across to Sicily and then to Naples and Rome, it had gained the loyalty and affection of officers and enlisted men—Air Force and Navy as well as Army. I saw its importance even to generals when American troops crossed the Arno and entered Pisa.

Naturally everyone wanted a close look at the leaning tower. I went there for a special reason; I was sure that the figures I had seen walking around its upper floors from across the Arno were German observers. I looked for a trace of their presence and found it in a piece of their orange-colored signal wire still hanging down. This, despite their claims that they were not using the campanile because it was church property. I was negotiating with an Italian official to enter the locked tower when, in a flurry of jeeps, General Mark W. Clark, the Fifth Army commander, drove up.

An affable general who was never shy about his personal publicity, Clark looked around for correspondents to cover him as he assumed the role of conqueror of Pisa. None had yet reached Pisa—except the correspondent from *Stars and Stripes*. The General cordially shook my hand and said, "Sergeant, why don't we go up and take a look?" The General and I became the first Americans to do so. At the top he posed his hawklike profile for a Signal Corps photographer—but a wise colonel on his staff killed the pictures on grounds that it might be used by the Germans as propaganda to show that *Americans* had turned the tower into an observation post.

Censorship and generals occasionally plagued *Stars and Stripes*. For the most part censorship was confined to military matters, such as making sure that fresh units were not identified until the enemy knew of their presence and strength. With this we, of course, did not disagree, since we were no more desirous of giving information to the Germans than was the censor. But when a story was held up for nonmilitary reasons, we complained.

I was impressed by the bravery, which almost reached the point of foolhardiness, of certain Italian partisans who were helping the Americans and British north of the Arno. When I wrote about them and their political radicalism, the story was stopped. I would resubmit it week after week, but that story never passed. On other occasions my colleagues and I learned how to circumvent censorship by planting in our copy certain obvious red flags that would be cut out in order to let other material stay in. These, in the main, centered on stories that revealed high-command clay feet.

While I was managing editor of the Sicilian edition of *Stars and Stripes,* probably the most sensitive story of the war fell into my lap. It was the incident in which General George S. Patton had slapped a hospitalized soldier. We knew about it, of course, but had a special problem (to put it mildly) in Sicily: General Patton and his Seventh Army headquarters were there. I had received a file of stories and matrixes from our weekly newspaper in North Africa and noticed that the Algiers edition had carried an AP story about the face-slapping incident. I thought this was the perfect solution. So I reprinted the wire-service story, put it under a fairly quiet two-column headline on the bottom of page 1, and submitted it to the major from Army headquarters assigned as censor. He gulped, read the story, and smiled weakly.

"This story presents a problem," he said. "Do you really want to run it?"

"Of course," I replied. "All I'm doing is picking up the wire-service report that already appeared in Algiers."

"But Patton is in Sicily," he said, "and he reads *Stars and Stripes* every morning with his breakfast. Can you imagine him reading this?"

I could, but argued, "The integrity of the paper is at stake. Because once this story appears in the States, families clip it out and mail it here. Then the GI's know we're suppressing news about their own theater."

The major seemed to see the light—for a moment. "I'd better check this with the colonel," he said. While I waited for my page proofs to be okayed, he called his next above. The major explained the story, then cupped the mouthpiece and whispered to me, "The colonel asked me to hang on while he checks with the General." I whispered, "Patton?" The major nodded and said, "Or Patton's chief of staff." Finally the voice came back on and the major signalled me to listen in with him.

"Major," I heard the colonel say coldly, "the answer is, It's *your* decision." The major hesitated, and then said, "Can you give me some guidance, sir?" The colonel replied, "Major, I would suggest that you use your own judgment based on what is best for the Army." He hung up. The major got the message. "My judgment is," he told me, "you can't run this story in Sicily." As I picked up my page proofs and left without a word, he said, "Dammit, I'm sorry."

Normally, being barless, stripeless, and in uniform had its advantages for the *Stars and Stripes* correspondent. The only instance in my own experience in which being an American soldier was the reason for not allowing me to cover a story occurred when the British reinvaded Greece in autumn of 1944. At the time I was covering Advanced Allied Force Headquarters (which wasn't very advanced—it was in Rome; the regular AFHQ was still back at the palace in Caserta). From a friend on the British *Eighth Army News,* our allied opposite newspaper, I learned that some civilian correspondents were going to be allowed to accompany the British, but no American soldiers would be included. The given reason was that Greece was to be strictly a British "show," on Prime Minister Churchill's orders. No American uniforms were desired on the scene to complicate the future political leverage that the Churchill government wanted to exercise there alone. Months later we discovered that this part of the world was being made safe for the "democracy" of the restored Greek royal house.

When I requested permission to accompany the British 2nd Parachute Brigade on the operation, I was politely refused. Then I heard that the U.S. 51st Wing would carry the chutists. I argued that they could not prevent me from covering just the American C-47's taking part in the jump. A compromise was worked out: I would be allowed to go along but not to land in Greece. We took off from a base in southern Italy, flew across the Ionian Sea and along the Gulf of Corinth, and arrived in sunlight at the drop zone—a small airfield at Megara, west of Athens. Apparently the retreating Germans knew we were coming and had mined the field, but the Greek partisans, who included many Communists, had saved many lives by unarming the mines. The quite wonderful British "red devils" (whose berets were maroon, actually) hit the silk (not nylon, then) and fell to earth without losing a man; I had the privilege of joining them—because who would know otherwise in Megara?

After interviewing people on the ground and getting such vitally unimportant information as the fact that most of the Greek partisans I spoke to seemed to have brothers who owned restaurants in the States, I wrote my stories. Later, at Advanced AFHQ, I had to honor my end of the bargain by such devious datelines as "With the 51st Wing over Greece"—which, curiously, included talks with Athenians on the ground. More important than the stories, however, I brought back one of the ripped silk chutes to Rome, and a seamstress there made dozens of scarves for my *Stars and Stripes* colleagues to wear around their olive-drab throats that winter of 1944-45 in Italy.

Nearly all staffers had come to *Stars and Stripes* from other outfits by hook, crook, or luck. The Mediterranean edition had begun to publish in Algiers on December 9, 1942, a month after the North African landings. It had been preceded by a London edition—the first of World War II—that started on April 18, 1942.

The British edition was Air Corps oriented, because that was the only war they had to write about for more than two years, until the second front was opened in Normandy. Our edition was, from the beginning, infantry oriented. Not being stationed in England, we were also more politically aware around the Mediterranean, because our basic story was the rise of France overseas and the fall of Italian fascism. By the time we reached Rome we were putting out a newspaper that was superior to many dailies in the United States to this day. It was eight pages long; later, twenty-four on Sunday, including a magazine, a news review, and color comics—a mechanical achievement we were proud of. All of us spent many a Saturday night folding in the comics by hand for the Sunday paper.

We were lucky to have two unusual men to guide the Mediterranean edition administratively and editorially—Egbert White, who had been a private first class on the First World War *Stars and Stripes* and, after an advertising and publishing career, had entered the Army a second time; and Robert Neville, a journalist who had specialized in foreign news as editor and correspondent for the New York *Herald Tribune, Time* magazine, and the adless newspaper, *P.M.* In retrospect, what made them outstanding was that they not only knew their business but also had a high level of tolerance about the staff. Many of the young men they took on had little experience, but White and Neville were willing to take chances, defend whims, and deflect the Army brass.

Around the Mediterranean the editions included personnel from every department of a newspaper but the pressroom. We had our own photographers, engravers, linotypists, and make-ups. In the mechanical area the GI printers and specialists often worked side by side with French and Italian craftsmen, and there was great mutuality of interest. The administrative officers and editors worried about the paper from the time it was raw stock, shipped from the States, till it was printed and distributed. The paper's circulation was handled by Sergeant William Estoff, who used everything from mules to C-47's for deliveries. Outfits near the city where the paper was printed usually picked up their quotas with their own transportation. Our own *Stars and Stripes* trucks rode through the night to deliver the paper to front-line divisions north of Rome and Air Corps wings south of Naples. The paper cost two francs or two lire in rear areas but was distributed free at the front.

Some of the soldiers who applied for transfer to *Stars and Stripes* came right out of combat units during the Tunisian and Italian campaigns. In the case of the GI printers, Sergeant Irving Levinson, our mechanical superintendent, went looking for them, but it was usually the other way around for correspondents and editors. In either case the men knew what they were writing, editing, or printing, for they had been in line outfits themselves.

The way I joined *Stars and Stripes* was typically untypical. I had been in southern Algeria with an Air Corps wing. When time allowed I put out a mimeographed paper called *The Bomb-Fighter Bulletin,* its news literally pulled out of the air by monitoring the BBC and Radio Berlin. I accidentally saw a copy of *Stars and Stripes* and decided to apply for a job. With the help of a kind lieutenant from my unit who covered up for me, I went A.W.O.L. for two days and showed up in Algiers, where *Stars and Stripes* had its office. I was interviewed by Neville, then a harassed lieutenant, who moaned that he was having trouble finding solid newspapermen (Which I certainly was not). Then he said, "Do you know that there are people on this paper who don't know how to spell Hitler's first name?" I trembled, fearing he might ask me, and I wouldn't know whether he wanted it to end in *f* or *ph*. Fortunately he didn't ask, and a month or so later I received my transfer.

The story of how William Estoff, our circulation chief, got on *Stars and Stripes* was cherished by his friends as the definitive exposé of shavetails and military foul-ups. One day in England a call came to a replacement depot for an enlisted man with newspaper circulation experience. A lieutenant dutifully examined the service records. He suddenly stopped at the name Estoff, private; age, mid-thirties; civilian occupation, bookmaker. (Estoff, a night-club and newsstand operator, as a lark had listed himself as a bookie.) "Bookmaker," the lieutenant is reported to have said. "That sounds close to what *Stars and Stripes* needs. Books—newspapers—can't be too different." This started a career for Sergeant Estoff that resulted in getting the ideal man for the complex assignment of making sure that the paper was circulated quickly to front-line divisions, plus the Air Corps and Navy.

As the war progressed, seasoned journalists—Hilary Lyons, Howard Taubman, John Radosta, John Willig, all past or future members of the *New York Times*—helped to turn the Mediterranean edition into a newspaper with a serious approach to U.S. and world events. Wire-service reports became available but were not accepted at face value. The major stories—our Italian front, northern Europe, the Russian counteroffensive, the Pacific theater—were handled on our own copy desk. The need was seen for better reporting from Washington and the home front slanted to an Army newspaper for men overseas, many of whom had missed three Christmases home. One correspondent began to be rotated every four or five months; from where we sat in Algiers or Palermo or Rome, we referred to our man in New York as the "foreign correspondent in reverse." Sergeant Bill Hogan was assigned to his home town, San Francisco, to report the founding of the United Nations there.

The *Stars and Stripes* in the Second World War leapfrogged the rear echelons. Thirty different editions were published; a number were dailies. Combined readership ran into the millions. As the Army freed each new island or town or country, editors, printers, and circulation men rushed into the nearest newspaper plant, occasionally at gunpoint, and took over. One of our lieutenants entered the plant of the *Giornale di Sicilia,* found the reluctant owner, and decided to put a fresh clip into his .45 at the moment of hesitancy. The owner relented, and *Stars and Stripes* began printing in Palermo. On the day Rome was freed, a dash was made for the plant of *Il Messaggero* by Sergeant Milton Lehman and several others, and a paper, headlined, "WE'RE IN ROME," was actually handed to some troops as they entered the city.

The news itself was supplemented by the two most popular features in the paper: "Puptent Poets" and "Mail Call." Although some distinguished poets in uniform were published, most of the men who submitted poems made no claim to expertise. There was humor ("Dirty Gertie from Bizerte/Hid a mousetrap 'neath her skirtie") and sentimental awareness ("This is the bridge. Dante stood in this place/And caught a fire that flamed Firenze town"). Corporal John Welsh III found himself doing little else but handling poetry on the Mediterranean edition; in two years one thousand poems were published, and fifteen times that were acknowledged with regret. In many cases poems were published posthumously. For the GI, poetry was the Greek chorus of his conscience, emerging in language of humor, protest, and even beauty.

The "Mail Call" column, edited by Sergeant Robert Wronker, exceeded the poetry in numbers received and printed. Initially, when *Stars and Stripes* published a new edition, the managing editor might write a few provoking letters under an assumed name to get the letters coming. What better way than to have a fictional "1st Sergeant McGonigle" demand more calisthenics for draftees overseas to keep them in trim as in the good old days of the prewar Regulars? What a private couldn't tell his supply sergeant and what a platoon lieutenant couldn't call a base-section saluting demon wound up in *Stars and Stripes* as a letter, poem, or article—and sometimes commanders listened, learned, retrained.

Bill Mauldin's daily cartoon reflected the paper's editorial attitude, yet he seldom editorialized. "Up Front . . . By Mauldin" was just that—a greatly talented soldier's view of what was on the combat GI's mind but not articulated until Mauldin expressed it for him in a simple sentence. He was in a direct line from the First World War's Bruce Bairnsfather, the British creator of the "Old Bill" cartoons and the play *The Better 'Ole*. One of Mauldin's early cartoons, showing the bearded Joe and Willie in an Italian foxhole, was captioned: "Th' hell this ain't th' most important hole in th' world. I'm in it." The Mauldin cartoons were not jokes; nor were they bitter humor. Rather, they were sardonic comments lifted out of the mouths and minds of front-line soldiers.

The cartoons invariably heroized the real dogface, often with a swipe at the rear echelon. In a cartoon that caused many soldiers to categorize themselves, Joe points to a couple of soldiers sitting at an outdoor cafe in France and comments, "We calls 'em garritroopers. They're too far forward to wear ties an' too far back to git shot." Mauldin's cracks were against oppressive authority, officer or EM.

Most of the generals—with a notable exception—enjoyed the Mauldin cartoons, defended them, sometimes asked for an original. But the cartoonist really stuck his neck out when he drew a cartoon ridiculing the tight discipline in the Third Army area—General George Patton's—that included a list of fines signed "By Order Ol' Blood and Guts."

An obligatory scene was played out between the General and the sergeant at Third Army headquarters. Captain Harry Butcher, General Eisenhower's naval aide, who arranged the confrontation, warned Mauldin to please wear a tidy uniform, stand at attention, and salute smartly. The General objected to the unkempt appearance of Willie and Joe; the sergeant said that he thought his characters faithfully represented the front-line GI. The meeting was a stand-off. Later, General Patton told Captain Butcher, "Why, if that little s.o.b. ever comes in the Third Army area again, I'll throw him in jail." Mauldin returned to Italy. Recalling the meeting long afterward, he told me, "I was frightened but steadfast."

Occasionally, in Naples, Mauldin would try out one of his caption lines on me. Rarely did I succeed in getting him to change a word—for a very good reason: his ear had perfect GI pitch. Who could improve upon the cartoon showing two stuffy officers overlooking a sunset and its accompanying line: "Beautiful view. Is there one for the enlisted men?"

There was a special reason why formal editorials were not

needed. A positive tone characterized the paper. *Stars and Stripes* was not an "Army" newspaper—it did not exist between the two World Wars—but, instead, a creation and expression of civilians under arms. A most important influence—more so than any general—was President Franklin D. Roosevelt, who voiced the American dream in language understood by the ranks. The President's popularity was shown by the soldiers' ballots in the 1944 election.

The Four Freedoms speech delivered by Roosevelt, the inspiring speeches of Winston Churchill, the organization of the United Nations, were all fully reported in *Stars and Stripes*. The civilians in uniform who put it out had wide interests and horizons. We were, many of us, fresh from the New Deal years, and some of the sociological thinking for the little man (temporarily called the enlisted man) pervaded the reporting, not only of staff members but of letter writers and poets.

Stars and Stripes achieved a historical place because it was an altogether human paper; it became the printed record of the emotions and passions of its readers. Had it been up to some of the generals and commands, especially the base sections in the rear, *Stars and Stripes* would have been reduced to little more than an Army house organ. Some of the brass considered it only a training manual, publicity release, or hot potato, and seldom just a newspaper.

Whenever a particular command wanted to disavow disputes in the paper, they would issue an order making the paper "unofficial." Nobody could logically explain how a newspaper run by sergeants, administered by captains and colonels, in turn drawing pay from the Army, could be unofficial. The other method of buck-passing by the Army was to keep shifting the command echelon above; an edition might be under a base section, special services, information and education, or Allied Force Headquarters staff.

From the Army's point of view—except for the brief existence of *Stars and Stripes* in World War I—there was no tradition of untrammelled expression; indeed, that was the antithesis of military discipline and unquestioning conformity. The serious *Stars and Stripes* editors were always aware of this apparently irreconcilable conflict. Yet they strove to turn the paper into the voice of men—like themselves—temporarily in uniform, to deliver the news professionally and idealistically, to reflect ideas under stress and our postwar aspirations.

The Second World War multiplied battles and ideals all over the globe. By contrast, the Vietnam folly diminished the United States in the eyes of even those peoples who once were freed by American soldiers. Correspondents and other observers caught up in wars past and present must still sit upon the ground and talk and write without sentiment of dictators and comrades; of the blacks and whites of conscience peering through the smoke; above all, of the need to escalate not the battles, but the ideals.

Stars and Stripes *in the First World War was the famous one, and justly so. From February 8, 1918, to June 13, 1919, its staff in Paris put out seventy-one fiercely independent, sentimental weekly issues. It was run by enlisted men—Private Harold W. Ross, Railway Engineers; Private John T. Winterich, Aero Service; Private Hudson Hawley, Machine Gun Battalion; Sergeant Alexander Woollcott, Medical Department—who were the editorial Big Four. Two officers—Captain Franklin P. Adams and Lieutenant Grantland Rice—for a time served as columnists. Many future journalists of distinction rounded out this brilliant staff, and outside poetry contributors included Sergeant Joyce Kilmer.*

The formal authorization came in a message from General John J. Pershing that appeared on the first page of Volume I, Number 1: "In this initial number of The Stars and Stripes, published by the men of the Overseas Command, the Commander-in-Chief of the American Expeditionary Forces extends his greetings through the editing staff to the readers from the front line trenches to the base ports. . . . The paper, written by the men in the service, should speak the thoughts of the new American Army and the American people from whom the Army has been drawn. Good luck to it."

It was only in the years after World War II that historical research uncovered casual editions of Stars and Stripes *that existed even before the famous World War I edition. The first issue of the* Stars and Stripes *as a military paper appeared in Bloomfield, Missouri, on Saturday, November 9, 1861. This edition was published by Union soldiers of the 18th and 29th Illinois Volunteer regiments. Unfortunately the paper only appeared once, probably due to the exigencies of the war in the Union's Department of the West.*

Other issues of soldier papers called Stars and Stripes *were put out by men in blue during the Civil War. Each one was independent, and no links existed between these short-lived issues and Washington. A group of Federal privates held in Confederate prisons in Richmond, Tuscaloosa, New Orleans, and Salisbury, North Carolina, for ten months before being exchanged in 1862 produced a hand-written* Stars and Stripes. *One of the offices where the paper was written was "Cell No. 9, third floor." Other independent editions of* Stars and Stripes *appeared in Jacksonport, Arkansas (the editor was post surgeon of the 3rd Cavalry Regiment of Missouri Volunteers), and in Thibodaux, Louisiana, in the local office of the Thibodaux* Banner *(whose owner had departed hurriedly) by Connecticut's 12th Regiment. Both editions were printed on wallpaper due to the shortage of newsprint.*

On the Confederate side of the lines, peripatetic-soldier papers were published, too. One was called the Daily Rebel Banner, *but there was no* Stars and Stripes.

—April 1971

WHEN I LANDED, THE WAR WAS OVER

by HUGHES RUDD

The high adventures and near misses of a Maytag Messerschmitt pilot.

T he idea is simple and sound and goes back at least to the American Civil War: to direct artillery fire intelligently, the higher you are above the target, the better. At ground level it's difficult to tell just how far short or long your shells are falling. In the Civil War they used balloons; in the First World War they were still using balloons, along with airplanes equipped with telegraph keys; in the Second World War the airplane had supplanted the balloon, but just barely. The United States Army of those days was not a hotbed of innovation, and when I reported for training as an artillery spotter pilot at Fort Sill, Oklahoma, in early 1942, there was still an enormous building on the post called the Balloon Hangar, even though no balloons were to be seen.

But before that, there was Fort Hays, which wasn't a fort at all in the 1940's but a town in western Kansas with a civilian airfield on the outskirts. I had enlisted in the Army Air Corps, hoping, like all nineteen-year-old American male movie fans, to become a fighter pilot, but one eye tested at 20/40, so the Army Air Corps gave me to the *Army,* period, to become what was called a "Liaison Pilot," meaning artillery spotter. At Fort Hays, the civilians taught us to fly, and it wasn't easy, for them *or* us.

The airplanes were Aeroncas, tandem two-seater monoplanes with sixty-five horsepower engines. They terrified us but aroused only contempt in our instructors, who were accustomed to heavier stuff. Sometimes, out of sheer boredom at the end of two hours in the air with me, trying to teach me crossroad eights, lazy eights, and all the other primer moves the beginning aviator learns, my instructor would seize the controls and put the lumbering Aeronca through snap rolls at an altitude of five hundred feet. The Aeronca, to him, was not an *airplane:* it was a sort of tricycle which occasionally found itself in the air. An Aeronca can kill you as well as an F-14, of course, but my instructor obviously didn't believe that, as witness the aileron-block affair.

Aileron blocks were two pieces of wood joined together with a bolt; when the airplane was through flying for the day, you shoved the bolt forward along the slot between the aileron and the fixed wing, to prevent the ailerons from flopping and banging back and forth in the wind, since that could damage something. A piece of red cloth ten feet long was attached to the aileron block as a warning *not* to take off with the block in place, since the ailerons control the banking and turning movements of the airplane: with block in place, no bank and no turn, a situation that could, as they said in the Army, ruin your whole day.

Nonetheless, one bright morning, as the first student out on solo in this particular Aeronca, I took off, thought the control stick a bit stiff, glanced out the window, and saw that awful red streamer, standing out stiff from the wing. Death, I thought, and I haven't even *seen* a German yet. There was, however, torque, the force exerted by the spinning propeller. Torque tends to turn the airplane, and sure enough, after a wide, wide circle of some twenty-five miles, I found myself lined up with the grass airstrip and landed. I instantly jumped out and threw the aileron block into a ditch before taking off again, but of course my instructor had seen the whole thing. After chewing me out for being just flat-ass *dumb,* he said, "Well, now you'll know what to do when they shoot your ailerons out." To him, clearly, there was nothing to fear in an Aeronca, not even the Luftwaffe.

After about twenty-five hours of solo at Fort Hays, we were shipped to Fort Sill, to the *real* Army, for sixteen weeks of learning to do the impossible with little airplanes. The "Short Field Course," it was called. Two hundred hours of instruction in what to expect in combat areas, and it took place in those little olive drab L-4s.

The L-4 was the Army's version of a Piper Cub: two seats,

one behind the other, a lot of Plexiglas all around, so you could see who was coming after you, and a sixty-five-horse-power, four-cylinder Lycoming engine which pulled the airplane along at a snappy seventy-five miles per hour, assuming no headwind. Speed wasn't the point. The L-4 was made of aluminum tubing with doped linen stretched over it: one man could pick one up by the tail and pull it along behind him. This lightness meant the airplane could land and take off from places unthinkable for *real* airplanes, and in combat, everybody knew we were going to be in a lot of unthinkable places.

The Army instructors at Sill were a lot tougher than the civilians at Fort Hays. The Army instructors had a terrifying habit of chopping the throttle back just as you lifted the airplane off the ground and then pounding on your shoulder and yelling, "Where you gonna put it? Where you gonna put it?" The answer was, in deeds, not words, straight ahead, even if straight ahead was a tree line. Attempting a turn at low altitude and low speed was *wrong, wrong, wrong,* and by God, don't you forget it. On these exercises the instructors would jam open the throttle again just as disaster loomed, and snarl, "All right, take it on up." You got to hate people like that, but of course they were right. The Army, I gradually learned, was *always* right.

Not all of us at Fort Sill *could* get it right. Much of the training involved taking off and landing over "obstacles," which required a certain judgment of height and distance. The obstacles were two upright bamboo poles with a rope tied between them, rags fluttering from the rope, and many a time one saw L-4s staggering through the air, trailing poles, ropes, and rags from the tail wheel. That meant the student had misjudged his take-off: those who misjudged their approach and landing were often saved by two haystacks, one on each side of the obstacle. If the airplane stalled out as the student was trying to slow it down as much as possible, the L-4 fell off on one wing and flopped into the haystack. Since the stalling speed was about thirty-five miles per hour, this was usually not fatal, although it put the instructors into a terrible temper, and people who fell into haystacks were washed out and sent elsewhere, never to be heard from again. Some 20 percent went that way, as I recall.

Others went the hard way. The Army did not make it a point to tell us about fatal crashes, and with some two hundred pilots in training it was hard to keep up with everybody, but young men died often enough in those harmless-looking little airplanes, without ever seeing a German or a Japanese. I was sitting in the waiting room of the base hospital one day, waiting to be treated for some minor medical problem, when I noticed a terrible odor. I asked the orderly what it was, and he said the lab was boiling the brain of a student who'd been killed that morning, to see if there was any alcohol in his system. Rumor had it that if you were killed with a hangover, your insurance was canceled. Since we were restricted to the post all week, this was rarely a problem.

On the weekends a lot of us *did* overdo it in the fleshpots of Lawton, Oklahoma, which has been catering to soldiers since before Custer and the 7th Cavalry were stationed at Sill. We even sang songs, just like soldiers in the movies. There was a song about *us,* to the tune of the "Artillery Song," the one where those caissons go rolling along, and so on, only our song went something like this: "Over trees, under wires, to hell with landing gears and tires, we're the eyes of the artillereeee. We don't mind the mud and sand, we don't need much room to land, we're the eyes of . . . et cetera."

Those of us who survived the Short Field Course were finally graduated, complete with a ceremony in which wings were pinned on our chests: it was pretty much the way Hollywood had told us it would be, except that we had to sign for the wings, as Government Issue property. That was a letdown, but before I had a chance to brood about it, I was assigned to the 93rd Armored Field Artillery Battalion, no longer a learner but a professional, or so the Army hoped, anyway,

Two pilots were assigned to each artillery battalion, but the other fellow gave me so much trouble I'm going to leave his name out of this. Anyway, the 93rd did not know what to make of two Piper Cub pilots, two airplanes, and a mechanic. The officers of the 93rd thought that L-4s were "vehicles," with the accent on the first syllable, and while we remained at Fort Sill they were forever after us to grease our *ve*hicles. Since we were only staff sergeants, we would look busy, but you don't really grease an airplane; you don't even wash it very often. Still, the 93rd believed in washing all *ve*hicles, including Sherman tanks, so we washed the L-4s. That did not end our stateside misunderstandings with the 93rd Battalion, however.

As pilots, we were issued aviator's sunglasses and leather flying jackets, and the 93rd didn't like that. The sunglasses were invaluable when you were called into the battery commander's hut to be reamed over some infraction or other, such as not wearing your leggins (and the word was *leggins,* not *leggings*). You stood there at attention in those dark glasses, your eyes roaming all over the room, avoiding the stern glare of the C.O. with no trouble whatever, and there wasn't a damn thing he could do about it: the glasses were, after all, Government Issue: G.I.

The leggins were a constant problem for a pilot, since they had little hooks along the sides to hold the laces, and those hooks caught in the exposed rudder cables in the cockpit of the L-4. You could *not* make an artillery officer understand that, or at least you couldn't within the continental limits of the United States, or Zone of the Interior, as the Army called it. Once outside the Z.I., the 93rd realized what the L-4s could do, and nobody cared what we wore.

In time, the 93rd Armored Field Artillery Battalion was sent to North Africa. The L-4s were packed into huge boxes like railroad freight cars, and I had my first real intimation that the Army might be asking us to perform out of our league: a manifest tacked to each enormous box said, among other things, "Aircraft, L-4, cost to US Govt., $800.; crate, 1942 M-2, cost to US Govt., $1200." The thought that our airplanes cost less than the boxes they came in was disquieting.

Our ship sailed from Staten Island. We had staged at a camp up the Hudson River, then taken the train for Staten Island, and we arrived at the Battery about five-thirty in the afternoon, just as all those commuters were boarding *their* trains, to go the other way. The nine hundred members of the 93rd Battalion streamed off our train, each man laden with two barracks bags stuffed to bursting ("place the contents of your A bag in your B bag and now proceed to pack your A bag with the following additional items") as well as various weapons hung about the person, and one and all suffering a certain nervous anxiety, mixed with equally nervous hilarity. Somehow a feeling swept through us that the ferryboats to Staten Island wouldn't wait for us—we would miss the war!—and we all started running. Just ahead of me my half-track driver tripped and fell, and lay in full view of all those commuters, pinned to the ground by those two barracks bags and two

Thompson .45-caliber submachine guns slung across his chest. As I stumbled past him I saw that Louis, in his nervousness, was, in his supine position, peeing great fountains up through his od's, and couldn't free his arms from those barracks bags in order to hide his shame from all those civilians. *La Gloire!* By God, we were off to war at last.

At Staten Island, the troopship, a converted banana boat, was modified to carry some eight hundred men. Through some mix-up or other, for which the Army and Navy blamed each other, twenty-four hundred men were at dockside, and all had to be crammed aboard. It was done, of course ("place the contents of your A bag in your B bag" et cetera). As we stepped on deck, a Naval officer buckled an inflatable life belt around each man's waist: below decks an officer of the 93rd, trying to shove me and my barracks bags and submachine guns into the topmost tier of an eight-high bunk rack, pushed me so hard the strings on the belt caught, the vest inflated, and I was stuck, half in, half out of the bunk. Somebody finally deflated the vest by puncturing it with a trench knife, and the next thing I knew, we were off.

The term "air section" perhaps requires explanation. It referred to the battalion's two pilots, the airplane mechanic, the armored half-track driver, and sometimes a 6 X 6 driver, a 6 X 6 being a two-and-a-half-ton truck used to collect gasoline and other supplies from appropriate dumps. The half-track was part of the air section only because we belonged to an armored battalion: its sole function for the air section was to beat down the grass in rough pastures we used for landing fields. We were *not* a fighting unit on the ground: attacked by German infantry, the half-track would have surrendered immediately, despite the fact it usually mounted one .50-caliber and three .30-caliber machine guns.

As a rule, we were not within range of even the most ambitious German infantry. At first, we located ourselves on farm fields as close to the battalion as possible, but a 105-mm. battalion must be pretty close to the front, since the effective range of the guns is only some ten thousand yards. The sight of L-4s landing and taking off within full view of German ground artillery observers was something those Germans could not resist, and they shelled those forward landing strips with such intensity, once night fell and we could not retaliate, that we learned prudence and stayed back a few miles. The L-4 was not built for night flying: it lacked the instruments and we lacked the training, and directing artillery fire at night is not easy in any case. You can't find the ground references, such as road intersections or bridges or farmhouses, which correspond to the references on your map. And without those, you can't tell the guns where to shoot. You did not say, "Jesus! There's a Panther tank over by the woods! Let him have it!" No, you said, "Baker One Able, this is Baker Three Able. I have a target for you, coordinates one niner niner three, six niner two, enemy tank, one round smoke when ready," assuming those numbers to be the coordinates nearest the Panther tank—or the artillery battery or the column of soldiers or the lone man on the motorcycle or the staff car of whatever it was you'd spotted. There was also the problem of German night fighters.

German fighters in the daytime were not a serious problem after North Africa, where the Luftwaffe lost air superiority forever. Some German fighter units did develop tactics to cope with the L-4s: two fighters attacked straight on, two from above, and two from below. This usually brought down the L-4, but there were never enough German fighters available on the Western front to make the technique widespread. The fact that it was used at all, tying up six scarce and valuable fighter aircraft against one feeble, eight-hundred-dollar L-4, is an indication of how the L-4s hurt the Germans. It was literally suicide for them to move anything in daylight within the eyesight of anybody in an L-4. My own battalion consisted of eighteen howitzers: at my command, all of them would pump a dreadful rain of high explosive on the target, and do it incredibly quickly. By the time the first shell reached the target from any given gun, the sixth shell was leaving the muzzle. The gun crews worked so rapidly that the ejecting shell casing had to be knocked out of the way by one of the gunners in order to make way for the fresh shell going into the breech. It was this quickness in getting on the target and rapid rate of fire that allowed the unarmed and unarmored L-4s to survive: a German antiaircraft battery knew it had to hit us with the first salvo, for we would surely spot their muzzle flashes and give them hell if they missed. Very few antiaircraft gunners are that sure of themselves, especially those with heavy-caliber weapons, since the heavier the caliber the bigger and more embarrassing the muzzle flash. Machine gunners and riflemen were not thus inhibited, but we usually flew at about three thousand feet, figuring a thousand yards was about the maximum unpleasant range of light weapons. Also, although the L-4s *were* unarmored as far as the Army was concerned, I had an iron stove lid in my seat beneath my parachute: that way I could at least avoid the worst.

The fact that we were unarmed was a constant annoyance. Many a tank or truck convoy got away because it was out of range of the 105s and the heavier guns took too long to get on target. Some attempts were made at firing bazookas from the wing struts, but accurate aiming was impossible. There was also a period when some L-4 pilots took to tossing out five-gallon cans of gasoline, which burst on impact like napalm, but that wasn't accurate either and was hard physical work besides, so we finally just left it to the guns.

The time I most regretted not having rockets or cannon aboard came somewhere north of Rome, when I was flying point for an armored column, with John Buckfelder as my observer. (You don't always take an observer: rarely, in fact. It depended on whether the landing field was long enough to let you take off with extra weight. It usually wasn't.)

Buckfelder and I had been having a quiet day, no targets, when about three in the afternoon we saw the impossible: a Tiger tank creeping along in the open on a narrow country road. The Tigers were monstrous: this one hung over the sides of the two-lane road and couldn't have been doing more than five miles an hour. We started calling fire down on it, but the 105 shells just popped like firecrackers against that heavy armor, so we "went upstairs," as the argot had it, and asked for 155-mm. Long Toms. They had more effect: a body suddenly appeared in the road behind the tank, apparently a crew member killed by concussion and dropped out the bottom, through the escape hatch. By now I had circled down to about three hundred feet above the road and Buchfelder and I were hollering into the microphones for more fire, more fire! You didn't get a Tiger tank in the open every day, and we felt sure he was going to get away because the high-explosive shells weren't penetrating his armor. But this Tiger had a gazogene unit bolted to the rear, one of those charcoal-burning contraptions the Germans used to save gasoline, and a 155 shell burst squarely in it. A small fire sprang up on the Tiger's rump. The tank kept moving in a straight line off the road and down a cliff, where it burst into real flame.

The L-4, which we came to call the "Maytag Messerschmitt," was not a comfortable airplane. You sat with your knees almost up to your chest, the aileron cable rubbed the top of your skull every time you moved the stick to left or right, it was unheated in winter, and you couldn't smoke because raw gasoline fumes filled the cockpit from the tank, which was right between your knees, just behind the instrument panel with nothing between the gasoline and a German bullet but air and thin aluminum. In summer it was often difficult to get the plane off the ground, because it didn't perform well in hot air; in winter you had to wipe the frost off the wings or it wouldn't take off at all. Unlike the glamorous folk flying real airplanes, we did not give our craft names: we named our jeeps and half-tracks, but not our L-4s. They had numbers, not names, and they were expendable: people set fire to them on beaches when it appeared the infantry was not going to hold the beachhead, they ran them into ditches trying to land on narrow roads, they flew them into high-tension wires, at least one ran headlong into a train, another hit the radio aerial on a German command car and barely fluttered back to safety, one collided with an aerial tramway in France, and at Anzio one ran into a 155 shell fired by the pilot's own battalion. There was even an L-4 that ran into a donkey on take-off, tearing off a wing and upsetting the donkey, without doing him any permanent damage whatever. The pilot in that case—me—was so enraged he ran to the tent for his pistol, intent on doing some damage to the donkey, but by the time he found the .45 in the bottom of his B bag, the creature had fled.

We lived, most of the time, in those tents, the pyramidal model, six or eight of us, and three months without a bath was not unusual. If you somehow went off and got a bath by yourself and then came back, your tentmates were intolerable: either everybody got a bath or nobody got a bath, and you could hardly have an entire air section off having a bath at one time.

We occasionally left laundry to be done in some village or other, but almost always the war moved on before the laundry was ready, and you moved with it. To this day I must have bundles of long johns and woolen shirts waiting for me up the length of the Italian peninsula and France, Austria, and Germany.

Monte Cassino: the first time I saw it, from about twenty

or thirty miles away, at three thousand feet, it was beautiful, a Disney dream of a mountain, rearing up from the floor of the Liri Valley almost as steeply as Yosemite's Half Dome. Not quite that steeply, of course: you could hardly make war on the face of Half Dome, but my God, how you could make war on Monte Cassino. It dominated the valley, which broadens at that point to a width of some thirty miles, maybe less. To the south, where the Americans, British, and French were, the mountains were smaller, the valleys narrower. The Germans had fought bitterly to keep us from the broad Liri Valley, which leads to Rome: once arrived at the mouth of that valley, we found ourselves fixed in place, the fierce glare of German observers on that mountain making us as naked and vulnerable as the L-4s made the Germans.

It was truly a beautiful mountain, in the beginning. At the foot, the town of Cassino, a highway intersection, red-tiled roofs, a provincial life, farms on the outskirts, and a hotel called the Continental. I did not enter the Continental Hotel until 1967, and by that time it had changed its name and the Tiger tank was no longer in the lobby. For months in 1943, the Tiger *was* in the lobby, while Americans and Germans fought each other in the rooms upstairs, tossing grenades back and forth, machine-gunning each other on the staircases. A sort of Italian Stalingrad.

But of course as an L-4 pilot I was not obliged to take part in that. Our mission was primarily counter-battery fire: the Germans had amassed large amounts of artillery in the valley, and we fired back and forth at each other, all day, every day, week after week, month after month, while our infantry tried to take the heights around Monte Cassino.

Much has been written about the infantry battle, one of the worst for both sides during the whole war in the West, but from the air, it was episodic; rarely did I have any sense of a planned campaign or even of massive effort. There were exceptions, of course: a regiment of the 36th Division crossed the Rapido River, which joins the Volturno at Cassino. A regiment was three battalions of infantry, roughly three thousand men. They crossed at night, on Treadway bridges, which were simple affairs, designed to carry trucks or tanks: two parallel strips of perforated steel planks. The regiment passed through the 93rd's area, which was just south of Monte Trocchio, the closest fold in the terrain to Cassino (that is, the closest large enough to shield 105-mm. howitzers), and a battery of the 93rd was scheduled to cross at daylight to provide close support, but at daylight all hell broke loose. The Germans shelled and destroyed the Treadway bridges, and when I arrived above the river about 5:30 A.M. that regiment of the 36th Division was flattened on the bare, naked, hostile ground on the wrong side of the Rapido. There was no cover, not even a bush, much less a ravine, and German artillery and mortar fire was landing on the area incessantly. We fired at dozens of muzzle flashes, but the effect was negligible: the German stuff kept coming, 88s, 105s, 150s, even *Nebel-werfers,* the short-range heavy German mortars that the infantry called "Screaming Meemies," because of the fierce howl the projectiles made as they came down. It was, for me, and God knows for the GI's on the ground, a horrible, helpless feeling. The German fire went on all day, and some of the infantrymen of the 36th broke and tried to swim the Rapido. I saw dozens plunge into the water of the river, which was only some fifty feet wide, but I saw none make it to the other bank. The Germans had, with superb military foresight, dumped coils of concertina barbed wire into the river to lie two or three feet below the surface, invisible from the banks. Military barbed wire, of course, is not like barbed wire you see on an American farm: the barbs are three or four inches long, very numerous, and they seize a soldier's uniform like steel cactus. I flew back and forth over the Rapido, directing fire all over the Liri Valley, wherever I could spot German batteries in action, and watched those little brown figures jump into the river and disappear. I'm not certain now, but I believe I cried: I was, after all, only twenty-two years old, and the 36th Division was the Texas National Guard Division. I grew up in Texas, and I had childhood friends in that regiment. Three of them never got back across the Rapido.

Oh, Monte Cassino, Monte Cassino! That beautiful, beautiful mountain: flying above Mignano, the destroyed town that dominated the approach to Cassino, the mountain loomed in blue haze, smoky: its peak appeared to be topped with eternal snow, but as one drew closer, the haze cleared and you saw it was not snow, it was the abbey, the abbey of Monte Cassino, white, white, *whiter* than snow, glittering, pure, high above the grunt and stink and killing of the valley. Founded some fourteen hundred years before our arrival, a marvel, a monument to God and man. Well, that didn't last long, once we got there.

After the war there was a great deal of argument about the abbey. The Vatican said no German soldiers were ever in or near it, and the Germans said the same thing. Well, that's bull: on several occasions I saw German machine-gun tracers coming from its northeast corner. The gun was either inside the abbey itself or firing from a position built into the exterior wall. I called fire on the spot each time, and the 93rd responded each time. After months of infantry assaults that broke against the mountain and the town at its foot, the Allies decided they would bomb their way through Monte Cassino. Though rarely mentioned in historical accounts, the first bomb attacks were made by P-40s based at a field near Naples: they dived with five-hundred-pound bombs. I was at three thousand feet, to fire the 93rd at any Germany flak batteries that opened up on the P-40s, and I can still see the fighters diving, their .50-caliber machine-gun bullets sparking on the mountain as they zeroed in, then the steep pull-up, followed seconds later by the geyser of smoke, flame, and dirt of the bomb's explosion. As they pulled out and away, headed for home and a hot shower, they zoomed all around me in my seventy-five-mile-an-hour machine, so close their slip-stream rocked and jolted the L-4.

But that bomb attack didn't work: the P-40s had concentrated on the mountainside, avoiding the abbey and the town of Cassino itself. They hit fortified German positions on the slopes and provided the Americans with a flood of bomb-shocked German prisoners, driven out of their minds by concussion, but bombing the mountain did not open the way to Rome. When the next attempt came from the air, it was a disaster.

If I ever knew what the tactical thinking was behind the second attack, I've forgotten. In those days, we all thought that heavy bomb raids were demoralizing and so destructive that nothing could survive in the target area, so, somewhere up the chain of command, the decision was made to bomb Cassino town *and* the abbey with medium and heavy bombers—B-25s, B-26s, and B-17s. I saw those types in the air: there may also have been B-24s, but they didn't cross my vision. What *did* cross my vision, floating over the abbey at three thousand feet—assignment: suppress heavy flak—was an oncoming and seemingly never-ending fleet of bombers, approaching from the south. The mediums were at about six or seven thousand feet; the heavies were way up there, just silhouettes. The heavy German flak, mostly 88s, went mad: the floor of the Liri Valley was sprinkled with red-orange muzzle flashes as the Germans threw everything they had at this incredible number of American bombers, a number seen up to then only over the *Heimat* itself. It must have struck the German flak crews as a splendid chance to get even, but they needn't have bothered. I saw not one American airplane hit by flak. I did see American bombs exploding all around the compass, twenty miles beyond the target, twenty miles short of the target, twenty miles to the left, twenty miles to the right. A fair number even landed on Cassino town and the abbey, but most landed in Allied territory. To watch a bombing run of that magnitude, involving hundreds of aircraft, was an awesome thing, to put it mildly; those heavy bombs sent up volcanoes of dirt and fire, the air shook, you could see ripples running across the surface of the earth as though an earthquake were in progress, and you felt the concussion even at three thousand feet. But my God, how inaccurate they were! The result of this second raid, which went on all morning, was that the town of Cassino was turned to rubble, making it impassable for American tanks, which were poised to attack, and the abbey also was turned to rubble, even though no Allied soldiers were near it. Fourteen hundred years were blown away that morning.

As I noted earlier, German flak crews were very cautious in shooting at the L-4s, but of course there were times when they thought the odds were in their favor and would let fly. Flak came in various calibers, from the big 88s on down to 20-mm. rapid-fire cannon, often mounted on half-tracks or flat-bed trucks. The 88s usually fired a "ladder" of six rounds, apparently hoping you'd fly into one of the three pairs, and people sometimes did. But the muzzle flash of the 88 was so large and bright that you couldn't miss it. In the Vosges in France I was flying near Bitche when six brown bursts appeared off my right wing, not close enough to do any harm. However, I had seen the muzzle flashes from a village across the Rhine, and when I radioed the 93rd's fire direction center and gave them the coordinates, they poured thirty-six rounds into the village; there were no more "ladders" from that quarter. On that mission, I became so intent on watching the effect of the fire that I made the supreme error of not keeping my head moving: you had to keep looking up, down, behind and on all sides. Although the Luftwaffe was occupied primarily at that stage with the Eastern front, there *were* fighter squadrons in the West, too. And sure enough, when I finally looked away from the target area, a Messerschmitt 109 was boring straight in at me, about a hundred yards away. I froze, unable to move the controls, and just sat there staring at the enormous, bright red spinner on his prop, certain this was it. But he zipped past beneath me, rocking the L-4, without firing a shot. I assume he was returning from a mission and had run out of ammo.

One of the strangest experiences I had with flak occurred near Dijon. The weather was atrocious—a cloud cover at about five hundred feet and misting rain. I was cruising back and forth near a village, at about three hundred feet, when I spotted six small, rapid muzzle flashes from the main street of the village. I depressed the button on the mike to give coordinates, but before I could speak, the six 20-mm. rounds burst around the airplane. I hollered into the open microphone, "Jesus Christ! The bastards are shooting at me!" The fire direction center said, very calmly, "Coordinates please." Very unprofessional behavior on my part. Anyway, I dropped down and hedge-hopped while I gave the coordinates, the fire direction center radioed, "One round smoke, on the way!" I pulled up to three hundred feet again, and the white phosphorus round burst alongside the flak wagon, which in this case was a flat-bed truck. I dived again, told the 93rd to fire for effect, again they radioed, "On the way!" and again I pulled up, to see six rounds of high explosives smother the truck. It's marvelous to be young and have reflexes which make you push the mike button before the enemy's rounds even arrive in your neighborhood: alas, those days and those reflexes are gone forever. Nowadays I can't even tell when a network vice-president is after my ass, until it's too late to take cover.

Our own antiaircraft fire was notoriously inaccurate, partly, no doubt, because the crews had very few targets to practice on, and we often had reason to thank God for that. I think most L-4 pilots were shot at by their own side at least once. The U.S. Navy found it impossible to distinguish between L-4s and German aircraft, and flying anywhere near a

U.S. warship during an amphibious landing was a hairy experience. At Anzio, where we sometimes had to fly courier runs from Monte Cassino, there was a rule that the L-4s had to enter the beachhead area precisely at the point where the front line curved down to the sea. This was supposed to tell the Navy that you were friendly, but it didn't, and the Germans *knew* you weren't friendly. The result was a sky filled with carpets of U.S. Navy gunfire, while the Germans below emptied machine guns and rifles into the air. Bill Leonard, who is now president of CBS News, was a gunnery officer on a destroyer during that war, and once when he and I were exchanging war stories, it gradually developed that he had personally shot at me all over the Mediterranean.

The Navy had nothing to do with my most upsetting experience with American antiaircraft, however. We were operating out of a cow pasture near the German village of Frankenhofen, attached to a fresh division whose L-4 pilots were very green. One morning hundreds of German soldiers started trickling out of the surrounding woods to give themselves up, since the war was obviously ending. We made them sit down in a corner of the pasture and went on flying missions, but at noon a German Red Cross nurse turned up on a bicycle and told us, in French, that an SS armored detachment was in the next village, about ten kilometers away, and the SS did *not* think the war was obviously ending. In fact, the nurse told us, the SS people were so annoyed by the soldiers who had surrendered to us that they were gearing up for an attack on their comrades and us. I immediately told the inexperienced captain commanding the division air section that we should get the hell out of there, but he pooh-poohed the idea, saying he didn't think the nurse was telling the truth, so we kept on flying missions throughout the afternoon.

Finally the sun went down, the flying stopped, and I braced myself for a very uneasy night. Then, just before bedtime, the nurse turned up again; this time she said the SS were on the way. Instant pandemonium. Gear was tossed into half-tracks and trucks, the captain pointed out on the map a bombed-out German airstrip to our front and said we'd fly there.

We took off in pitch darkness. Over the radio I heard the other aircraft calling, trying to establish the compass course and warning one another to stay out of the way. These were fruitless instructions, since you couldn't see any other airplanes. The radio traffic was heard by our battalions, of course, and all the fire direction centers came on the air, demanding to know what was up. We told them they'd get details later and meanwhile to stay off the air. I kept droning along at about two thousand feet, hoping I had the proper compass course and wondering how I would spot the bombed-out airfield even if I *was* on course. A half-moon came out from behind some clouds, which helped a little: you could see reflections on rivers and ponds, but not much else. Suddenly, there was a great burst of orange flame on the ground below us, and what seemed like every antiaircraft weapon in the U.S. Army opened up, spouting tracers in all directions. I dived, hoping my altimeter was reasonably accurate and that there were no high-tension lines in the neighborhood, and hollered into the radio to the 93rd to tell the antiaircraft people to cut that out. A German bomber had unloaded on a bridge that was heavily defended against aerial attack. Presumably he had picked up our L-4s on his radar and had sneaked in under cover of those radar reflections, knowing American radar couldn't distinguish him from us.

We got past that and actually found the bombed-out German airfield: the concrete of the ruined runways gleamed in the moonlight, and there was just enough left of one of them to put down an L-4. One pilot did get lost for about an hour and called frantically and constantly over the radio for help. Finally the division captain told him we would fire a .50-caliber machine gun and he could home in on the tracers. We fired into the air, and instantly every other .50-caliber in the neighborhood did the same, apparently under the impression that another air raid was in progress. Some of their rounds came quite close to the lost pilot, to judge by the squeaking tone which came from him over the radio, but he finally found us and landed. It was a very busy night, and we never did find out if the SS detachment made a run at our Frankenhofen strip.

German artillery, tanks, and flak batteries could not avoid giving away their positions as soon as they went into action, of course, but the German infantrymen were wizards at the art of cover and concealment. From the air, they were almost never to be seen, either in attack or retreat, but I do recall one remarkable exception. Flying under a heavy overcast at about five hundred feet in Burgundy, I was astonished to see a column of some fifty German soldiers riding bicycles along the shoulder of a secondary road, not a quarter mile away. They must have heard my engine, but there they were, pedaling along at a leisurely pace, rifles slung across their backs. The road ran straight for about two miles, then bent into a horseshoe curve around a small hill. I radioed the coordinates of the horseshoe bend to the fire direction center, adjusted the smoke rounds until they were landing in the bend, then waited for the bicycle column to arrive at that spot. When it did, we fired six rounds from each gun in B Battery, making thirty-six high-explosive shells in all. An officer of the 93rd visited the area the next day and found some twenty mangled bicycles lying alongside the road.

Compared with the Germans, we were prodigal with our artillery ammunition. They had to be rather miserly, but we shot at anything that moved or even looked suspicious. On several occasions I chased solitary motorcycle riders with 105-mm. rounds that cost about ninety dollars each, without ever hitting one, so far as I know. The motorcyclists were considered worthwhile targets because the assumption was they were dispatch riders carrying orders back and forth between various headquarters, so we would pump out dozens of shells at them. I was doing just that one day north of Rome when, with that marvelous peripheral vision granted the young and healthy, I saw a horse run out from the woods with a man hanging on to its bridle, struggling to drag the horse back under cover. I was low enough to see he was wearing *Feldgrau,* so I called for a round of smoke in the woods. It burst, and immediately dozens of horse-drawn artillery pieces, caissons, field kitchens, and wagons came plunging out of the trees onto the road, headed north at full gallop. They had obviously holed up there waiting for nightfall before moving into new positions, but they now found themselves on a straight stretch of road in broad daylight. The horse-drawn column was thoroughly raked, and all because one horse had bolted into the open, driven berserk, no doubt, by the noise of our shells chasing the motorcycle rider.

During the week-long battle of Montélimar, in the Rhone Valley, I came as close to ground combat as I ever care to get. We were operating from a farm near the village of Loriol. The farm family had fled, leaving the place in the charge of a hired hand, who was clearly not right in the head. The battle had developed when a combat command column of armor, artillery, and infantry had raced northward from southern France along roads paralleling the Rhone, then turned westward north of Montélimar, cutting the main highway. The German 19th Army was trying to go north to support the German defenses in Normandy, so this created a problem. The highway was soon littered with shot-up tanks, trucks, and artillery pieces, burning hulks strung out over ten miles. From the air we could see a German counterattack starting up from the northeast, and since the infantry was heavily engaged along the highway to the west, there was nothing to stop the German attack but artillery. The shooting was frantic and incessant: on one day I flew more than ten hours, landing every two hours or so for gasoline, but the German armored cars and light tanks kept edging closer and closer and by nightfall of that day were within about two miles of our farm. Assuming they would push on during the night, we built a hollow square of hay bales in the barn, and crawled inside it, pulling another bale over the entrance. The idea was that the German infantry, when they came, would go right on by. And sure enough, they did come, Schmeisser machine pistols burping bullets in every direction, but we were perfectly safe in our hay-bale cave. Unfortunately, however, we had given that hired hand a cup of instant coffee during the day, the first he'd had since the war began, no doubt, and he chose this moment to come into the barn with a kerosene lantern to thank us for it. In horror we watched the light get brighter through the cracks between the hay bales, then he pulled away the one covering our entrance hole, leaned in, and said, with the beautiful smile of the idiot, "Nescafé est bon!" We waited for the Germans to jump him and us, but they didn't. By the time the night was over, we were ready to shoot the hired hand ourselves, since he repeated the same stunt four more times. Years later, my mother heard from the mother of our mechanic that he had recurring nightmares in which he woke, shouting, "Nescafé est bon!" and she wondered if my mother could ask me about it. You just don't need civilians at a time like that.

There were exceptions, of course: when I landed my L-4 in a field in southern France, after taking off from an LST which had been fitted with a plywood flight deck, I jumped out of the airplane before it stopped rolling and crawled into a clump of bushes. The situation was, as they say, "fluid," and I didn't know where the infantry line was located. Lying there, I heard somebody running in my direction and puckered up considerably, expecting to see a German rifleman. Instead it was a French farmer carrying a bottle of red wine and a smeared glass. He filled the glass, handed it to me, and shouted, "Bienvenue! Bienvenue!" I fell in love with La Belle France on the spot and have remained in love with her ever since.

We went on through France, finally crossed the Rhine near Strasbourg, turned southeast through Germany and on into Austria. Taking off one morning from a field outside Imst, I was astonished to find the roads crammed with German vehicles of every description. Paradise for an artillery spotter! But when I began radioing fire directions, the battalion called back, "Wait." This happened several times, and I got angrier and angrier, until finally the fire direction center radioed, "Cease all forward action." When I landed, I discovered that meant the war was over. It was a terrible letdown: I had assumed the war would *never* end, or that I wouldn't be there when it did. According to my logbook I had flown 368 missions and turned a lot of beautiful German hardware into scrap. Aside from falling in love with the perfect woman, nothing has ever seemed so important or exciting since.

—October 1981

PURSUIT: NORMANDY, 1944

by CHARLES CAWTHON

An infantryman remembers how it was for the 2d Battalion of the Stonewall Brigade.

Victory in Europe seemed sure and near for the Western Allies in late summer, 1944, as their armies broke out of a shallow beachhead on the Channel coast of France and rolled, seemingly unstoppable, across Normandy, Brittany, Flanders, on to Paris, and up to the borders of Germany itself. But here, braked by worn-out men and machines and an outrun fuel supply, the advance slowed and halted. The dark winter of the Ardennes followed, and it was spring before Germany was finally reduced to the smoking, starving ruin that constituted defeat.

During the August progress of arms across France, however, any suggestion that the end to five years of devastating war could be so delayed seemed pessimistic, even unpatriotic. No liberation of towns and destruction of enemy formations (unfortunately the two often overlapped) was proclaimed in stark black and white; valor and daring versus, at best, a diabolical cunning. A sense of swashbuckling abandon was conveyed; something of a game of Allied hounds coursing the German hare.

Perhaps a distant perspective of the giant scene gave this impression. Close up, however, at the armor and infantry points of the pursuit, the sensation was not that of chasing a hare, but that of following a wounded tiger into the bush; the tiger turning now and again to slash at its tormentors, each slash drawing blood.

This is a personal account of one of those pursuing points

of infantry; the 2d Battalion, 116th Regiment (the Stonewall Brigade), 29th Infantry Division. We joined the battle on July 28, three days after the massive Allied air bombardment that launched the operation called COBRA, designed to rupture the German lines on a four-mile-wide front west of St. Lô. COBRA developed into a breakout from the beachhead, and then into the great pursuit that at its height involved upward of two million men on the two sides. On August 15 the Allied invasion of southern France added another front to the massive battle.

On a battlefield of such enormous proportions, the actions of a single infantry battalion can provide only a small, closely cropped scene from a giant canvas of fire-breathing columns, writhing and twisting across a fair French countryside, trailing behind them broken men and machines, smoking villages, and trampled fields. This battalion scene, so relatively minute in time and space, covers fourteen days and some fifteen straight-line miles from the village of Moyon to the ancient town of Vire; in width it rarely measures more than two hundred yards. But it was not composed without pain, and I believe it to be a fair sample of much of the great pursuit. No swashbuckling column we, but a dogged, trudging one, at times creeping and crawling.

The Stonewall Brigade's fifteen miles cost over a thousand killed and wounded, of which the 2d Battalion bore its about one-third share. This cost was not excessive by Normandy standards, and it was light compared to the more than thirty-five hundred Stonewallers left along the twenty-mile stretch from Omaha Beach through St. Lô. Yet to lose within two weeks nearly half of the battalion's seven hundred officers and men was enough to cause an immediate hurt militarily, and a lasting one personally.

The 116th is a Virginia National Guard regiment. Its hereditary title, Stonewall Brigade, was gained at the First Battle of Manassas in the Civil War under General Thomas J. Jackson. The regiment was mustered for World War II in 1941. By August, 1944, relatively few Virginians remained; many were in the military cemetery at La Cambe; more were in hospital or had been invalided home. These losses were made good with draftees from across the country and resulted in ranks as much Yankee as Virginian.

With the seniority gained from chance survival of its

battles, I had advanced from company commander to battalion major and executive officer. The battalion commander was of tested combat worthiness. He was a professional product of West Point, but unorthodox and irreverent enough to lead amateurs whose approach to soldiering was aggressively temporary.

The eight days between the taking of St. Lô and joining COBRA were spent by the 29th Division in corps reserve, refitting with men and material. The 2d Battalion's bivouac was among orchards of ancient, gnarled apple trees outside the village of St. Clair-sur-l'Elle, which we had taken in a night attack just over a month before. The luxury of hot meals, showers, clean uniforms, and being away from the immediate vicinity of death and destruction obscured the discouraging fact that the crusade in Europe had advanced little more than three miles during that month of hard fighting and heavy losses. (There were vague reports of the July 20 attempt to assassinate Hitler, and a momentary hope that this might mean the collapse of the German army, but nothing came of it, and it was accepted that the war would have to be fought out the hard way.)

The weather that since D-day had alternated between damp cold and sultry heat turned pleasantly warm and bright. The sickening smell of cordite with which war infected the countryside had blown away, and our orchard was green and summer-smelling. For recreation, motion pictures ran all day in a blacked-out barn, the film spotty and jerky from constant use. These wartime films, like wartime writing, projected a streak of blatant unreality, but they were enjoyed, for this was the tenor of the times and we were all attuned to it.

A Red Cross canteen truck also appeared at intervals with two representatives of American womanhood to dispense coffee, doughnuts, and paperback books. The doughnuts had the weak flavor of rationing, but some of the books were full bodied. There is a pleasant memory of lying in the orchard grass on soft summer evenings reading MacKinlay Kantor's *Long Remember,* a novel woven into the historical fabric of the Gettysburg battle.

A chasm of time and circumstance separated Gettysburg, 1863, and Normandy, 1944, but I found it bridged by the casual and mindless unconcern with which the armies at the two places and times wreaked havoc on each other and on all about them.

The tension and fatigue of the forty-five days of battle just behind us gave way to lethargy. The major general commanding the 29th, however, was a detector and eradicator of lethargy, and on the second day in reserve a training schedule was ordained that included close-order drill. The battalion dutifully and profanely tramped by platoons and companies over rough pasture sharing sweat and temper that helped meld the new men in with the veterans. This was well, for in the long stretch at St. Lô there had been instances of new men being wounded or dying as strangers without names to those around them.

Lethargy got its comeuppance on a dull July afternoon at a training session on hedgerow assault tactics. Little attention was paid to this requirement other than to assign a company to run a squad demonstration for the battalion. The company commander was new and relied on a sergeant who had been in the hedgerow fighting to stage it. The demonstration was not a model for the infantry school. The battalion, trailing along in worse array than the gallery at a golf tournament, could see little and hear less. An awareness of not having given enough direction to the assignment peaked as the general arrived unexpectedly, with his usual velocity, took it all in with a glittering eye, and delivered several pungently phrased judgments. The price for such a lapse during pre-D-day training would have been harsh and immediate, but as a battalion that had pulled its combat weight, we got off with blisters. It was enough to get us back on the job, and to give the troops further cause to wish the war over.

Other scenes emerge from the shifting memories of that eight-day interlude. One is of sending a detachment of veterans to represent the battalion at the division's memorial service at La Cambe Cemetery. On their return, I thought I had never seen such somber young men. Each had a friend or more in the newly mounded graves; a corporal told me in a controlled voice that it looked as though a whole division were being buried there.

This seemed a possibility, for so far as we could foresee, the small, deadly battles for one hedgerow at a time would continue indefinitely. Superiority in manpower, fire power, and air power assured the taking of that next hedgerow, provided the price was paid; but then there would be another and another. This was the close-up, ground-level view of the war. At First Army Headquarters, which dealt in larger views, plans were being completed for COBRA. Central to these plans was a massive air strike that was to blast a corridor through the German defenses that fronted on the St. Lô-Périers highway. Four infantry and two armored divisions of VII Corps were then to attack to complete the breach.

COBRA was to be launched on July 24, but, once a portion of the bomber force was airborne from England, it was decided that dangerously poor visibility over the target required a postponement. A number of formations did not get the recall signal and made their runs, some bombs falling short into the attack assembly areas and causing casualties and disruption. The next day, with better visibility and added precautions, the air strike went in again in full force. Once more, however, human error showed its amazing versatility; bombs were again dropped into the assembly areas, resulting in more deaths, including that of a ranking general.

Despite this, the infantry advanced and wedged a way into the bomb-wracked defenses. COBRA was under way and soon promised significant results. The sulphurous war of words between the ground and air staffs over fault for the bombing errors was overladen by the sweet smell of success.

I recite this well-worn history to develop a facet of the infantry battalion's image of itself: that all things somehow work against it, even those designed to help. We had constant occasion to appreciate Allied air power, but were also wary of it; some claimed it safer to be *on* the bombing target than near it.

Still ignorant of COBRA, we watched the planes go over, and heard the distant rolling thunder of their carpet bombing. Then came word of the offensive, and an alert order to join it on July 28. Camp was struck early, and late that afternoon trucks arrived to convoy us to the front, the exact location not known.

I closed the rear of the motor march, and so watched the trucks pass at careful sixty-yard intervals, each loaded with serious-faced young men seated on benches on either side, rifles between their knees and packs stacked in the middle. I was again impressed by how little of the "old," pre-D-day battalion, remained; those who did stood out by indefinable expression and posture.

The convoy trundled slowly down the dusty road that was

bounded on both sides by tangles of communication wire, wrecked farm buildings, broken hedgerows, and into St. Lô, itself, a barren desert of broken masonry through which a roadway had been 'dozed. Here we stalled in the enormous traffic that trails a major advance. The 2d Armored Division had been committed to the growing prospects of COBRA, and the pressure of its supply train compressed the column until the trucks were head to tail, lurching forward a few yards at a time. Sitting in the middle of such a bountiful target was uncomfortable, but proved uneventful; the German artillery still within range was apparently more concerned with the forward edge of COBRA than with its rear.

After two hours, and about five miles south of St. Lô, we were deposited by the roadside, where again we waited while a warm, still, and very dark night came on, the southeastern horizon glowing red at intervals with gun flashes. It was near midnight when our destination order arrived by a jeep that crept toward us, its cat's-eye blackout lights glowing evilly. The battalion formed up and started down the dusty road that in places stank of burned cordite. After two hours the march became a plodding column, more asleep than awake. All traffic had disappeared; we were in a dark void treading a shade lighter line of roadway; even the war had stopped growling in the distance. About 0300 the assembly area was reached and the companies stumbled off into the fields.

Then it was discovered that Headquarters Company, bringing up the rear, was missing. I told the commander that I would find it and, without going into my performance in closing the column, he observed that this was a damn good idea. I started back over our route looking for what amounted to a moving black dot in a vast expanse of darkness. Sleep was becoming the end of all desire when I literally collided with the captain at the head of his trance-walking company. There was a mumbled exchange over not having gotten the start signal at the last break, and we trudged on to the assembly area. The battalion commander was relieved that the lost had been found, and on this happier note I left the world and its foolish war for the incalculably greater attractions of oblivion.

Awakening came shortly after dawn with the blast of a rifleshot from an adjoining hedgerow, where, it developed, one of the new men had wounded himself in the foot. He moaned in shock and pain that it was an accident; whether so or not, he was our first, and inglorious, casualty of COBRA. The condition of his foot indicated poor premeditation, if such it was.

Drifting away and out of any battalion portrait are the furtive shapes of the stragglers; a few with self-inflicted wounds; many more simply quitting through physical and emotional weariness. These latter, called combat-fatigue cases, were tolerated, I believe, to an unnecessary and disturbing degree.

By 1944 the infantry battalions were composed largely of draftees. But, given the low degree of coercion applied to keep them there, they were draftees for the army, and volunteers for the fight—as good company as a man could wish, but tragic in that so many were doomed by their own courage.

The 2d Battalion started southward that morning, feeling its way through a milky-white ground fog that lay over fields and orchards, damp and cool. The regiment's objective was a sector centering on Moyon, reported sparsely held by the 2d Armored Division. Battle groups of German tanks and infantry were in front of and behind Moyon.

Our advance found one of these battle groups as we closed in on our objective south of the village. Two newly assigned lieutenants and the scouts of the two leading companies went down in the first blast of machine-gun fire. The Stonewall Brigade's three battalions deployed along the line of opposition; we had again grappled with the enemy, and whatever our individual reluctance, corporately, we would not let go.

That night, the *Luftwaffe* mustered a lone plane to drone along the front, dropping flares whose white glare created a feeling of unwholesome exposure.

Intermittent shelling continued the next morning. In the midst of it we were ordered to send a company to a crossroads, called La Denisière, to the rear of our right flank where there was an uncertain report of a roadblock of German tanks. G Company was given the mission, and around that inconspicuous crossing of dusty Normandy roads waged one of those small, bloody battles that leave their mark on those in them, but hardly a whisper in history.

The day, July 30, also left its mark on me; late in its afternoon I received word that the battalion commander had been hit in the forearm and was being evacuated. I was to take command. My first sensation was one of such complete inadequacy that it seemed important to share it with the regimental commander. I took a jeep back to his command post and advised him that there were undoubtedly officers standing around better qualified for the job. The colonel did not dispute this, but told me that I had accepted the promotion to executive officer, and I would now go back and command the battalion. My reluctance, however, must have raised doubt as to my qualities of dynamic leadership, for that evening he sent up a senior captain from his staff as executive officer and potential replacement.

So I shouldered the full weight of the war, going first to La Denisière where G Company had gained control of the crossroads. A German half-track, its radio still crackling Teutonic military jargon, was tilted into a ditch, the bodies of the crew strewn about.

The crossroads lay across the route of a new division being committed to COBRA, and the German command thought enough of its tactical value to waste scarce armor trying to block it. G Company had paid the price: lying near the half-track was a lieutenant who had joined us the week before, unconscious and breathing with the heavy snoring characteristic of head wounds. Other still forms were collected in the shade of a hedgerow.

The day's cost didn't end with G Company: the veteran F Company commander and another new lieutenant from H Company were also killed; wounded men and emotional casualties amounted to another squad or so. Add the loss of the battalion commander, and the toll for the pursuit was mounting, though we had hardly started.

That night the German flare plane was accompanied by a bomber but disturbed nothing in the 2d Battalion except rest. With this second appearance, the flare plane naturally acquired the title of "Bed-Check Charlie."

The next day was spent in place. Throughout the morning seven Panzers probed across our front, then suddenly turned and began blasting the hedgerows held by E Company. The company claimed disabling bazooka hits on one that was towed away by the others. Later a young German officer in the black Panzer uniform was brought in, his lower jaw a bloody mess of smashed teeth, bone, and flesh. He was on his feet but could make only gurgling noises and hold his head in obviously harrowing pain. Compassion for an enemy, I found, diminishes as a battle drags on—in the Western theater it was to reach a nadir in the misery of the Ardennes—but enough remained that day for me to send him back to the aid station by jeep.

Patrols that night found the Germans gone. The reason, though we did not know it, was that VIII Corps, on the right flank of COBRA, was breaking through to the coastal town of Avranches. Through this corridor, the U.S. Third Army was to sweep westward into Brittany, and eastward to form the southern side of the Falaise-Argentan pocket. The effect was immediate: a pullback of German tank and infantry groups began all across the front.

A departing army, taking menace with it, leaves a palpable void. Into this void the 2d Battalion advanced the next morning encountering wrecked vehicles and freshly dug roadside graves; in retreat, we found, the Germans buried their dead where they fell.

The great pursuit was on.

The 2d Battalion's advance was through full-blown summer fields and orchards, and at times along country lanes marked by tank tracks that posed the constant question of where they might stop. They did not stop that day, and we covered more than two uneventful miles, digging in at dusk and hugging the shadows of hedgerows as the flare plane came over on its nightly swing.

The day had been a rare one of no casualties. My most anxious moments had come on seeing a rifle company trudging in file across the enemy side of a grassy slope, resembling nothing so much as moving targets in a shooting gallery. Company commanders' careers in Normandy were apt to be brief and allowed little chance to accumulate experience—but this particular tactical rashness was not called to account by the German rear guard.

The next morning we started again over the rolling hills, and in a wide swale passed the debris of a tank battle. The scorched hulks of three Shermans and two Mark IV's were tumbled about, their guns tilted at odd angles. A blackened body lay halfway out of the driver's hatch of a Sherman, arms extended and fingers crooked, clawing for escape. The passing files barely glanced at the scene; even the most morbid curiosity must have been satisfied long before.

That afternoon the enemy added to their delaying force a large-caliber, long-range mortar that lobbed its huge shells in at intervals to avoid being located by our Cub artillery spotter. The mortar immediately became a dreaded thing, its shells able to blow apart anything in a field. One of the first rounds did this to a squad and further dampened any exhilaration of the chase.

The battalion pushed on late into the soft evening of that day, and started again the next morning through a white ground mist. Along the way, German stragglers came out of holes or houses and surrendered. They supplied very little useful information, being too anxious to tell what they thought we wanted to hear about the sad straits of the German army, and their personal anti-Nazi sentiments.

Also uncovered was a young American paratrooper who had been captured on D-day but had escaped to hide out with a farm family. He wore the beret and faded blue work clothes of the French farmer, but remained unmistakably American to more than a glance.

Signs of the retreat abounded, but all the weapons and equipment we passed were smashed; there was none of the litter or usable material that trails a routed army. A farm where we paused briefly had been a depot for bicycle troops, and dozens of the heavy, cumbersome machines in various stages of repair were ranked in the barn and sheds. We admired much of the German equipment: their lower-slung tanks made our Shermans appear awkwardly high and vulnerable; the P-38 pistol was highly sought; their machine pistols and machine guns had a higher cyclic rate of fire than our Brownings and seemed more deadly. I don't think, however, that any of our lads considered those bicycles as a desirable way to war, or practical as a souvenir. Some probably were repaired by the thrifty Norman farmers and are still in use.

Our zone of advance now centered on the town of Vire, which we found, in due time, to be on the eastern side of a deep ravine cut through the hills by the Vire River. Vire, like St. Lô, is a road and market center, its origins dating back into the Middle Ages. Also, as at St. Lô, the hills and ridges around it are adapted for defense, and the nearer we drew, the harder and more costly became the going.

Late on August 3, near the village of Landelles-et-Coupigny, a heavier than usual volume of artillery, mortar, and tank fire exploded across the front, and we went to ground. Our artillery blasted back, and the stained stretchers were carried to the rear with their loads.

So reminiscent was this of the approaches to St. Lô that I was convinced the rest of the way to Vire would be equally costly. This outlook grew darker with the evening until it developed into genuine gloom, a not unfamiliar emotion for me in the manic-depressive atmosphere of war. Usually able to dissemble it, I knew that I would have to come to grips with it now, for I had seen soldiers led forward by desperation, but I had never seen them follow gloom in any direction other than to the rear.

Even the small forward command-post group—all steady veterans—was too much company for this mood, so, with the radio operator, I went forward through the gloaming to a frontline hedgerow where a small squad of riflemen was dug in, resting or watching. Similar squads were in the fields to either flank, but so compartmented by the hedgerows that each had reason to feel alone in the war.

The evening had grown quiet except for the far-off rumble of heavy traffic as German armor and trucks pulled back from the developing pincer arms. Now and then the rumble was interrupted by the dull crash and dim red glow of shell fire as our artillery sought out the retreat. I stood for a few minutes watching this and the landscape just ahead, hazily lighted by some small phase of the moon. Then, on impulse, I told the radio operator to stay behind while I went up to the next hedgerow. He did not protest, nor did the squad leader, who probably saw no reason to object to a gratuitous outpost. After arranging return signals, I clambered over the hedgerow and crossed the narrow field to the front.

Here, indeed, was a rare solitude that I think can be found only in the dead space between two resting armies. It could be violated by patrols, but this was unlikely considering the German posture of retreat. I felt no fear of disturbances as I leaned into the rank growth of the chest-high hedgerow and tried to think away gloom. There was no military reason for it: we were winning the war. The 2d Battalion was a responsive command, becoming more effective by the day as the new men turned veteran. Making decisions involving lives was a heavy burden, but it was now an accustomed one, and less a moral weight in that my hide was also at stake—there is little impersonal decision making in an infantry battalion. Besides, these decisions were bounded by what we were ordered to do. For tomorrow, the order was to attack at 0530. Following a brief artillery preparation, the riflemen would maneuver forward, and if the Germans had not pulled out, some would be killed, and more wounded.

To this relentless pattern we were committed by discipline, training, pride, and by—I think—a generally held conviction that for Americans in 1944 there was no alternative. It was while groping in this dark maze of the mind that a dimly perceived movement materialized on the opposite side of the hedgerow to the left. As fiction the scene that then developed would require only ordinary imagination; to claim it as fact would be absurd. I offer it as a particularly vivid hallucination arising from fatigue long sustained and from the effect of continuing violence on an essentially nonviolent nature.

The scene that came into dim focus was a German patrol moving in my direction. This in itself would have been a sufficient shock; compounding it was a developing awareness that this patrol was not exactly of the Wehrmacht with which we had been in deadly embrace for the past two months, and its movement was as noiseless as the gathering of white ground fog in a low swale to the front.

All of this was registered under the impact of known proximity to an enemy whom I never regarded with detachment at any range. The identification that developed in more detail was with the sepia-toned pictures of the Kaiser's army in an illustrated history of the Great War that I pored over as a boy.

Soldiers of the Kaiser's Imperial Army and those of Hitler's Third Reich both wore helmets described as "coal scuttle," for their resemblance to a household implement of the era of the coal-burning stove. There were marked differences, however, between the cloth fatigue caps worn in the two wars. The cap of Hitler's army had a long bill and low crown, while the one the Kaiser's soldiers wore was round, high standing, and had no visor at all—looking something like a modified chef's bonnet, but distinctively German. Each member of the patrol that I eventually made out wore the round cap of the Kaiser's army.

Further, as the scene developed, each appeared to be

shod in the calf-high jack boots which were universal in pictures of the World War I German army. Jack boots were also favored in 1944, but I had noted that most of the prisoners we had been taking wore heavy shoes and short canvas gaiters. There was another difference. The German rear guards and patrols favored the machine pistol over the rifle, and I don't recall encountering one not so armed. But this patrol carried only rifles, the barrels slanting alternatively right and left.

Old men do indeed forget; memories merge, shift, and take nonesuch shapes. So strong, however, was the impact of the antique figures and the aura they projected that they have remained with me intact down the years. It was a hallucination of uncommon power and shock effect.

I have said that the dark figures (there were seven or eight of them) materialized suddenly and silently in space that had been empty. Countering an immediate imperative to leave was a conviction that before I lumbered a few yards those rifles could be leveled for execution as if I were a condemned man tied to a stake. I don't recall considering my service automatic adequate to the odds.

My uncalculated response was to crouch to eye level with the top of the hedgerow and stare through the rank growth at the darker figures moving toward me in the general darkness, only their upper bodies and rifles visible from my level. Seconds more and they would have been abreast. But then, without signal that I discerned, they stopped and bent below the level of the hedgerow, out of my vision. One can withhold breathing for an eternity, and I did, before the dark battle frieze again materialized above the hedgerow. But now, instead of continuing toward me they turned hard left in single file and in a predatory crouch moved the short distance into the ground fog filling the swale to become dark blobs on its white surface, and then to disappear. The turn had brought each figure into the silhouette, and I got the full effect of the caps, rifles, and the jack boots that moved without a whisper through the grass. Thus, the hallucination passed. Gradually I became aware again of the distant rumble of the retreat, and of the summer rustlings and green smells of the hedgerow. The impressionist landscape to my front, with the coal-black line of the next hedgerow drawn across it, and lighter splash of ground fog athwart its center, held mystery more haunting than menacing.

I do not know how long I stood so, and it was without conscious decision that I turned back across the narrow field to our lines, tapping the return signal on my helmet—probably unnecessarily, because the sentries and radio operator must have been able to make me out dimly the entire time.

No comments were made as I rejoined them, and self-preservation as a commander argued against mentioning that a German patrol from another war had passed by a field away.

The radio operator and I returned to the command post where, except for the man on telephone watch, all were asleep along the hedgerow. The night had the hazy, dreamlike aspect of the glade scene in *A Midsummer Night's Dream;* but here a different sort of folly was afoot.

I was aware, though, that my burden of gloom had lifted; lacking another reason, I attribute it to the shock of seeing a sight that never was. None of this says much for my emotional balance, but then there is not much to say for it at that point. Wrapping myself in a raincoat against the dew, I slept.

We were up in the dawn mist, each eating whatever part of the cold field ration he could tolerate. The artillery preparation descended, and we moved forward. Here the script departed from the one I had gloomily foreseen, for the Germans had pulled out, except for a few stragglers waiting to surrender.

Now we were pointed straight for Vire, but across the path loomed Hill 219 (its meter height) dominating the western approaches. We had advanced little more than a mile when the enormously destructive shells from the heavy mortar and artillery fire exploded along the route. More men went down, and the companies dispersed along the hedgerows. The shelling subsided, but hit us again each time we came under observation from the hill. Early in the evening we dug in, and the 3d Battalion advanced through our positions for an attack on the hill the next morning. The evening was quiet except for tank-gun fire off to the left, where the 2d Armored was battling for a bridge over the Vire.

The next day, August 5, was also costly. The 3d Battalion attacked, along with 2d Armored tanks, and gained the hill. We were ordered up on the right and reached the hill's broad, flat top just at dusk. A thin line was organized among the tanks already deployed along the eastern edge overlooking the deep, dark ravine of the Vire River and the town on the opposite side. Now and again an ear-splitting exchange of tank-gun fire cracked across the ravine.

The command post was in an ancient barn that held penetrating smells of musty hay, animals, and untold generations of mice. The seriously wounded were sent down the rough hillside by stretcher, and the lesser hurt were collected in the barn for the night.

We remained on the hill throughout the morning and afternoon of August 6, dug in against the intermittent artillery and tank fire. Late in the afternoon the tankers, after communication among themselves, abruptly cranked up and roared away without so much as a wave. The 2d and 3d Battalions were now the battered kings of 219. Shortly thereafter came a warning order to prepare to assault Vire.

I had spent the day at the forward edge of the hill where there was a clear view of the town on the opposite and slightly lower heights. From here it looked like a picture postcard, the backs of the closely set houses, with red tile roofs, making a varicolored wall above the ravine.

Vire was acquainted with calamity: it had known terrible passages of the Black Death plague in the fourteenth century; innumerable local conflicts of feudal lords; and in the fifteenth century the devastation of the Hundred Years' War. An Allied air raid had hit the town on D-day, leaving many of its citizens dead or wounded. Now, on a beautiful August evening, its ancient stones were again to be tumbled about, this time in a contention between the Stonewall Brigade, sometime of the Army of Northern Virginia, C.S.A., and a conglomerate of German paratroopers, infantry, and armor. It was, I suppose, an incident of history neither more nor less likely than any other.

I had not expected the attack order. The ravine and river, I thought, must be recognized as too formidable an obstacle for our depleted ranks. It seemed logical that the attack be made in greater strength along some less precipitous approach. This wishful logic was exploded by the arrival of the regimental commander with the order that in just over two hours the 2d and 3d Battalions were to take Vire and block the five roads converging there.

The colonel was not quite able to conceal his apprehension over the prospect. A big, heavyset man who had taken over at St. Lô, he was having a difficult time pleasing the divisional commander who was his opposite in stature and temperament. The clash building between the two already pointed to the colonel's departure.

The general kept tabs on his three regiments by posting liaison officers to each to report developments directly to him without waiting for the slower staff channels. The young lieutenant with the 116th was a bumbling type, and in his zeal to hear what the colonel was telling me he stumbled and fell against him—sending maps and overlays spinning.

The colonel, anxious over the mission, and probably resentful of what he considered the general's snooping, delivered a loud bawling out that left the lieutenant riddled. It also served as comic relief for the dark prospects of the attack.

While the rest of us brought our coughing under control, the colonel straightened out his rumpled dignity and, apparently feeling better, laid out the battalion boundaries and objectives. Then with a blessing of "Good luck, and don't fail," he departed with a final admonishment to keep him informed.

I went over the order with the company commanders and, in turn, assigned boundaries and objectives, which they accepted without expressed misgivings. Then, there was a surprise call from the general asking how long I had had to prepare for the attack. He actually sounded a little uncertain, and I found myself foolishly trying to reassure probably one of the most assured men in the army that all would be well.

By now, evening shadows were stretching out, leaving our west side of the ravine dark and highlighting the opposite side. Vire appeared in this light as a medieval town under siege, black smoke rising above it and artillery fire echoing along the ravine. A short stretch of the road entering the town from the southwest was visible, and on this a squat German tank lurched into view, traversed its gun, and began pumping shells down the ravine at a target we couldn't see, possibly the river bridge. The artillery observer brought in the fire of a battery on it, the first shell hitting directly in front of the turret in a splash of flame. Through field glasses, I saw the tank rock like a poleaxed steer, its tracks shedding dust and its gun silenced; then slowly it crawled out of view toward the town; followed by more shell splashes. So we knew there was at least one tank in Vire, the crew probably with monumental headaches, but counting themselves lucky at having been hit by a high explosive rather than an armor-piercing shell.

The two assault companies started in columns abreast down the steep hillside and were immediately lost to view in the underbrush and dark shadows. The battalion command group followed, slipping and sliding, holding on to brush and trees. At the bottom, we passed one of the first wounded, a rifleman bandaged and lying beside the river. He raised himself on an elbow and asked to be helped back to the aid station. I had to tell him that none of our small party could be spared, but that the stretcher bearers with the reserve company were following directly behind and would take care of him. He sank back without complaint; a recurring and troubling wonder is whether he was ever found in the fading light.

We forded the shallow river and started up the opposite slope toward a racket of gunfire beyond the wall of houses. A number of stragglers were drifting back toward the river, each announcing himself to be the sole survivor of this squad or platoon. They were added to our party, and we entered the town through a narrow lane that opened between the houses. The scene inside was worthy of a witches' sabbath: the night lit by the undulating red glow of burning buildings, all overhung by a pall of smoke. The only orgy under way, however, was that of destruction; parties of Germans were trying to surrender, others were trying to withdraw and doing a lot of yelling; tracer bullets crisscrossed and ricocheted off the rubble. In the general madness and confusion, some who had surrendered undoubtedly changed their minds and slipped away.

The two assault companies had dissolved in the debris, and the only usable force still in hand was the reserve company, which pushed along the main street to the eastern exit of the town. On this street was a massive, two-storied stone building, and here the command group stopped and tried to get the battalion into some sort of order. Little was achieved that night. There was no radio contact with the regiment, or with the two assault companies, both of whose commanders were casualties. Delayed word came that the executive officer had also been wounded and evacuated. This was a loss, for while he was ambitious for command, he had been loyal and energetic in helping me.

The night finally grew quiet, and with what seemed undue reluctance, gave way to the usual milky dawn. Vire by day lost its dramatic appearance and became just a dismal place of gray, smoking rubble. The scattered battalion was gradually pulled together and the roadblocks were established. The principal one, farther along the street from the command post, centered around a heavy machine gun of H Company set up in a bomb crater. I was talking with the crew about the field of fire when directly to the front a close column of German troops debouched from a wooded area onto the road and marched away eastward. In the haze of fatigue, and the uncertain visibility, we failed to react to this ideal machine-gun target, the long axis of the marching column being directly in the long axis of the gun's cone of fire. By the time the gunner had squeezed off a burst, the column was vanishing down a slope into the mist, much luckier than it deserved to be. At the time I regretted this lost opportunity, but not now.

Returning to the command post, I found the wounded had been gathered in the cobbled courtyard, but that the battalion surgeon was not yet there to care for them. I had become accustomed to surgeons who put the job above their skins, and I only now realized that this one, who had joined after St. Lô, was not of that cut. He had been slow getting up on Hill 219, and he was now long overdue in Vire. I sent him word to get there immediately or report to the colonel under arrest. He soon faded completely, and we were assigned a young Puerto Rican doctor who remained a bright spot in the battalion throughout the war.

While I was still boiling over the surgeon's absence, a German medical officer and his aide men were brought in as POW's. I asked him to give emergency care to our wounded. He agreed, and with the efficiency of long practice his crew cleared a table in a bright room and set out instruments and bandages from field medical kits. With assembly-line precision a dozen or more of our wounded were stanched, cleaned, bandaged, and injected. Along with everything else I had seen of the enemy, this work was professional and competent; there was a sinking feeling that the German army would take much more destroying.

It was now mid-morning. There had been quiet since dawn, but now a shell from the heavy mortar slammed into one end of the building, followed by artillery fire that stirred the rubble once again. The explosions continued walking through the ruins at intervals. The German surgeon called attention to his rights as a POW to be moved from the danger zone, and during a lull in the shelling he was sent to the rear with the wounded.

Late that afternoon the regimental commander again arrived with an order. This time it was to take Hill 251 that loomed over Vire to the east and was probably the observation post for the shelling. The 1st Battalion was to assault a similar hill to the south. A battalion of the 2d Infantry Division arrived to take over in Vire, and we advanced to the base of 251 for the attack the next morning, August 7.

The move uncovered a German rifleman who had sniped several Stonewallers during the day; he waited too long to pull out and was cut down as he ran along a narrow garden lane. The night at the foot of the hill was quiet, although German artillery continued to rend the town.

Preparation for the attack was automatic: One rifle company—now about fifty men—and the heavy weapons would form a fire base on the right, while the other two companies—with a combined strength of less than one—attacked on the left along a farm road. The morning mist cleared by jump-off time at 0630, and the hill's great round shape reared above us in the light of another bright August day. The artillery and fire base opened on the moment and created their own haze around the crest. The two assault companies started up and had not gone far before machine-gun fire clipped the hedge tops. Among the first casualties was an Indian from the Southwest, naturally called "Chief," who had been at the front of every attack starting with D-day. I had tried several times to talk to him as one of the remaining veterans, but got only monosyllables in answer. What his thoughts were on fighting at the front of what was essentially white America's war I was unable to determine. Now he stumbled down the slope blinded by blood streaming from a scalp wound. He did not return to the regiment and became another of the hundreds who shed blood in its ranks and then disappeared.

After this show of opposition the defenders pulled out and the attack went up with a rush to find the hill's broad top divided into fields and orchards. The riflemen coalesced along the hedgerows fencing in a brick farmhouse where a number of German wounded had been left behind—something that had not happened before.

Suddenly, from a field beyond the house, came sounds of

a loud argument in German, apparently between those who wanted to surrender and others who wanted to retreat and shoot at us another day. More artillery fire was called in to encourage surrender, and one of our men promoted the idea in Milwaukee German.

Apparently the die-hards among the arguing enemy prevailed, for the loud voices faded. The communications platoon labored up with the latest extension of a telephone line that they had started laying on Omaha Beach two months before. I got through to the regimental commander to tell him that the objective was taken, and he sounded surprised and relieved. There is a flamboyant tradition that on such an occasion one announces that his command awaits further orders. Not wanting further orders, I didn't ask for any.

Checking around our perimeter, I stopped at a post that looked across another ravine to Hill 203, taken by the 1st Battalion that morning in an action that won for it a presidential citation. A stretch of farm lane along the ravine was in view, and as we watched three or four Germans appeared trudging along it in single file, apparently in retreat from Hill 203. Very much as in a shooting gallery, one of our riflemen crumpled them into gray bundles. Presently, another figure appeared on the lane, as if from the wings of a stage, waving a large Red Cross flag. He examined the bundles and, apparently finding them lifeless, exited slowly again into the wings, still waving his flag. The rifleman who had done the sharpshooting was grinning; the rest looked on without speaking.

I continued around the perimeter and toward its northern part followed a high stone wall that ended ahead in the side of a farm building. Laboring along this wall, vastly weary, I became aware of thumping sounds behind me, and just before reaching the building there was a louder thump in front and stone chips flew from the impact of a bullet. Only then did it dawn that I was being tracked by a distant sniper; the next shot would likely be on target. The only exit from the situation was through an open window directly in front of me in the side of the building. The sill was at least shoulder high; without conscious thought and from a standing start I dove through the window into the building—the outstanding athletic achievement of my life, and not a mean one by any standard. A sergeant and some riflemen in the room where I landed in a heap were apparently beyond surprise, for they did not comment on this unorthodox entrance by the battalion commander. I cautioned them about the sniper and left by the other end of the building, following the protected side of the wall, and on down to the command post on the western slope of the hill.

It was early afternoon. I was certain that we had reached a stopping point; that nothing more could be asked of the now truly decimated 2d Battalion other than to hold where it was. With this comforting conviction—for which there was no basis in experience—I lay down in the cool grass and drifted into a half doze. This pleasant state did not last long: sharp explosions of M-1 rifle fire from the top of the hill brought me up with a start, and set the field phone buzzing. In a few moments word came down that two German motorcycles with sidecars had been driven into our lines and had been promptly bushwhacked. Shortly afterward four POW's were marched into the command post carrying a young staff captain wounded in the foot.

The captain looked the part of a German war poster: handsome, blond, and tall. He and his party had been on reconnaissance and had driven into our lines unaware that the hill was no longer German-held. This happened often enough on both sides to constitute a prime hazard to staff service.

While the intelligence officer was collecting material from the motorcycles, I offered the captain a field ration and we talked about the war, he speaking heavily accented but adequate English. I handed him one of the leaflets that had been showered on the Germans pointing out the hopelessness of their situation and urging surrender. He said, pleasantly enough, that it was silly to expect an army that had fought as the German army had fought for the past five years to surrender to such pieces of paper.

I observed that as far as he was concerned, this was academic. He agreed, but advised me not to expect the German army to fall apart. He complimented the field ration, and I said that if he found that palatable, his army was in worse shape than he realized.

The conversation was drifting into banter as the S-2 arrived with maps and papers from the sidecars. The captain looked at the bundle ruefully as he was carried away by the other POW's on a stretcher improvised from a door. I warned him that our rear-area people often stripped POW's of watches, medals, and anything else removable. He said that German troops did the same, and that I should get the good Luger that had been taken from him. It would have been hard to wish so pleasant a fellow reduced to another lifeless heap on a dusty Normandy hilltop. One of the motorcycles was undamaged, and I used it for a few days, until the regiment heard about it and ordered it turned in.

The rest of the day and night was quiet. The next morning, August 9, patrols found no sign of the enemy other than fresh graves and wrecked equipment. We did not know that two days before, some fifteen miles to the southwest, the last German offensive in Normandy had been launched to sever the breakthrough corridor at Avranches through which the U.S. Third Army was rolling. This futile effort was drawing all their resources.

The battalion that had relieved us at Vire now took over Hill 251, and we marched back to join the rest of the regiment in corps reserve in an area southwest of the town, the whole battalion on the march looking like one full-strength company. There was a hot supper waiting, and the next day clean uniforms were issued to replace those we had sweated, fought, and slept in for the past ten days. Current editions of the *Stars and Stripes* arrived and told of a booming Allied war effort. The German counterattack had been stopped at Mortain after hard fighting, with never a pause in the Third Army columns that were pouring into Brittany and also curving in toward Falaise.

New men arrived to bring the companies up to over half strength, and training was resumed. A white-haired lieutenant colonel from a reinforcement depot also came by saying, very businesslike, that he wanted to observe at first hand the "maintenance job" on the battalion. I am sure that he meant well, and was dedicated to his job of fairly allocating badly strained infantry manpower. The inference, however, that those we had left along the road to Vire, so many of whom I knew so well, were simply worn-out parts to be replaced, struck me as intolerable. I have an unfortunate tendency to sputter incoherently when angry, and I did so then to the astonishment of the well-meaning officer, who must have left thinking that his maintenance work would soon have to include a new battalion commander. But if he reported this unmannerly reaction to his innocent jargon, the regimental commander never mentioned it.

During those few days in bivouac we were visited by the divisional commander, and at a formation the regimental commander presented Purple Hearts and Bronze Stars. They told us that we had done well, and I don't recall any disclaimers.

There had been losses in all ranks, and reorganization was constant. The one remaining captain was moved up to executive officer, to be killed the following month at Brest. A new operations officer, the fourth in two months, arrived and was to prove a mainstay and a friend. We were both wounded the same day near Aachen, he losing a leg, but never a warm and generous nature. Two surviving lieutenants, and one returning from the hospital, became company commanders. (Newly assigned lieutenants seemed to be mostly Texas A&M graduates.)

Such a litany of change must run through any account of a battalion in combat. It is remarkable that through it all the battalion's personality remained so constant. The reason must be that despite the losses, enough of the past always remained to provide a continuity of character. New men tended to regard the veterans with respect, and adopted their attitudes and actions. Thus, even a relatively few veterans in a battle-worthy battalion had great influence in keeping it so; by the same token, a hard-luck outfit with a background of failure was very hard to turn around.

The third day in reserve ended in a spurt of activity as we were ordered back to Hill 251, some higher command having decided that the Germans might turn and strike at Vire as they had at Avranches. This proved a farfetched concern that might better have been saved for the Ardennes situation four months hence. Some of the old men pointed out that being deployed had its advantages, for had we stayed in bivouac another day we would have been doing close-order drill.

The battalion marched back to the hill that evening and was dug in by midnight, ready for a counterattack that became more remote by the day. Training was resumed in the form of rerunning the attack on the hill. Doubtlessly, the tactics were embellished with practice, and each veteran probably gilded his part a bit, also. I did not re-enact my leap through the window. The new men seemed impressed and intent on learning from so recent an action.

Meanwhile, the war rolled eastward, taking along its fancy lady, Glory, who has never been any better than she should be. Little of the German Seventh Army escaped; their Fifteenth Army was nearly routed in Flanders; the Parisians rose against their occupiers; and the Allied invasion of southern France gained momentum. For the 2d Battalion, I think, this was all one; our small, violent scene in the giant canvas of the pursuit was done; we were in no rush to start another.

—February 1978

BLOODY HUERTGEN: THE BATTLE THAT SHOULD NEVER HAVE BEEN FOUGHT

by GENERAL JAMES M. GAVIN

For the Germans, holding the Huertgen Forest was Phase One of the Battle of the Bulge. For the Americans, trying to occupy the forest was a ghastly mistake.

T he Battle of the Bulge came to an end in the closing days of January, 1945. The combat divisions were immediately redeployed to resume the offensive into Germany, and the 82nd Airborne, which I commanded, was ordered into the Huertgen Forest, a densely wooded area astride the Siegfried Line, just inside the German border. In the fall of 1944 there had been many grim stories in the *Stars and Stripes,* the army newspaper, about the fighting in the Huertgen. We were not looking forward to the assignment.

I opened the division command post in the midst of the forest in the small town of Rott on February 8, and a few hours later stopped at corps headquarters to get an outline of our next mission. Then, traveling by jeep, I started through the Huertgen Forest to the clearings on the far side where our jump-off positions would be. I learned my first lesson about the Huertgen. It could not be traversed by jeep. The mud was too deep and the jeep bellied down. In addition the forest was heavily fortified and highly organized for defense. Although I had seen heavy pillbox fortifications in Sicily, they were nothing compared with those in the Huertgen Forest. In the Huertgen they were huge (frequently consisting of several rooms). They were dark, and landscaped to blend with the trees—so well covered by leaves and pine needles that they were hardly visible. I was startled when I first realized that I was looking right at one only a short distance away and hadn't realized that it was a pillbox. In addition to the pillboxes, concertina barbed wire was stretched across the forest floor. This, with trip wires, antipersonnel mines, and antitank mines, reduced the fighting to its most primitive form: man against man at grenade distance.

Having been preoccupied with the Battle of the Bulge, the Allies had paid little attention to the Huertgen Forest for the past several months. I found a road that a jeep could travel on, and went to the town of Vossenack on reconnaissance without meeting any enemy. The Germans presumably had withdrawn to the Roer River or very close to it. I left my jeep in the town and started down the trail that crossed the Kall River valley. I was accompanied by the Division G-3, Colonel John Norton, and Sergeant Walker Woods. It really was a reconnaissance, since I did not know what the lay of the land would be, and what, if any, enemy might still be there. Our orders for the following day were to attack across the Kall River valley from Vossenack and seize the town of Schmidt. By now most of the snow had melted and only small patches remained under the trees. I walked down the trail, which was obviously impassable for a jeep. It was a shambles of wrecked vehicles and abandoned tanks. The first tanks that had attempted to go down the trail evidently had slid off and thrown their tracks. In some cases tanks had been pushed off the trail and toppled down the gorge among the trees. Between where the trail began outside of Vossenack and the bottom of the canyon there were four abandoned tank destroyers and five disabled and abandoned tanks. In addition, all along the sides of the trail there were many, many cadavers that had just emerged from the winter snow. Their gangrenous, broken, and torn bodies were rigid and grotesque, some of them with arms skyward, seemingly in supplication. They were wearing the red keystone of the 28th Infantry Division, the "Bloody Bucket." It evidently had fought through there in the preceding fall, just before the heavy snows. I continued down the trail for about half a mile to the bottom, where there was a tumbling mountain stream about six feet wide. A stone bridge that once had crossed it had long since been demolished, and a few planks were placed across the stone arches for the use of individual infantrymen. Nearby were dozens more dead men.

Apparently an aid station had been established near the creek and in the midst of the fighting it had been abandoned, many of the men dying on their stretchers. About fifty yards off to the right, a hard road appeared. Across it were six American antitank mines. On the near side of the mines were three or four American soldiers who apparently had been laying the mines and protecting them when they were killed. Beyond the American mines, about ten feet away, were some German Teller mines, connected like beads on a string. And on the other side of these were three or four German dead, a dramatic example of what the fighting must have been like in the Huertgen. It was savage, bitter, and at close quarters.

I made my way up the far side of the canyon. One had to be extremely careful because the trail had not been cleared of mines. I assumed that the woods were infested with them and hence did not even get near the edge of the trail. As we approached the top, all the debris evinced a bitter struggle. There were more bodies, an antitank gun or two, destroyed jeeps, and abandoned weapons. We emerged from the top of the trail into a wide clearing. A few miles away we could see the small German town of Kommerscheidt. So far, we had not been challenged by any Germans, but I knew they were supposed to be in Kommerscheidt and in the town of Schmidt, beyond. The sun was setting and I was anxious to get back to the other side of the valley before darkness. As evening descended over the canyon, it was an eerie scene, like something from a low level of Dante's *Inferno*. To add to the horror, a plaintive human voice could be heard calling from the woods quite some distance away. We continued on down and up on the other side, reaching Vossenack in the darkness. During the night, troops were moved up to the town, and I went back down the trail with the leading battalion not long after daylight. I remember vividly the battalion stopping for a short break. A young soldier, a new replacement, was looking with horror at the dead. He began to turn pale, then green, and he was obviously about to vomit. I knew his state of mind: every young soldier, upon first entering combat, is horrified by the sight of bodies that have been abandoned. They always imagine themselves dead and neglected. I talked to him, calmed him a bit, and assured him that our outfit never abandoned its dead, that we always cared for and buried them. Soon the battalion continued down the trail and up on the other side. It attacked across the open land, seized Kommers-cheidt and then Schmidt. The fighting was moderate to heavy, and after capturing Schmidt we continued to receive artillery fire.

It seemed obvious to me that the regiment could not be supplied across the Kall River canyon, certainly not if the enemy interfered or if artillery fire covered the trail. In addition, the trail was impassable for vehicles. A catastrophe must have occurred there in the fall of 1944. I could not understand why the bodies had not been removed and buried. Neither the corps nor the army headquarters could have been aware of the conditions in the canyon. Otherwise the corpses would have been interred and the disabled tanks recovered. As soon as I returned to the command post, I called the chief of staff of V Corps and explained the situation to him, emphasizing the need for an alternate supply route. There was a good one from Lammersdorf to Schmidt and that was under V Corps. He listened to my story, then laughed and asked, "Have you tried pack mules?" It made me furious. There is nothing that angers a combat soldier more than a higher headquarters staff officer belittling the problems of the combat infantryman. It is as old as soldiering.

The following morning I went to Lammersdorf to meet the commander of V Corps and the commander of the division whose headquarters was in that town. Obviously, the attack on Schmidt should have been made straight down the ridge from Lammersdorf. Lammersdorf and Schmidt are connected by a paved road, the terrain was a mixture of woods and open farm land—good tank country—and it would have been a much simpler tactical undertaking than crossing the Kall River. The question in my mind was how in the world did they ever get involved in attacking across the Kall River valley in the first place? Why not stick to the high ground, bypassing the Germans in the valley, and then go on to the Roer River? I raised this question with a corps staff officer present, but he brushed it aside. Apparently that was a "no-no" question, not to be talked about.

In the meantime I noticed that the corps commander and the commander of a new division were bent over a map. The corps commander occasionally drew a short line with a blue grease pencil. The line represented an infantry battalion, and he was suggesting to the division commander a tactical scheme by moving battalions about. I realize how remote they were from the reality of what it was like up where the battalions were. The thought crossed my mind that the disaster that had befallen the 28th Division may have been related to the lack of understanding in higher headquarters of what the actual situation in the Kall River valley was. That turned out to be true.

Optimism was widespread in the Allied high command in Europe in the late summer of '44. As the summer waned, the world was treated to the spectacle of the German 7th Army and the 5th Panzer Army fleeing from the battlefields of Normandy. Handcarts, horses and wagons, bicycles, baby carriages, anything that they could lay their hands on were used to help in their escape. Eisenhower's staff seemed convinced that the war was over. His chief of staff, Lieutenant General Bedell Smith, announced to the press in early September, "Militarily the war is over." Most astounding, post exchange officers sent orders back to the States to stop all Christmas packages. The war would be over by Christmas. And the optimism went beyond the generals. Meeting with President Roosevelt at Quebec on September 10, 1944, Winston Churchill remarked, "Victory is everywhere." And later he added, "I would not be surprised, now that the American 3d Army is standing on the border of Germany, if the enemy surrendered within weeks." But the very success of Eisenhower's armies contained the seeds of trouble. By September he had outrun his supplies. Trucks bringing gasoline and ammunition to George Patton's army, for example, had to travel 360 miles back to the Normandy beaches. And by the end of August, 90 to 95 percent of the supplies for Eisenhower's armies lay in depots near the beaches.

The northernmost of the U.S. armies was the 1st U.S. Army, commanded by Lieutenant General Courtney Hodges. I had known General Hodges when he was Chief of Staff of the Philippine Division from 1936 to 1938. He was an intelligent, thoughtful, studious sort of officer. Unlike the other U.S. Army commanders, he was not a West Pointer. He attended the military academy but dropped out during his plebe year, enlisted, and earned his commission from the ranks. He was a veteran of World War I and knew his trade well; some thought him rather colorless—certainly he was when compared with Patton—but those who knew him had great respect for the consideration he showed for his troops; he was always careful not to waste his men and was cautious in his tactical deployments.

The 1st U.S. Army was a veteran command. It had made the Normandy assault and promptly accomplished its first mission, capturing Cherbourg. Thereafter, it endured very heavy fighting in the Normandy hedgerows for almost two months. In July, Patton's 3d Army came ashore and was committed to battle on the right of the 1st. It rampaged through Brittany and directly contributed to the defeat and rout of the Germans in mid-August. Both the 1st and 3d armies pursued the enemy vigorously, and by mid-September they were up to the German frontier. The U.S. 1st Army was still in pursuit, with all three of its corps in line across a front of more than 120 miles—far too widespread to engage in heavy combat—as they considered themselves to be still in pursuit of a beaten enemy. Furthermore, during the long trek across France, maintenance of vehicles, especially tanks, had been badly neglected. For example, the 3d Armored Division had only 75 serviceable tanks out of an allotment of 232. Then, too, some combat divisions had dropped their artillery far behind in order to use the artillery tow trucks to carry infantry.

As they neared the German frontier, there was much speculation about the Siegfried Line. Rumor had it that the pillboxes and fortifications were unmanned. But General Hodges anticipated heavy fighting and he thought it best to delay his advance for about two days to permit his forces to regroup. The corps commanders were impatient, however, particularly Major General Joe Collins, commander of the VII Corps; they wanted to get on with the attack while they had momentum and before the Siegfried Line could be manned. Collins reasoned that if he penetrated the line, so much to the good, but if unexpected resistance occurred, he still would not have lost anything. However, the Germans were far from defeated. Indeed, they were preparing a major counteroffensive.

On September 5, 1944, Hitler called back Field Marshal Gerd von Rundstedt. He had dismissed him earlier, in July, after von Rundstedt, upon being queried by the German high command on what they should do, replied, "End the war, you fools." Now he was forgiven in the hour of need. He was respected throughout the German army and was the one soldier who could rally the Wehrmacht. His problems were many, but he went about solving them in a very businesslike manner. To begin with, he managed to bring General Gustav von Zangen's 15th Army from Calais by barge and boat to positions in Holland to confront the Allies. Systematically, efforts were made to round up and reassign individuals and small groups of German soldiers that had made their way back from the battlefields of France. Fortunately for von Rundstedt, the high-command structure down to and including some of the combat divisions was generally intact. While von Rundstedt was assembling troops, Hitler took additional steps to bolster the defenses. About a hundred "fortress" infantry battalions were hastily re-equipped and hurried to the front. These had been used in rear areas and they were made up mostly of undertrained and overage individuals. They were to give a good account of themselves in manning the Siegfried Line.

While these moves were under way, Hitler made one of his intuitive decisions. On Saturday, September 16, 1944, he had a conference in his East Prussian headquarters, the Wolf's Lair. Field Marshal Jodl was ticking off the depressing statistics: shortages of ammunition, shortages of tanks, German troops withdrawing from southern France. Suddenly, Hitler interrupted, "I have just made a momentous decision. I shall go over to the counterattack, that is to say," pointing to the map unrolled on the desk before him, "here, out of the Ardennes, with the objective—Antwerp." The counterattack was scheduled for a launching within two months, although, as it finally developed, it took three months. To deny the Allies the type of information that they had obtained by radio intercept in the past, Hitler insisted that all communications would be by wire, written messages, or staff visits. There would be no radio communications among the higher formations. Thus he undertook to organize a counteroffensive that would involve three field armies, consisting of twenty-one divisions, including eight Panzer divisions.

Opposing the U.S. 1st Army was the German 7th Army commanded by General der Panzertruppen Eric Brandenberger. His mission, once Hitler's decision had been made, was to hold off the U.S. 1st Army until the counteroffensive could be launched. At this point another factor entered into the German thinking. Behind the Siegfried Line, in the Huertgen Forest area, were a series of major dams that controlled the flow of water into the Roer River. By opening these dams, General Brandenberger could effectively block the U.S. 1st Army from crossing the Roer and thus making its way to the Rhine at Cologne. So, Brandenberger's mission was to protect the dams, using the Siegfried Line and all the odd-lot troop formations that he could find, as well as one or two battle-experienced formations. And finally, the German positions were to be held at all costs to permit the build-up of a great counteroffensive, which Hitler was convinced would split the Allies and bring about a petition for peace. Thus the stage was set for the battle of the Huertgen Forest.

"The Huertgen," the GI's called it. To the soldiers the word "Huertgen" was synonymous with getting hurt. It was to be known as one of the most costly battles in our history. Yet, when the fighting in the Huertgen Forest began, no one, neither American nor German, had a clear idea of how intense and costly it would be. The Americans wanted to seize the eastern edge of the forest and in so doing protect the right flank of the U.S. 1st Army, which was moving on to Cologne. But neither side could guess the other's objective and both sides were surprised by the intensity and heavy cost of the fighting that followed.

The Huertgen Forest is part of a heavily wooded area of about fifty square miles. It begins about five miles southeast of Aachen. As the official *U.S. Army History* described it: "Looking east from the little German border villages southeast of Aachen, the Huertgen forest is a seemingly impenetrable mass, a vast undulating blackish-green ocean stretching as far as the eye can see. Upon entering the forest, you want to drop things behind to mark your path, as Hansel and Gretel did with their bread crumbs."

After traversing the forest for three or four miles, one came upon open farming country on higher ground. Two ridges thrust like fingers toward the distant Roer River. On the north, extending to the northeast for three miles, was the ridge containing the towns of Huertgen, Menhau, and Grosshau. To the south was a longer ridge, extending from the town of Lammersdorf toward Schmidt, the town which overlooked the principal dam on the Roer River. Between these cleared ridge lines lay the deep Kall River gorge.

The famed Siegfried Line, or West Wall, consisted of two

lines of fortifications, running parallel and several miles apart, directly through the Huertgen Forest. Each line had to be taken in turn, and each contained a large number of pillboxes with interlocking fields of fire, bunkers, and command posts.

As General Hodges prepared plans for his move across the Roer River and on to Cologne on the Rhine, he looked with some concern at the Huertgen Forest. General Hodges and General Collins were both veterans of World War I. They recalled the heavy fighting in the Argonne Forest, and they knew that the Huertgen could provide cover for a German force that might seriously threaten their right flank. So far, they had not given any thought to the dams. They believed, however, that their present widespread deployments could sweep through the forest without too much delay, and in so doing seize the high ground overlooking the Roer. The veteran 9th Division was chosen for the task. Its 38th Infantry Regiment was given the principal mission. It crossed the German border and entered the village of Lammersdorf on September 14. It was protected by the 47th Infantry Regiment, which was about seven miles to the north, and the 60th Infantry Regiment, also of the 9th Division, about five miles to the south. This deployment of the three regiments was far too widespread to break through serious resistance. The 39th learned quickly that the Germans were manning the pillboxes of the Siegfried Line. It was the toughest defense situation that they had encountered since Normandy. After three days of costly, bitter fighting, they had advanced only about a mile and a half. The Germans continued gradually to build up their defenses, and the battle raged back and forth through the pillbox area. It was a special kind of warfare for which our troops were not well trained or equipped. As it turned out, the 9th Division was the first of a steady procession of American units which in subsequent weeks would learn to equate the Huertgen with gloom, misery, wounds, and death. General Collins decided to stop the attack and to regroup his forces. The forest remained unconquered.

Early in October the decision was made to attack once again, using the same 9th Infantry Division. At last, the higher staff were beginning to attach some importance to the dams. Some prisoners told them of the German plans for the dams and that arrangements had been made to ring church bells in the villages downstream when the flooding began. The 9th

Infantry Division launched its attack on October 6 with Schmidt, which overlooked the Schwammenauel Dam, as its objective. Again the German resistance stiffened. The Infantry found themselves widely dispersed, and their losses were appalling. Vehicles and tanks bogged down in the forest. The dense tree cover denied them support from their own air force. German artillery projectiles burst in the tops of the trees, hurling shell fragments earthward. Replacements were lost by the hundreds before they could even join their outfits. When they did arrive, they found that the problem of the tree bursts made it necessary for them to cover their foxholes with logs. When caught in the open, the soldiers learned that the safest defense was to stand or to crouch rather than to lie flat on the forest floor. By late October the Huertgen had taken its toll. The 9th Division had gained no more than three thousand yards, which they paid for in one and a half casualties per yard. The division had lost about forty-five hundred men, and according to the official report, "The real winner appeared to be the vast, undulating, blackish-green sea that virtually negated American superiority in the air, artillery, and armor to reduce warfare to its lowest common denominator." The forest refused to yield, and now there were the dams.

Toward the end of October General Hodges set the date of November 5 for the main attack that would take his 1st Army across the Roer and on to the Rhine. The principal effort was to be given to Joe Collins' VII Corps. His mission was to clear the Huertgen Forest and seize the high ground to the east. The dams were transferred to General Gerow's V Corps on Collins' right. Hodges was anxious that the V Corps get started as soon as possible and he set the date of November first. Its mission was to clear the Vossenack-Schmidt-Lammersdorf triangle down to the headwaters of the Roer River, so as to protect the right flank of the 1st Army. To increase the V Corps' strength, it was given the 28th Division and a combat command of the 5th Armored Division. The 28th was the Pennsylvania National Guard Division. It had made the Normandy assault and was fresh and experienced in every respect and ready for its difficult mission. By now, the Huertgen was recognized as a tough nut to crack. Considerable pressure was put on the 28th Division commander, Major General Norman D. Cota. His principal mission was to seize Vossenack, cross the Kall River gorge, seize Kommerscheidt, and then Schmidt, enabling the V Corps to command a position close to and overlooking the Schwammenauel Dam. The 112th Infantry Regiment (of the 28th Division), commanded by Lieutenant Colonel Carl L. Peterson, was assigned the central position. It was supported on its left by the 109th Infantry, which moved toward the village of Huertgen, and on the right by the 110th Infantry, which moved to the south in the direction of the village of Raffelsbrand. It should be noted that the three regiments diverged from the beginning and, in fact, uncovered the flanks of the middle regiment, the 112th Infantry, which had a difficult mission at best and one that could have been catastrophic if its flanks were attacked in the Kall River gorge. The division was opposed by the German 275th Division, which had proved its mettle against the 9th Division earlier.

By this time heavy autumn rains and dense fogs and mist plagued the attackers. Soon there would be snow. The infantry could expect little air support.

The attack on Schmidt was launched on November second in characteristically bad weather. Despite poor conditions, however, both V Corps and VII Corps supported the forthcoming attack with artillery barrages. By H-hour, the 28th Division artillery had fired 7,313 rounds. The high command had at last learned respect for the German defenses and they were taking no chances. The attack went off on schedule and the second battalion of the 112th Infantry captured Vossenack by early afternoon and soon were digging foxholes on the forward slopes overlooking the forested valleys below. The two remaining battalions of the 112th Infantry moved through Vossenack down the trail across the Kall River gorge, virtually unopposed, until they were all the way across the Kall and crossing the open farm country in sight of Kommerscheidt.

Kommerscheidt and Schmidt, in turn, were seized with little opposition. There was elation in the 28th Division Headquarters, and the division commander, General Cota, was to say later that he felt like "a little Napoleon." But the elation was short-lived. Actually, the Germans were in the process of replacing the forces that had been defending Schmidt.

The following day the Germans counterattacked with armor and drove the defenders from their water-filled, icy foxholes around Schmidt back on Kommerscheidt, and later pushed the survivors of Kommerscheidt to the edge of the Kall River gorge. In addition, they attacked all along the gorge, thus cutting off the remnants of the two attacking battalions that had just been driven from Schmidt and Kommerscheidt. Repeated orders by the 28th Division to recapture Schmidt were meaningless, as the survivors were incapable of mounting an attack. The regimental commander was directed to report to division headquarters. Although he was physically exhausted and twice had been wounded by artillery fire, he started down the trail of the Kall River gorge. He was in bad physical shape when the engineers on the trail found him, put him in a jeep, and started him back. He must have been a sight to see when he walked in on General Cota. At the sight of him, Cota fainted. Before the engagement was through, the 28th Division suffered over six thousand casualties.

The 28th was followed in turn by the 4th, the 8th, and the 83rd infantry divisions, and a combat command of the 5th Armored Division. Tragically, before it was over, not only were the casualties frightful, but the real objective turned out to be not the Huertgen Forest itself but the dams over the Roer River on the far side of it.

Over twenty-four thousand Americans were killed, missing and captured, or wounded in the fighting in the Huertgen and another nine thousand succumbed to the wet and cold with trench foot and respiratory diseases, for a total cost of thirty-three thousand men. In retrospect it was a battle that should not have been fought. Once we were in it, the higher command did not seem to appreciate the incredible conditions under which the infantrymen had to fight. Unlike other battles in Europe up to that time, we sacrificed our ground mobility and our tactical air support, and we chose to fight the Germans under conditions entirely to their own advantage, in which they fought from strong fortifications on ground they knew very well. In an interview after the war, General Major Rudolph Gersdorff, chief of staff of the German 7th Army, said, "The German Command could not understand the reason for the strong American attacks in the Huertgen forest . . . the fighting in the wooded area denied the American troops the advantages offered them by their air and armored forces, the superiority of which had been decisive in all the battles waged before, etc." But the Huertgen was over and I think it fair to say that little was learned from it and less understood.

From October until mid-December the Germans had fought hard to protect the assembly of the armies that Hitler had earmarked for his great counteroffensive—the Battle of the Bulge. The Germans had fought with skill and courage and took heavy casualties. The Allies had no idea of the coming counteroffensive, so one must judge the German defense as having been entirely successful. On December 16, 1944, Hitler launched three field armies against the Allied center, on a seventy-mile front. At once the Huertgen lost its importance as all attention was focused on the Ardennes.

Military critics have argued about the battle of the Huertgen Forest ever since World War II. Today, at the Command and General Staff College at Fort Leavenworth, Kansas, it is presented by the faculty to each new incoming class as a case history. Particular emphasis is placed upon the attack of the 28th Infantry Division across the Kall River gorge, and on to Kommerscheidt and Schmidt. They point out the disastrous consequences that can befall a command when the generals do not know the environment in which the troops must fight. A troublesome aspect of the Huertgen battle is that it was fought by inexperienced, courageous battle leaders who made few other mistakes during the war in Europe. So why did it happen?

In the first place there was the optimism that was so pervasive throughout all echelons of the Allied forces in the late summer of 1944. It seemed clear that the Germans were beaten, badly beaten. Then there was the unbelievably poor intelligence of the Allied high command. Up to the fall of 1944 the Allies depended heavily upon ULTRA SECRET, that priceless information that came to them from radio intercepts of German communications to and from tactical headquarters.

When the intercepts were suddenly brought to a stop by Hitler's ban on all radio communications, no one seems to have questioned what was going on. Hitler therefore was able to assemble twenty-one combat divisions, including eight Panzers, without the Allies knowing anything about it. In retrospect, this seems unbelievable, but all three events were closely related—the unbridled optimism of the high command, the discontinuance of the radio traffic of the German formations, and their ability to organize a major counteroffensive. Thus, to the Germans, the battle of the Huertgen Forest was Phase One of the Battle of the Bulge.

That battle was Hitler's last gamble. The bitter, costly fighting by the Germans in the Huertgen Forest in October and November of 1944 was essential to their chance of success. But for us, Huertgen was one of the most costly, most unproductive, and most ill-advised battles that our army has ever fought.

—December 1979

THE MAN WHO COULD SPEAK JAPANESE

by *WILLIAM MANCHESTER*

Private Whitey Dumas and the march to victory in the Pacific.

In the spring of 1944 the United States Marine Corps formed its last rifle regiment of World War II, the 29th Marines, in New River, North Carolina. The first of its three battalions was already overseas, having been built around ex-Raiders and parachutists who had fought on Guadalcanal, Tarawa, and Saipan. Great pains were being taken to make the other two battalions worthy of them. The troops assembling in New River were picked men. Officers and key noncoms had already been tested in battles against the enemy, and though few riflemen in the line companies had been under fire, they tended to be hulking, deep-voiced mesomorphs whose records suggested that they would perform well when they, too, hit the beach. There was, however, one small band of exceptions. These were the nineteen enlisted men comprising the intelligence section of the 29th's second battalion. All nineteen were Officer Candidate washouts. I, also a washout, led them. My rank was Corporal, acting Platoon Sergeant—Acting John.

We were, every one of us, military misfits, college students who in a fever of patriotism had rushed to the Marine Corps' Officer Candidate School at Quantico, Virginia and had subsequently been rejected because, for various reasons, we did not conform with the established concept of how officers should look, speak, and act. Chet Przystawski of Colgate, for example, had a build like Charles Atlas but a voice like Lily Pons; when he yelled a command, the effect was that of an eerie shriek. Ace Livick of the University of Virginia had no sense of direction: at Quantico he had flunked map reading. Jerry Collins, a Yale man, was painfully shy. Stan Zoglin, a Cantab, had poor posture. Mack Yates of Ole Miss wore spectacles. Tom Jasper of Brown and I had been insubordinate. I had refused to clean a rifle on the ground that it was already clean, and I suffered the added stigma of being scrawny. I've forgotten the order Jasper disobeyed, though I knew that he too had another count against him: he admired the Japanese enormously.

Sy Ivice of Chicago christened us "the Raggedy-Ass Marines." That was about the size of it. Love had died between us and the Marine Corps. The rest of the battalion amiably addressed us as "Mac"—all enlisted Marines were "Mac" to their officers and to one another—but there was a widespread awareness that we were unsuitably bookish, slack on the drill field, and generally beneath the fastidious stateside standards established in the Corps' 169-year history. If there had been such a thing as a Military Quotient, the spit-and-polish equivalent of an Intelligence Quotient, our M.Q. would have been pegged at about 78. It is fair to add that this rating would have been confined to our parade-ground performance. We were regarded as good combat prospects. All of us, I believe, had qualified on the Parris Island, South Carolina, rifle range as Sharpshooters or Expert Riflemen. It was thought (and, as it proved, rightly so) that we would be useful in battle. Our problem, or rather the problem of our leaders, was that we lacked what the British army calls Quetta manners. We weren't properly starched and blancoed, weren't martially prepossessing—weren't in a word, good for the 29th's image.

We were rarely given liberty, because our company commander was ashamed to let civilians see us wearing the corps uniform. Shirttails out, buttons missing, fore-and-aft (overseas) caps down around our ears—these were signs that we had lost our drill-field ardor in OCS and were playing our roles of incorrigible eccentrics to the hilt. We looked like caricatures from cartoons in *The Leatherneck*, the Marine Corps equivalent of *Yank*, and the only reason our betters allowed us to stay together, setting a bad example to one another and damaging battalion élan, was a provision in the official Table of Organization for an intelligence section and our qualifications for membership in it. Between Quantico and assignment to the 29th we had all attended something called intelligence school.

Theoretically we were experts in identifying enemy units by searching Jap corpses, recognizing the silhouettes of Zero fighters, reconnoitering behind the lines, etc. It was all rather vague. If we proved useless in these tasks, our commanders knew that we could always be used for odd jobs.

Meanwhile we carried out exhausting training exercises in the Carolina boondocks, inflating rubber boats, getting snarled in bales of communications wire, carrying out simulated patrol missions at night. Whenever it was Livick's turn to keep the map, we would vanish into the piney woods, subsisting on K and D rations for hours until we were found thrashing around in the bush and led back by a rescue party from the battalion's 81-millimeter platoon, our long-suffering neighbors in New River's Tent City. For the most part it was an uneventful time, however. Nothing interesting seemed likely to happen before we were shipped overseas.

Then one morning the battalion adjutant summoned me.

"Mac."

"Sir."

"You will square away to snap in a new man."

Marine Corps orders were always given this way: "You will scrub bulkheads," "You will police this area," "You will hold a field day." There was only one permissible response.

"Aye, aye, sir," I said.

"He's a Japanese-language interpreter," he said.

"A *what?*"

In 1944 virtually no one in the Marine Corps spoke Japanese. Unlike the ETO, where plenty of GI's were bilingual, Americans were at a severe linguistic disadvantage in the Pacific. It was worsened by the fact that many Japs spoke English; they could eavesdrop on our combat field telephones. As a result by the third year of the war the headquarters company of each Marine battalion carried on its roster a full-blooded Navaho who could communicate over radiophones in his own tongue with the Navahos in other battalions. After the outbreak of war Washington had set up several crash courses to teach Japanese to bright young Americans, but the first graduates wouldn't emerge until the spring of 1945.

"We'll be the only outfit with its own translator," he said.

"Sir."

"Private Harold Dumas will be coming down from post headquarters at fourteen hundred."

That was too much. "He's only a *private?*"

"Knock it off!"

"Aye, aye, sir."

A noncom wasn't supposed to question higher wisdom, but clearly there was something odd here. Back in our pyramidal tent I passed the word among my people, whose astonishment matched mine. Their first reaction was that I was snowing them, but within an hour the dope was confirmed by the sergeant major, a bright little sparrow of a man named John Guard. Guard had some intriguing details, including an explanation for the translator's low rank. Until very recently—two days ago, in fact—Harold Dumas had been locked up in Portsmouth naval prison. The nature of his offense was unknown to Guard, but the sergeant major knew where Dumas was believed to have learned Japanese. He was a native of California; his neighbors had been Issei (first-generation Japanese-Americans) and Nisei (children of Issei).

The fact that the newcomer was a Californian is important to an understanding of what happened later. The Marine Corps maintained a rigid geographical segregation. Every man enlisting east of the Mississippi was sent to boot camp at Parris Island and shipped to New River after his recruit training. West of the Mississippi, boots went to the San Diego base and, once they had qualified, to nearby Camp Pendleton. Virtually none of us in Tent City knew anything about life on the West Coast. We had never seen a giant redwood, or the Grand Canyon, or Hollywood. We had never even met anyone from California until Harold Dumas arrived that afternoon at two o'clock.

He made a great entrance. He was wearing a salty barracks (visored) cap, a field scarf (necktie) so bleached that it was almost white, heavily starched khakis, and high-top dress shoes. The shoes were especially impressive. The Marine Corps had stopped issuing high-tops after Pearl Harbor, and they were therefore a great status symbol, signifying membership in the elite prewar Old Corps. Dumas was the only post-Pearl Marine I ever knew who had them, but then, he was unusual in lots of ways.

Prepossessing is the word that best describes him, though it is really inadequate. The moment he strode into Tent City with his elbows swinging wide, every eye was on him. Six foot two, with a magnificent physique, he carried himself like

Randolph Scott in *To the Shores of Tripoli,* the movie that had conned thousands of Marines into joining up. His face was freckled, his eyes were sky-blue, his expression was wholly without guile; he was a man you trusted instinctively, whose every word you believed, for whose reputation you would fight, and whose friend you longed to be. When he removed the barracks cap, he was a towhead; and even before we had met—before that firm, hearty handclasp that characterized all his greetings—he was known to us simply as "Whitey."

"The name's Dumas," he said in a rich, manly baritone, looking straight at you with an expression that, in those days before Madison Avenue had corrupted the word, could only be called sincere. Sincerity emanated from him; so did an air of achievement. Whitey was in his mid-twenties, a few years older than the rest of us, and it developed that he had used his time well. No one could call him a braggart—he was in fact conspicuously modest—but over the next few weeks particulars about his background slipped out naturally in normal conversation. He had been a newspaperman and a professional boxer. The fact that he had made money in the ring had been his undoing, accounting for his imprisonment; he had slugged a bully in a San Francisco bar, and under California law, he explained, a blow by a professional fighter was regarded as assault with a deadly weapon. If it hadn't been for his knowledge of Japanese, which he had disclosed to the authorities in Portsmouth, he would still be in the dreary exercise yard there.

"Isn't it typical of the Marine Corps to keep him a private?" Yates said scornfully. "In the Army he'd be at least a major."

The more we saw of Whitey the more we admired him. He was everything we wanted to be. He even had a sexy wife, a Paramount starlet. After much coaxing he was persuaded to produce a picture of her, an eight-by-ten glossy print of a beaming blonde in a bathing suit; it was signed "With all my love—Laverne." Even more impressive, Whitey, unlike most of us, was a combat veteran. He had been a machine gunner in the 1st Marines during the early days on Guadalcanal. This was a matter of special interest to Sy Ivice, who had landed on the 'Canal later with the 2d Marines. Sy wanted to reminisce about those days with Whitey, but Whitey politely declined. He had lost two of his best buddies in the fire fight along the Tenaru River, he told us, and he didn't want to talk about it.

Whitey's greatest achievement, of course, was his mastery of the enemy's language, the attainment that had sprung him from Portsmouth, and it was far too valuable to be confined to my section. Shortly after we crossed the country by troop train and encamped at Linda Vista, north of San Diego, preparatory to boarding ship, our gifted ex-con attracted the attention of the 29th's commanding officer, Colonel George F. Hastings. Hastings was the kind of colorful hard-charger the Marine Corps had always valued highly. Reportedly he was a native of an Arizona town named Buzzard's Gulch. Myth had it that his middle initial stood for "Flytrap," which was absurd, but it was quite true that between the wars he had designed the Corps' standard M1A1 flytrap. Until the 29th was formed, this device had existed only on paper, but over one weekend in training he had ordered one built. It didn't work. Not a single insect ventured into it. Nobody had the courage to tell the colonel, and on a Sunday of punishing heat the first sergeants had turned everybody out to catch flies by hand and put them in the trap so that Hastings wouldn't feel crushed.

The colonel was a great gray weasel of a man who always wore a bleached khaki fore-and-aft cap pushed to the back of his head. He was also the hoarsest and most redundant man I have ever known. His normal speaking voice can only be described as throaty, and he was forever saying things in it like "Here in Dixie we're in the Deep South," "Keep fit and healthy," and "Eat lots of food and plenty of it."

One sunlit morning—heavily handsome as only southern Californian weather can be—I was summoned by the sergeant major into the C.O.'s august presence. Hastings was standing beside a Lister bag in Officers' Country, slaking his thirst.

"We're going to sail aboard ship tomorrow," he barked after draining a canteen cup.

"Sir."

"The first day out I want Private Dumas to hold Japanese lessons. Just some fundamental key phrases. All officers and staff N.C.O.'s will meet on the fantail in the stern. I'm requisitioning a blackboard from ship's stores. Make sure Dumas is ready."

When I passed the word to Whitey, he gave me what we called a thousand-yard stare—a look of profound preoccupation. Then, while we were mounting the gangplank of the U.S.S. *General C. G. Morton*, lugging our seabags on our left shoulders and saluting the ship's colors as we boarded her, word was passed of our voyage's destination. We were headed for jungle maneuvers on Guadalcanal. "Oh, Christ, not that goddamned island," Ivice groaned. As Acting John I had been the first to reach the deck, and I happened to be looking at Dumas when the news reached him. He gave me a two-thousand-yard stare.

The next morning all designated hands fell out aft, with notebooks and pencils in hand. First the colonel pointed out that the blackboard was there, with lots of chalk and plenty of it, and that we were about to get some dope that would improve our efficiency and competence. Then he introduced Dumas. It was, I later thought, one of Whitey's finest hours. Arms akimbo, head high, with just a trace of a smile on that rugged face—the look of the learned teacher addressing eager neophytes—he proceeded with such assurance that one momentarily forgot he was outranked by everyone else there. Like English, he observed, Japanese was two languages, the written and the spoken. We would be chiefly concerned with the second, but it might be useful if we acquired some proficiency with the first. Turning to the blackboard he chalked with stenographic speed:

"That means 'Put your hands up, Nip!'" he said easily. "The best phonetic rendition I can give you is *'Zari sin toy fong!'*"

We wrote it down.

The next phrase was:

" *'Booki fai kiz soy?'*" said Whitey. "It means 'Do you surrender?'"

Then:

" *'Mizi pok loi ooni rak tong zin?'* 'Where are your comrades?'"

"Tong *what?*" rasped the colonel.

"Tong *zin,* sir," our instructor replied, rolling chalk between his palms. He arched his eyebrows, as though inviting another question. There was one. The adjutant asked, "What's that gizmo on the end?"

"It's called a *fy-thong,*" Whitey said. "It looks like a quotation mark, or a German umlaut, but its function is very different. It makes the question imperative—almost a threat. In effect you're saying, 'Tell me where your comrades are or you're a dead Nip.' "

"Right on target," the colonel muttered, writing furiously.

Next Whitey scrawled:

大 下 令 彐 題 自 中 内 死 上

"Means 'I want some water,' " he explained. "You say it *'Ruki gack keer pong tari loo-loo.'*"

Then:

覬 屮 乞 闋 ⁊ ㄸ 枒 心 木

" '*Moodi fang baki kim tuki dim fai?*' That's a question: 'Where is your commander?' "

A company commander raised a hand. "Why no *fy—fy* . . ."

"*Fy-thong,*" Whitey prompted. He spread his hands. "I really can't explain it, sir. The imperative just doesn't exist in certain conjugations. They call it a narrow inflection. It's a weird language." He grinned. "But then, they're a peculiar people."

"Murdering ****heads," hoarsed the colonel, flexing his elbow and scribbling on.

The battalion operations officer—the Bn-3—cleared his throat. He was a squat gargoyle of a man with a thick Brooklyn accent, the comic of Officers' Country. He asked, "How do you say 'I got to take a crap?' "

Into laughter Whitey said earnestly, "That's a good question, sir. The Japanese are very sensitive about bodily functions. You have to put it just right."

He chalked:

⁊ 勺 彑 兆 弾 彼 嬰 ナ

He said: " *'Song foy suk-suki kai moy-ah.'* "

The Bn-3 shot back, "What about saying to a Nip girl *'Voulez-vous coucher avec moi?'* "

Colonel Hastings thought that was hilarious, and once his guffaws had sanctioned the joke, everyone joined in lustily. Everyone, that is, except Whitey. Nursing his elbows and rocking back on his heels, he gave them a small, tight enlisted-man's smile. Slowly it dawned on the rest of us that he had not understood the operations officer, that his foreign languages did not include French. There was much coughing and shuffling of feet; then the Bn-3 said in the subdued voice of one whose joke had been unappreciated, "What I mean is—how you say you want your ashes hauled?"

Now Whitey beamed. He turned to the blackboard and scrawled:

車よろ都な空信ゾま

"How do you *say* it?" shouted the quartermaster.

" *'Naka-naka eeda kooda-sai,'* " Whitey said slowly. There was a long pause while we all made sure we had that one right. Thirty years later I can read it clearly in my yellowing notes, carefully printed in block capitals.

The colonel stood up, yawned, and prepared to shove off. He was bushed, he said, and he looked it. Doubtless this was his most intense cogitation since the invention of the flytrap. But then, we were all stretching ourselves. Although Marine Corps routine can be exhausting, it is rarely cerebral. The only man there who looked fresh was Whitey. Of course, he already knew Japanese.

The colonel was nothing if not dogged, however, and every day thereafter we assembled on the fantail for more skull sessions. By the end of the second week we were jabbering at each other with reasonable fluency, and the more enterprising platoon leaders were drilling their men in the basic idioms. Hastings, now well into his third notebook, was a bottomless source of questions. ("How do you say 'Put down your weapon' and tell them to do that?") We all felt that the 29th had a distinct edge on the other twenty-eight Marine regiments. Even the jaded members of my intelligence section were roused to pride—Jasper, a particularly apt pupil, marvelled at the exquisite nuances of the tongue, at its Oriental

precision and delicacy of phrasing—though Zoglin dampened
our enthusiasm somewhat by pointing out the unlikelihood
that we would ever have an opportunity to use our new skill.
Japanese soldiers were notorious for their refusal to surrender.
They considered it an honor to die for their emperor and a
disgrace to be taken alive; when defeat loomed for them at the
end of an island battle, their officers would round them up for
a traditional *banzai* (hurrah) suicide charge, and our people
obligingly mowed them down. (Banzai, Whitey explained in
response to a question, was spelled " 万歳.")

On the morning of the seventeenth day we climbed
topside to find ourselves lying off the 'Canal, that lush,
incredibly green, entirely repulsive island that for most of us
had existed only in legend. Ivice had a lot to say about its
banyan trees and kunai grass, but Whitey continued to be
reticent about his recollections of it. Toward the end the
journey had been a great strain for him. Of course, he had a lot
on his mind. Rising in the night for a trip to the scuttlebutt or
the head, I would see him lying awake on his bunk, sweating in
his skivvies, preparing the next day's lecture.

Slinging our 782 gear over our field packs, we scrambled
down the cargo nets thrown over the side of the *Morton*,
landed in the waiting Higgins boats, and raced in them toward
the shore. There we found that we were to make our training
camp on the banks of a river. And there Whitey committed
what seemed to be a peculiar blunder. As he looked down on
the stream his eyes misted over. "Sweet Jesus," he said
feelingly, picking up a corroded old cartridge case. "I never
thought I'd see the Matanikau again."

Ivice looked at him in disbelief. "The *Matanikau!*" he
said. "What the **** are you talking about? This is the
Kokumbona. The Matanikau's four miles to the east!"

Whitey hesitated and wet his lips. It was the first time any
of us had seen him shook. Finally he blinked and said, "Man, I
must be Asiatic." He shrugged. "All these goddamned rivers
look the same to me."

The rest of us accepted that—this tangled island bewildered us too—but Ivice said nothing. Throughout that day I
caught him eyeing Whitey strangely from time to time, and

the following morning, when I hitched a ride to Lunga Point on a DUKW and crossed the coconut-log bridge spanning the Matanikau, I understood why. The two rivers were entirely different. Compared to the mighty Matanikau, the Kokumbona was a shallow brook. Whitey's error was inexplicable.

Ivice was the first to entertain doubts about the star of our intelligence section, and I was the second. One evening over a joe-pot I mentioned to the sergeant major that Mrs. Dumas was a movie starlet. The sparrow chirped, "There ain't no Mrs. Dumas. If there was one, there'd be an allotment for her on the books, and there ain't none. I keep the books. I *know*." Shortly thereafter I saw a pinup of Betty Grable in a slop chute near Henderson Field. I recognized the style immediately: an eight-by-ten glossy print. What Whitey had been passing off as a photograph of his wife was a publicity shot of some Hollywood aspirant. Probably he had never met her. I never learned for sure.

Bit by bit the elaborate structure he had erected so adroitly and so successfully was beginning to come unstuck. Working on the Point Cruz dock, Yates met a port battalion officer who had been an Oakland lawyer before the war and who hooted at the idea of California law defining a boxer's punch as an assault with a deadly weapon. Then a gunnery sergeant, arriving as a replacement from Pendleton, recognized Whitey and revealed the true reason he had been stripped of rank and sent to prison. While still in boot camp, it turned out, he had been arrested for impersonating an officer in downtown San Diego. Since he hadn't become a recruit until the fall of 1943, Whitey had been a civilian during the battle for the 'Canal. Ivice was confirmed; our prodigy had never seen the island before he had landed with us. There was another thing: Whitey had told us that he had been a reporter. Journalism was something I knew about—in college I had been an Amherst stringer for the Springfield *Republican*—and when I started a camp newspaper, I invited him to contribute to it. He tried; he really tried. For days he struggled with a pencil, but when the result came in, it was functionally illiterate, almost incomprehensible. If he had ever been a reporter, the paper hadn't been published in the English language.

Of course, it might have been a *Japanese* newspaper. Whitey's claim to be a linguist was the last of his status symbols, and he clung to it desperately. Looking back, I think his improvisations on the *Morton* fantail must have been one of the most heroic achievements in the history of confidence men—which, as you may have gathered by now, was Whitey's true profession. Toward the end of our tour of duty on the 'Canal he was totally discredited with us and transferred at his own request to the 81-millimeter platoon, where our disregard for him was no stigma, since the 81-millimeter musclemen regarded us as a bunch of eight balls anyway. Yet even then, even after we had become completely disillusioned with him, he remained a figure of wonder among us. We could scarcely believe that an impostor could be clever enough actually to *invent* a language—phonics, calligraphy, and all. It had looked like Japanese and sounded like Japanese, and during his seventeen days of lecturing on that ship Whitey had carried it all in his head, remembering every variation, every subtlety, every syntactic construction.

Whitey stayed out of jail, and in the 29th, because the one man who never lost confidence in him was Colonel Hastings. The colonel continued to believe, not because he was stupid, but because Whitey staged his greatest show—literally a command performance—for the regimental C.O. I was there, yet to this day I don't fully understand how he pulled it off. What happened was that the First Marine Division, while securing Peleliu in October of 1944, had bagged five Japanese prisoners. That sort of thing happened from time to time in the Pacific war, usually under freakish circumstances. A Jap was dazed by a shell or otherwise rendered unable to kill himself. Seized by our troops, he was physically restrained from making amends to the emperor. Five months after their capture these failed suicides were ferried to the 'Canal from the First's base on the Russell Islands. Clad in loincloths and penned behind maximum-security concertinas of barbed wire, they passively awaited the pleasure of their conquerors. But nobody with jurisdiction knew quite how to dispose of them. Then word of their presence reached the C.O. of the 29th. Hastings knew exactly what to do; he announced to their wardens that he would interrogate them through his very own interpreter, Private Harold Dumas. Whitey greeted the news with a ten-thousand-yard stare and utter silence. There was, it seemed, nothing he could say.

The POW stockade was at Koli Point, and one morning

at 0800 hours we set out for it in a convoy, with Colonel Hastings and his private translator leading in a jeep and the rest of us trailing in a green crocodile of DUKW's, six-by trucks, and various other military vehicles. This was a big day for the colonel; he wanted every officer and staff N.C.O. to remember it. Since Whitey was riding with him, I didn't see the interpreter during the trip, and I have no way of knowing how he behaved, though I'm sure he retained his poise. Anybody who had the guts to snow his way through those classes on the *Morton* would be equal to almost any crisis; it was not crises, but day-by-day, round-the-clock testing that had led to our disenchantment with him. When I arrived at Koli, Hastings' jeep was already parked beside the huge barbed-wire coils. The colonel was outside, glaring in wrathfully. The prisoners were squatting miserably on their haunches, and Whitey, dressed in Marine dungarees and a raider cap, was squatting alongside them.

Apparently an exchange of some sort was going on. Obviously the colonel thought so; his eyes darted alertly from Whitey to the Japs, and his right ear was cocked, trying to pick up a thread of sense by using the vocabulary he had learned on the voyage from San Diego. It was, of course, impossible. Whitey was ad-libbing with his brilliant double-talk, which, however Oriental it sounded to us, was utterly devoid of real meaning. What the Nips were saying is a matter of conjecture, since no one there was equipped to understand them. My own belief is that they were replying to Whitey, "We only speak Japanese." All that can be said with any certainty is that the POW's and their interrogator had reached an impasse. After a long lull in the nonconversation Whitey came out with a hangdog look.

"What's happening?" the colonel asked anxiously.

"Sir, I goofed," Whitey said wretchedly.

"What? Why? How?"

With a swooping gesture Whitey swung out his right forefinger and pointed to the Marine Corps emblem printed on the left breast of his dungaree jacket. "I should never have worn this," he said in his guileless voice. "You see, sir," he explained, looking directly at Hastings, "they know what the globe-and-fouled-anchor means. They know what the Marine Corps is. They realize that the corps is destroying their emperor and their homeland, and they just won't answer my questions."

For a long moment the colonel stared back at Whitey. Then he squared his shoulders, and his pouter-pigeon chest swelled. "Goddam right," he grated, his voice like a coarse file. He peered contemptuously into the pen and said, "Those sons of bitches are a bunch of bastards."

With that he strutted back to his jeep and soon, it developed, out of our lives—Whitey's, mine, and the 29th's. That week the battalion boarded the APA (attack transport) *George C. Clymer* for Okinawa, where the colonel left us after the first few days of battle. He was relieved of his command on Motobu peninsula after the divisional commander asked him the whereabouts of his first and third battalions and received no satisfactory reply. I happened to be there when the question was raised, and I can still see the look of utter bewilderment on Hastings' face. He had always been vague about the rest of his regiment; his heart had belonged to our second battalion; he had allowed his lieutenant colonels to run the others, and in the excitement of combat he had neglected to update his situation map. "Inexcusable!" said the general, clearly outraged. "I'm sorry. I regret it," the colonel croaked brokenly. Later I heard that he had been shunted back to the corps staff, where he was awarded the Bronze Star "for excellence in keeping records during combat."

Whitey had vanished at about the same time during a sick call. Quite apart from gunshot wounds, there was a pattern of bizarre casualties in the island battles of World War II. Some poor bastard wading toward the beach would stumble off a reef, and with eighty pounds of hardware on his back he would sink like a stone. A BAR man in Easy Company disappeared that way in the early hours of Love Day, as Okinawa's D-day was quaintly called. Other people went rock happy—"combat fatigue," it was called. The sergeant major did; he was carried off cackling nonsense even less intelligible than that of Private Dumas. Then there was always some sad clown who, the first night on the beach, would forget that he had to stay in his hole until dawn, or "morning twilight," because the Japs were ingenious at night infiltrations. We scratched one Fox Company 60-millimeter mortarman at 2 A.M. that April 2; he was up relieving himself over a slit trench when a sentry drilled him through one cheek. ("A good shot in the bull's eye," said our callous colonel the following morning, just before he was deprived of his command.) Finally, there were the back cases. Whitey became one of them.

Every salt knew that you could get surveyed if you complained long enough about chronic back pains. Back on the 'Canal I lost a Philadelphian who had enlisted at the age of twenty-eight—we called him "Pop"—and who, fed up with jungle training, used that excuse to get stateside. Whitey followed his ignoble example. To the disgust of the gung-ho 81-millimeter mortarmen, he kept insisting that his spine was killing him, and finally the skeptical medical corpsmen sighed and took him away for a check.

It was months before I learned what happened to him after that, because after the battle began in earnest, my people became extremely active. Okinawa turned out to be the bloodiest engagement of the Pacific war, eclipsing even Iwo. After it was all over, a Presidential citation commended the division "for extraordinary heroism in action against enemy Japanese forces" and for "gallantry in overcoming a fanatic enemy in the face of extraordinary danger," but all I remember is mud and terror. Years later I learned from reading Samuel Eliot Morison that the 29th had sustained the heaviest casualties of any regiment in the history of the Marine Corps— 2,821 out of some 3,300 riflemen. My section was cut to pieces. Once the slaughter began, we were used as runners, carrying messages between battalion staff officers, company commanders, and even platoon leaders whose walkie-talkies had conked out. It was exceptionally perilous work. In 1918 someone computed the life expectancy of a German machine gunner on the western front at thirty minutes, and I don't believe that of a Marine runner along Okinawa's Machinato line could have been much longer. We were rarely in defilade, usually exposed, and often had to spend long periods lined up in some Jap sniper's sights. I myself was hit twice. The first time was May 17 on the northern slope of Sugar Loaf Hill. It was only a flesh wound, and I jumped hospital to rejoin the battalion, but on June 5 I was decked again. That one was almost for keeps, a massive chest wound from fourteen-inch rocket-mortar shrapnel. For five months I was on and off operating tables on a hospital ship, on Saipan, in Alewa Heights Naval Hospital overlooking Honolulu, in San Francisco, and finally at San Diego's naval hospital in Balboa Park.

A letter from Jasper—who survived the war to marry a

Nisei—reached me in Balboa that October, filling me in on Whitey's last adventure in the 29th. I was wearing a buck sergeant's stripes by then, or rather they were sewn to the sleeves of my greens, for I was still bedridden. I have a hazy memory of church bells tolling the previous August, and my asking a chief petty officer what it meant, and his answering, "The war's over," and my saying "Oh," just "Oh." Within a few months the 29th's people began heading home. Whitey, however, was not among them. His complaint about his back hadn't deceived the mortarmen, but then, they, like us, had known him. The physicians at the regimental aid station, on an LST offshore, had been seduced by his earnest charm, though the ultimate result was not quite what he had had in mind. The docs put him in a Higgins boat and sent him back to a corps clearing hospital. All badges of rank having been removed before we hit the beach—Nip sharpshooters liked to pick off officers and N.C.O.'s—the hospital's medical corpsmen had no way of knowing the military status of casualties, so they usually asked them. They asked Whitey, and he repeated his bootcamp lie. He said he was a first lieutenant, reasoning that life would be more comfortable, and the chow more edible, on an officer's ward.

He was right, but there were special hazards for him there. A captain in the next bunk asked him what his job in the Marine Corps was. "Japanese-language interpreter," said Whitey. They shot the breeze for a while, and then the captain asked Whitey for a lesson. Ever obliging, our man rattled off a few phrases and jotted down some of his Oriental hieroglyphics on a slip of paper. "Very interesting," the real officer said slowly. Then he yelled: "Corpsman! Put this man under arrest!" It developed that the captain was one of the first graduates of the Japanese-language schools that had been set up after Pearl Harbor. They were arriving in the Pacific too late to do much toward winning the war, but this one had turned up at exactly the right time to nail Whitey. Our confidence man had tried to dupe one mark too many. He was shipped straight back to Portsmouth.

I never saw him again, but I heard from him once. Five years after the war, when my first stories were appearing in national magazines, I received a letter postmarked Hollywood and written in a familiar scrawl. It was on MGM stationery. God knows where he had picked it up, but he certainly hadn't acquired it legally. Letters from studio executives—for that is what it claimed to be—are typed. They are also spelled correctly and properly phrased. This one was neither. I have never seen a clearer illustration of Whitey's own aphorism that we have two languages, one we speak and one we write. He was entirely verbal; when he lectured, it was with easy assurance and an impressive vocabulary. On his pilfered MGM stationery he was another hustler. Gone were his casual references to conjugations, modifiers, inflections, and the imperative mood. Not since his stab at journalism on the 'Canal had he been so incoherent.

His missive ran:

> Dear Bill,
> Caught your artical in this months Harpers. Real good. Always knew you had it in you.
> Look—could you give yours truely a break? Am now doing PR for Sam Goldwyn & Co and am trying to promote to stardom a real cute chick, name of Boobs Slotkin. (Boobs—ha! ha! I gave her the name & when you glim her knockers you'll see why.) Give me the word and I'll shoot you some pix. Some for the public and some for your private eye if you get my meaning—ha! ha!
> Sure miss the old gang on the Canal and all the good times we had. I don't hear from any of them, do you?
> Let me know about Boobs. This is a real good deal and I can put you next to her roommate whose no dog either next time your in this neck of the woods. Brunette 37-24-30 and hot pants. A real athalete in the sack. You won't regret it believe me.
> > Your old ******* buddy,
> > Harold V. Dumas
> > Chief of Public Relations
> > Metro-Goldwyn-Mayer Studios
> P.S. Don't write to me at the office as this is kind of personal. Just send it to me care of General Delivery L.A. and it will get to me Okay.

I never replied, but I found the note strangely moving. Whitey had climbed the Parnassus of his calling, and evidently he had now slid back down all the way. He was pathetic on paper, and his assessment of the kind of material that interested *Harper's* was unbelievable. (How on earth had he even *seen* the magazine?) He had entered the shadows; for all I know, he never emerged again. It is of course quite possible that he staged a stunning caper under another name—as G. Gordon Liddy, say—yet somehow I doubt it. His big sting with us had a one-shot air about it, like the flight of an exotic bird that dazzles for a single season and is never seen again. But on the *Morton's* fantail, and outside that POW stockade at Koli Point, he had been magnificent. And to this day I feel a tingling at the base of my scalp when I think of that towheaded prisoner in his Portsmouth cell dreaming up what must have been the most imaginative con of the war, saying in that straightforward voice, "Guard, I want to speak to the C.O.," and then, "Sir, I know I deserve to be here, but my country is threatened and I want to do my share. I can really help in an unusual way, sir. You see, I speak Japanese."

—*December 1975*

LOOKING FOR THE GOOD GERMANS

by DAVID DAVIDSON

The victors divided the Germans into three groups: black (Nazi), white (innocent), and gray—that vast, vast area in between.

E ven before the last shots were fired in Europe in World War II and the dust had begun to settle over the ruins of Hitler's Thousand-Year Reich, teams of Americans in Army uniform were moving into Germany to begin sitting in judgment of the defeated enemy.

Not content with simply enjoying the relaxations of victory, the conquerors now went to work with a moral yardstick to measure the degree of iniquity of which some millions of the conquered were guilty.

I do not refer to the spectacular Nuremberg trials in which the fabled monsters of the Nazi leadership were arraigned and convicted as war criminals but to the ethical code that American Military Government, the interim ruler of the U.S.-occupied zone in southern Germany, applied day by day to all Germans holding, or hoping to assume, positions in government and public communications.

I was one of these moralists in khaki. A newspaperman and radio writer in civil life, only a few days after the German surrender in May, 1945, I took my place behind a battered pine desk in a bomb-cracked building in Munich that originally had served as an old-folks home and later as headquarters for the German army service of supply.

An hour earlier, having driven in from Paris over a poppy-carpeted landscape, I had been confronted with a perfect, up-to-date expression of the ancient German conflict of "two souls in one breast." Across the façade of the Rathaus, or city hall, somebody had chalked, "Dachau, Auschwitz, Belsen—I am ashamed to be a German!" Directly below, another hand had scrawled, "Beethoven, Schiller, Goethe—I am proud to be a German!"

In the city of putsch and pact, where in 1923 Hitler launched an abortive uprising and in 1938 ensnared Neville Chamberlain, German work crews were still digging up corpses from ruins estimated to cover 60 percent of the town. But on Renatastrasse, at my second-story window, still hung with ragged chintz from the old-folks era, I looked out on eye level at pretty girls in Bavarian dirndls standing on ladders to pick the surviving blossoms from half-charred trees to make linden tea.

Below, at a narrow side door, a sign explained that here was the headquarters of 6870 DISCC, a unit of the Supreme Headquarters Allied Expeditionary Forces. Translated, this was District Information Services Control Command, a part of the Information Control Division (ICD), which later became an arm of American Military Government.

My unit, in which I was assigned to the press section, covered Bavaria. A similar outfit operated out of Frankfurt, to the west.

Our mission, as the military called any operation from taking Iwo Jima to obtaining a new batch of paper clips, was to suspend immediately every activity in public communications—press, book, and magazine publishing, radio, theater, opera, and even the circus—and root out all practitioners tainted with Nazism. Next we would search out, investigate, and license provably anti-Nazi Germans to build up a whole new democratic establishment of communications over which there would be no need to exercise censorship.

At the start it was a matter of conducting merciless interrogations and investigations of all who came to apply for licenses—editors, publisher, actors, musicians—and making determinations of how they had behaved under Hitler. (To permit a soprano who had been a particular favorite of Hitler's to give a lieder recital would be taken by the Germans, in our estimation, as signifying we were not at all serious in our condemnation of Nazism.)

The procession of Germans who came before us were, by our rough-and-ready rule of thumb, soon classified as falling into one of three categories: black, white, or gray.

Black denoted applicants with an out-and-out Nazi background and on whom little time need be wasted except for a few calculated insults to themselves and their fallen Fuhrer. White denoted "good Germans," those who had never given in to Nazism during the Hitler era.

Gray was the tragic group, consisting of good Germans who had gone bad under pressure; people of decent anti-Nazi convictions who, because of the necessities of making a living, pursuing a career, or even staying out of the Gestapo dungeons, had finally caved in to one degree or another. They had written pro-Nazi articles they didn't believe and had joined organizations such as the Nazi auto club, contributed to Nazi charity funds, or even, a last resort, joined the Nazi party.

Interrogating the grays was always the most painful—for the interrogator as well as for the applicant. To the grays we represented the conscience they had betrayed. And the consequences of these interrogations could be painfully dramatic. One applicant, after being faced with the record of his concessions to Nazism, killed himself.

In my case, an applicant whom I had accused of fighting Hitler "with your fist in your pocket" turned on me and shot a barbed question that stings to this day: "How do you think *you* would have behaved under Hitler?"

On the average I conducted ten interrogations a day. Often I felt so emotionally exhausted that I would have to knock off by 4:00 P.M. and hoist three or four stiff drinks to relax. Always there was the odd sensation of sitting on a stage as a character in a play under the spotlight of history.

Our basic aim was to limit operations in all media for the first years to proven anti-Nazis and thus give them a solid head start against the day when the Germans would resume self-government and open the field to all comers.

Our occupation of Germany was certainly the first broad experience for Americans as conquerors of a foreign power. At the end of World War I, a token force of U.S. troops had occupied the Rhine city of Koblenz, but since that war had stopped short of the German borders, few doughboys of the American Expeditionary Force even set foot inside the country. And in spite of all the wartime cries about German atrocities and the threats to "hang the Kaiser" and punish the Huns, there were no serious efforts at holding any kind of trials.

Now, in dealing with the remains of Hitler's empire, our attitudes were sharpened by the discovery of gas chambers and piles of corpses as Allied troops took the concentration camps.

But, in fact, the blueprint for Information Control was drawn long before V-E Day. It was the product of a team of political scientists, psychologists, and sociologists under the command of Colonel William Paley, who had taken leave from his radio empire of Columbia Broadcasting System to go to war with the Psychological Warfare Division, the predecessor of Information Control.

Our mission—to "re-educate the Germans and save the peace"—was described by our top military command as "of the highest priority" and "second to none." We were given authority to travel anywhere to carry out our orders, were permitted to meet with any and all Germans at a time when fraternization was forbidden to the rest of the Army, and were empowered to requisition any property, including printing presses, radio stations, and theaters, necessary "to carry out the mission."

The manual assembled by the Paley team for the indoctrination and guidance of Information Control officers, of whom I was one, proved remarkably realistic for our dealings with the German applicants, serving as a combination book of etiquette and Geiger counter for detecting Nazism.

For instance, we were instructed to speak only German during interrogations and to resist all attempts to draw us into English. This was for two reasons: to demonstrate our know-how on the job and to keep a cool, censorious distance from the applicant until he was proven to be anti-Nazi.

Before each interrogation, the applicant was required to fill out a formidable *Fragebogen,* or questionnaire, of 131 piercing questions about his politics, education, employment, affiliations, and general social outlook.

The manual also told us to look for giveaways such as dueling scars on the face, betokening membership in the university student "corporations," centers of political reaction from the mid-nineteenth century; filling out the application in gothic script, commanded by Hitler as a badge of true Germanism, as against roman script; the use of Nazi-favored expressions such as Gefolgschaft ("crew" or "staff") and *Begegnungsgefecht,* the characteristic supposedly reserved for Germans of fighting spirit and initiative.

Another symptom was the sycophantic custom of knocking not only on the outside of the office door when seeking entrance but, once in, of knocking again on the inside, which was always followed by excessive bowing from the waist, making the applicant look like a wind-up toy.

It was almost an unvarying rule that the less polite, less subservient, and more badly dressed the applicant was, the less likely he was to have a Nazi taint.

In search, like Diogenes with his lamp, of honest men, during my twelve months with Information Control I traveled twenty-five thousand miles around Bavaria by jeep and a commandeered Mercedes and interrogated twenty-five hundred Germans. In that period I lost one pound of weight for each hundred Germans and each thousand miles, shrinking from 175 pounds to 150. Partly this was because of the grueling travel over washboard back roads, bombed-out highways, and manure-heap barnyards following even the faintest clue to the whereabouts of reputedly anti-Nazi editors and publishers. And partly it was because of the wearing intensity of feeling in my outfit that if only we succeeded in finding the right people we would "save the peace."

There were a couple hundred of us in the Bavarian division—officers, enlisted men, civilian specialists, and German employees—and by the end of the first year a considerable amount of work had been accomplished. The press section established amid the ruins twenty-one newspapers with a total circulation of 2,000,000 to serve a population of some 10,000,000 Bavarians and refugees from other areas of Germany.

The book section launched a program equivalent in output to a major U.S. publishing house. The theater section opened as many legitimate theaters as in the largest American chain. As many movie houses were licensed as there were in Manhattan, and more musicians were cleared to perform than were under contract to Columbia Artists and the Metropolitan Opera.

My own job was to serve—first as co-chief with Joseph Dunner, a brilliant political science professor from Grinnell College, and then as sole director—on a Munich-centered press detachment of ten Americans and Germans, which eventually set up and supervised six new German newspapers in southern Bavaria. Their combined circulation was over a million.

Our jewel was the *Süddeutsche Zeitung* of Munich, in which we first made a bold experiment. German journalism had always been strictly oriented to political parties and had angled the news coverage accordingly; but here we proposed a mixed editor-publisher team of a Social Democrat, a member of the Bavarian Peasant party, and someone from the Catholic Center party.

We put them together in a room, asked them to decide whether they could work with each other to put out a newspaper dedicated to objective news coverage, and locked the door.

An hour later they came out and began publishing a newspaper that very soon became and remains to this day the "*New York Times* of Germany."

It was not easy finding these men. Immediately upon Hitler's accession, they had left journalism rather than make any compromise with Nazism. August Schwingenstein, the Peasant party man who became publisher, had created for himself during the Hitler era a weird business of attending funerals, taking down the eulogy in shorthand, then printing it up as a handsomely designed plaque and selling copies to the family of the departed. Edmund Goldschag, Social Democrat and managing editor, had lost himself in the far reaches of the Black Forest, working variously as a dairyman and printer. Dr. Franz Josef Schoeningh, cultural editor, had drifted into the haven of church publications.

The day they came in for interrogation, each at once displayed the right political symptoms. Each wore shoes that were down at the heels and suits that were frayed. Goldschag was missing several front teeth and could not afford to replace them. All were underweight. All had been picked up for questioning at one time or another by Hitler's police. The *Fragebogen* of each read *Nein!* up and down the columns of questions about Nazi affiliations.

Once publishing teams had been selected and licensed, I began to take on a host of new duties.

I would confiscate printing plants that had belonged to the Nazi party and individual Nazis and lease them to the new publishers, search out supplies of newsprint and ink, arrange for the salvage of bombed presses, supervise a swap of wheels of Bavarian cheese for British-zone zinc needed for making photographic plates, wake up the Munich publisher in the middle of the night and authorize an extra edition of a million copies on the Nuremberg trial, scrutinize each issue of every licensed newspaper and make suggestions about brightening up the contents and format, and—of prime importance— protect the publishers when their zeal for free and critical expression, even of the conquerors, brought them into conflict with the Army occupation command.

My military status was an ambiguous but highly desirable one as a civilian specialist with the "assimilated," or honorary, rank of major. Such specialists constituted almost half the executive personnel of ICD because of three stiff requirements that made it difficult for the military to fill the tables of organization from its own commissioned ranks. These requirements were an ability to speak German fairly fluently, a knowledge of German politics, and professional experience in at least one medium of communication.

The great advantage of my status, as I soon learned, was that civilians with the Army could not be court-martialed—for disobeying orders, insubordination, disrespect, or anything else. In consequence, the real military among us, nearly all combat veterans, soon learned to make cunning use of me. Whenever they found themselves at odds with the top brass, they would send me in to do battle, as, for instance, when the whole outfit was ordered to move to a fairyland castle forty miles away from Munich, where we could not possibly have functioned. And, when other officers in Military Government began jeering at us because one of our top people had taken as his mistress the widow of an SS general, I was delegated to take this up with the offending leader.

In good military style I drew up a memo in which I recounted the "surely unfounded gossip," expressed the loyal conviction that the offender could not be guilty of such conduct, and proposed that he avail himself of the white lists of potential German mistresses that our intelligence section had prepared for the use of the outfit.

On the day before I left Bavaria for home, the offender called me in for a red-faced, stuttering apology, but whether this changed the contents of his bed I was never able to find out.

If my status often puzzled the military, it absolutely bewildered my German interviewees. In accord with their national habit they would try to pile rank on me, with no clue to guide them, because we civilian specialists did not wear any insignia. Thus I would be addressed by such obscene exaggerations as "Colonel-Director-Commander," upon which I would frown darkly and declare this was not enough.

"Your Honor. . . . Your Excellency . . .?"

"Still not enough. Remember that as far as you are concerned, I sit here representing the United States of America. Therefore you must address me by the same title you would address the President of the United States."

"Your Eminence. . . . Your Worship . . .?"

"No! As 'mister.' Just plain 'mister.' The same title as the President of the United States of America."

Another linguistic curio was my discovery, after the first dozen interrogations, of a phenomenon with which I am still able to surprise professional philologists: namely, that the German language has no words for "fair" and "gentleman." Again and again I would find interviewees, especially those with bad conscience, declaring hopefully that I would be "fair" in my treatment of them because I was assuredly a "gentleman."

Why, I inquired finally, keep using the English words instead of German?

Because, it turned out, the nearest German word to "fair" was *gerecht*, meaning "just, granting the exact letter of the law," something very different from the relaxed, compassionate concept of fairness. And the nearest German word for "gentleman" was *Herr*, connoting merely a man of noble birth or elevated social position.

In these daily confrontations one never knew when to expect extremes of drama. In our music section, Captain Edward Kilenyi, an international concert pianist in civil life, found himself facing a pre-war colleague who had given in totally to the Nazis. Kilenyi, now in uniform with a Colt .45 on his hip, told the man he could not possibly grant him clearance to perform in the U.S. zone but suggested that he might do better among the French, known to be cynical in these matters, or the British, who were tired and indifferent, or the Russians, who would probably clear him for the price of joining the Communist party.

Instead, the man went home and hanged himself.

I had a similar experience upon being informed by our

intelligence section that one of our approved editors had in fact knuckled under during the Hitler era, writing numerous unsigned pro-Nazi editorials. With a thought for his wife and large brood of children, we permitted him simply to transfer to a modest church weekly.

One of Military Government's major problems in this area was none other than Richard Strauss. The great musician had let himself be made the figurehead chief of the Nazi Culture Chamber. Loving the comforts of home, he simply could not pick himself up to go into exile as had Thomas Mann and other of his peers. Week after week, Strauss's do-nothing son would descend on Military Government head-quarters in Garmisch-Partenkirchen to demand extra rations of coal and roast beef in the name of his father. "Do you want to be responsible for the death of the greatest genius of the twentieth century?" he would declaim. We solved the problem very neatly by obtaining for Strauss the first exit permit for a German from the American zone. Once he was safely on his way to Switzerland, the gloves were off, and the next time Strauss Junior went to Military Government to make demands, he was booted out of the building.

In the course of my interrogations, even in that stern soul-searching atmosphere, there was a host of weird conversations that I came to catalogue as "Dialogues from Walpurgisnacht," the German equivalent of Halloween. One day a German newspaperman, whom I still identify in my mind as "Camel Face," entered my office. He duly double-knocked on the door, then turned to me to utter his first, truly astonishing words: "My mother was a bastard."

"Very sad," I said, "but wherein is that relevant?"

He proceeded to explain a closely guarded family secret. His mother had been fathered by a Jewish traveling salesman, which made her half-Jewish and Camel Face himself one-quarter Jewish, a horrendous infirmity in the Nazi era. But one day, alas, a homely female cousin whom Camel Face jilted after a long engagement gave away the secret to the authorities.

"At once," said Camel Face, "I was made to suffer."

"In what regard?" I asked.

"Immediately," said Camel Face, "I was expelled from the SS."

There was an inevitable answer. "In your family," I said, showing him the door, "there are two bastards."

As a companion piece to this, a woman interviewee one day told me how the Nazis had discriminated against her family. "My mother," she said, "bore eight children for the Führer, but he never sent her the Mother's Medal to which she was entitled."

Another bizarre tale, but a sunnier one, developed when I glanced through the *Fragebogen* of a very blond young German, the very model of the super-Ayran, who was applying for a job as a driver with our outfit. His record was absolutely flawless; he had not even been enrolled in a Nazi kindergarten.

"Wonderful," I said, "but how is this possible?"

"Ach," he said, "didn't you notice my given name?"

I looked more closely this time. Bizarre, in so perfect a Teutonic type. The name was Isidor. Yes, Isidor.

"My father," the young man went on, "being a farmer and a devout Catholic, named me for the patron saint of the peasant, Saint Isidor. But every time I was enrolled in some organization, the Nazis expelled me. 'Send him home, the Jew Isidor.' So I stayed on the farm all through the war and dug potatoes, and my father couldn't have been happier."

But for me the most dramatic confrontation, one which became a turning point in my professional life, occurred with my very first interrogation. I had just set down my duffel bag on arriving from Paris when I was told to talk with a noted German travel writer, Kasimir Edschmid, who had published abroad in a dozen countries but had chosen to remain in Hitler's Germany. He had engaged, he said, in an "inner emigration," keeping his thoughts and soul apart from the Nazi regime.

(Later, when Edschmid published an apologia under this title, he was jeered by critics throughout the two Germanys, East and West.)

It was Edschmid who, when I chided him, flung at me the shattering question, "How do you think *you* would have behaved under Hitler?"

It was a question I could not shake off. It troubled quite a few of my fellow Americans, to a greater or lesser degree, who had to judge the Germans. In an attempt to answer it, I found myself latching on to the dossier of a young German newspaperman, exactly my own age and with a similar history as a journalist, who was described by informants as having been a fervent anti-Nazi and a gadfly to Nazi big shots in Bavaria before Hitler's accession. But now he had been swallowed up somewhere in a French POW camp.

For the next year, in every moment I could steal from my assigned duties, and often going AWOL with self-forged orders, I tried to locate him and to learn how he had behaved under Hitler. He had become my alter ego. His story had become my story. When I learned how he had conducted himself under Nazism, I would find out how I myself would have stood up, or failed to.

Bit by bit, even before I finally located him, I uncovered his record in the Nazi era. It was a story of daring underground activities and practical compromises, of rough handling by the Gestapo and occasional capitulation, presumably for tactical reasons.

Finally, on the eve of my leaving the Army and Germany, he came before me. To my surprise, he bore not the slightest physical resemblance to myself. After a hearty handshake and exchange of pleasantries, he told me something that made my heart sink—for both of us. He told me that after an unbearable accumulation of pressures on himself and his new young wife, he had agreed to fill out an application for membership in the Nazi party. Before this could be acted upon, war broke out and he was drafted into the army.

Would that have been my own fate as a German? Would they have worn me down too in the end?

In my self-decreed identification with this German, I was forced to accept that as the judgment on myself. In practical terms, the ICD rules made it impossible for me to clear the man (or myself) immediately for a top editor's job, as I had hoped, but I did manage to obtain enough of a dispensation for him to start work again as a reporter.

Altogether it was a year of intense feeling and being. But, of course, the role also brought with it all sorts of compensations: easy living, inexpensive booze, cut-rate merchandise at the PX, good company, and the shelter of authority. For instance, at the last moment, as I was saying good-by to my German (and provenly anti-Nazi) secretary, she told me it had been most interesting to work with me, especially because of the dozen new German words I had created during my speeches at the opening of various newspapers.

"I made a lot of mistakes in German?"

"Well," she said, "those were words that didn't exist

before you came to Germany, but I found them very interesting and even useful."

"Why," I demanded, "didn't you tell me I was making mistakes?"

Her answer went to the heart of the whole matter. "What," she said, "tell a conqueror . . .?"

—June 1982

CONTRIBUTORS

CAPTAIN EDWARD L. BEACH retired from active naval service in 1966. He is the author of numerous books including *Run Silent, Run Deep*.

JOHN R. BURROUGHS was a construction engineer who spent three and a half years in captivity in prison camps in China and Japan.

CHARLES CAWTHON stayed on in the army through the Korean War and, after his discharge, worked as a newspaper editor. He is the author of *Other Clay*.

ADMIRAL J. J. CLARK commanded the *Yorktown* before his promotion to Rear Admiral in 1944.

DAVID DAVIDSON was a novelist and television documentary writer. His novel *The Steeper Cliff* was based on his experiences in postwar Germany.

LEWIS ELLIS is now retired and lives in Washington, D.C.

GENERAL JAMES M. GAVIN commanded the 82nd Airborne Division during World War II.

ALLEN HEYN was a seaman aboard the *Juneau* during the Battle of Guadalcanal.

G.D. LILLIBRIDGE is a professor emeritus of history at California State University at Chico.

WILLIAM MANCHESTER has written biographies of John F. Kennedy, Douglas MacArthur, and Winston Churchill.

HERBERT MITGANG is a reporter for *The New York Times* and the author of *Dangerous Dossiers*.

LESTER F. RENTMEESTER retired from the Air Force as a colonel and is now a professor at Florida Institute of Technology.

HUGHES RUDD has been a correspondent for both CBS and ABC News, and is the author of *My Escape from the CIA (and other Improbable Events)*.

REAR ADMIRAL KEMP TOLLEY, now retired, was a 1929 graduate of Annapolis and was assistant naval attache in Moscow from 1942 to 1944.

STEPHEN BOWER YOUNG served as a seaman in the Guadalcanal and Georgia campaigns. Later he returned to action in the Korean War.